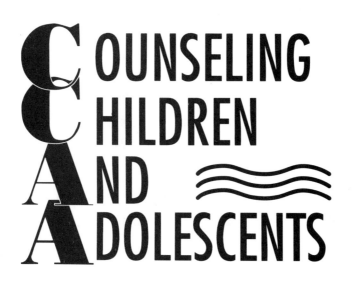

COUNSELING CHILDREN AND ADOLESCENTS

ANN VERNON
University of Northern Iowa

LOVE PUBLISHING COMPANY®
Denver, Colorado 80222

Library of Congress Catalog Number 92-74808

Copyright © 1993 Love Publishing Company
Printed in the U.S.A.
ISBN 0-89108-228-X

Contents

5 Counseling with Exceptional Children   119

Thomas V. Trotter
School Psychology and Counselor Education Program
University of Idaho, Moscow

6 Counseling with Young Multicultural Clients   137

Thomas V. Trotter
School Psychology and Counselor Education Program
University of Idaho, Moscow

7 Counseling with At-Risk Students   157

James V. Wigtil
Counseling Program
The Ohio State University, Columbus
JoAnne M. Wigtil
Doctoral Candidate, Family Relations and Human Development
The Ohio State University, Columbus

10   Counseling with Families   271

Larry Golden
Counseling and Guidance Program
University of Texas, San Antonio

11   Consulting with School Staff and Administration   291

Brooke B. Collison
Counselor Education Program
Oregon State University, Corvallis

Preface

At a recent conference for school counselors, participants were asked to describe a problem presented by one of their clients. Next, they were instructed to think of themselves at the age of this client and to describe a problem they recalled having. After sharing the responses in small groups, the summaries clearly showed most of the problems the counselors identified for themselves were normal developmental problems: conflicts with friends or parents, anxiety about school or extracurricular performance, or concerns about their future. The issues they specified for *their clients*, on the other hand, included abuse or neglect, living with an alcoholic parent, teen pregnancy, substance abuse, or depression and suicide.

Today's school-age population faces far different challenges in growing up than many of us did. Consequently, the school counselor's role has changed primarily in two ways: (1) Counselors are working more with serious issues, and (2) preventive, developmental counseling programs are more prevalent. In turn, counselor educators recognize that training programs have to be modified. Counselors-in-training need to learn specific strategies that work with children, rather than watered down adaptations of adult interventions. They also must know how to implement developmental counseling programs, work effectively with at-risk and special populations, and be skilled in small-group facilitation, consultation, and working with families. In addition, they must be able to develop programs that emphasize development and prevention, understand developmental concerns of school-age children, and respond to the needs of a multicultural population.

This book is intended for students taking courses in counseling techniques for children and adolescents. The contributing authors have provided up-to-date information that will increase the reader's knowledge about effective counseling strategies for school-age children. Each chapter contains practical information, often interspersed with case studies, to illustrate specific application of content. The book addresses the current national emphasis on developmental counseling versus the traditional responsive services model. Because no text can adequately include all topics relevant to working with children and adolescents, the focus here is on child-specific topics that may not be covered in other courses.

The text is divided into two parts. Part One, The Counseling Process with Children and Adolescents, covers individual counseling approaches, developmental considerations and interventions, and creative counseling techniques. Also included are chapters on working with multicultural children, children with exceptionalities, and youth at risk. Part Two contains chapters on group counseling, developmental guidance curriculum, consultation with school personnel, and working with families.

We have made a concerted effort to provide practical information that will enhance readers' ability to work with children and adolescents. We hope this text will be a valuable resource that can help make a difference for today's youth.

Ann Vernon

To my son,

Eric J. Vernon,

with pride and appreciation

for the person he is.

The Counseling Process with Children and Adolescents

Part *I*

1 An Introduction

Ann Vernon

Department of
Educational Administration and Counseling
University of Northern Iowa, Cedar Falls

Dear Dr. Vernon,

I used to get upset because when I had a problem, you never *told* me what to do. You just tried to help me figure it out. Now I'm glad you didn't give me the answers, 'cuz I learned that I can solve a lot of my problems myself!

Love, Yolanda

This letter was written by a sixth grader and given to me several years ago when I was an elementary school counselor. Yolanda's note epitomizes what counseling children is all about—helping them learn to help themselves. In our contemporary society, counselors must help children and adolescents identify healthy ways to deal with increasingly complex issues and challenges.

GROWING UP IN THE 1990s

During practicum supervision a student raised a concern about how to handle a case with one of her clients, a third grader. This eight-year-old was seeing the student counselor because she was trying to decide whether to "have sex" with her boyfriend, an eighth grader. "If I don't, he'll get mad and he might hit me," was what we heard on the tape my supervisee presented. This *child* was being confronted with choices far beyond her comprehension. The tape reflected her sense of powerlessness, dependency, fear, and confusion.

Applying what she had learned in skills classes, the supervisee had empathically and attentively listened to this young client, all the while identifying with the client's sense of powerlessness because she herself was overwhelmed with an issue that she hadn't expected to be helping a third grader deal with. "Where do I go from here?" was not an easy question to answer.

This is just one example of what many counselors confront regularly. Today's youth are growing up in a world characterized by changing family structures, AIDS, rampant substance abuse, teen pregnancy, family and societal violence, cultural diversity, alternative lifestyles, homelessness, and increased incidence of depression and suicide (Gerler, Ciechalski, and Parker 1990). In assisting young clients with their personal development, counselors must understand the ramifications of these issues.

Contemporary Stressors

Recently I switched on the radio, which was tuned to a rock station that my teenage son had selected. As I listened, I realized that this medium is an extremely powerful source of "information" about sex, drugs, violence, relationships, and suicide. The prevalence of these themes, and the frequency with which young people are exposed to unhealthy, self-defeating messages about life, is sobering.

Unfortunately, the themes in these songs do represent reality. Adolescent suicide is the second leading cause of death in the eleven to twenty-four-year age group, and six teenagers kill themselves every day (Capuzzi 1988; Glosoff and Koprowicz 1990). Although suicidal behaviors are widely believed to be restricted primarily to adolescence and adulthood, Stefanowski-Harding (1990) stated that child suicide is a reality and that suicides in this age-group continue to rise. According to Hipple (1990), approximately 200 suicides are reported annually for children under age twelve, but 25,000 children are hospitalized yearly for suicidal ideation.

Children and adolescents are both perpetrators and victims of violence. Youths between ages ten and seventeen commit more than half of all serious crimes in the United States, including rape, assault, murder, robbery, larceny, and motor vehicle theft (Winbush 1988), and 135,000 children bring guns to school every day (Glosoff and Koprowicz 1990). Winbush noted that the forms of violence among youths are more deadly and diverse and often spontaneous and difficult to predict.

School-age children are victims of physical, emotional, and sexual abuse. An estimated one of every four girls and one of every seven to ten boys will have been sexually abused by an adult prior to age eighteen (Hackbarth, Murphy, and McQuary 1991). Although judging the extent of victimization is difficult, Thompson and Rudolph (1992) stated that more than two million cases were reported in 1987. The psychological wounds resulting from these traumatic experiences will have a major impact on subsequent development.

Drug experimentation often begins in elementary school, leading to chemical abuse and addiction in adolescence (Gerler et al. 1990). Furthermore, as many as 44 percent of school-age children live in alcoholic families, and 60 percent of these children will ultimately misuse substances or develop another form of compulsive behavior (O'Rourke 1990). William Bennett, coordinator for drug policy under President Bush, stated that "the most serious threat to the health and well-being of our children is drug use" (in Gerler et al. 1990, 79).

According to Hayes and Cryer (1988), "Of the more than 29 million teenagers in this country, approximately 12 million have had sexual intercourse. Of this population, more than 1.1 million girls are expected to become pregnant this year and bear nearly 500,000 infants" (p. 22). In recent years, the birthrate for girls age fourteen and under has increased, as has the likelihood that they will give birth subsequently during the teen years when sexual activity begins so early (Lachance 1985). Hayes and Cryer (1988) noted the domino effect of teenage pregnancy—incomplete education, psychological and developmental difficulties, unemployment, social isolation, and poverty—which in turn impacts the way future children are raised.

Cause and Effect

These facts speak for themselves. Far too many youths are experiencing traumatic events when they are most vulnerable and least able to cope. Whether problems result from these events or whether violence, substance abuse, teen pregnancy, and suicide are responses to societal changes during the last two decades is difficult to know. Whichever the case, young people are facing challenges of a culturally diverse, technological society characterized by changing values, insecurity, instability, and life on the "fast track."

A DEVELOPMENTAL PERSPECTIVE

As Barbara Kuczen (1987) pointed out, "Growing up has never been easy, but it has never been harder than in today's society" (p. xi). Not only do growing numbers of children and adolescents have to deal with an increasingly stressful society, but they also have typical developmental problems. To varying degrees, children still worry about performing well in school, being included with peers, looking "just right" for the opposite sex, or getting teased for being "different."

A fourteen-year-old explained growing up by saying, "Just when I thought I had all my problems solved, like being scared that I wouldn't be picked first for a team or that kids would make fun of me when I got my glasses, now *I hate* the way I look and I'm embarrassed to be seen with my parents because they act so *dumb.*"

Although these developmental problems may seem minor in comparison to those of the victimized child or the adolescent growing up in an alcoholic family, the issue isn't really *which is* more serious. Rather, the question is: What are the issues, and *how* can we most successfully help children lead healthy, satisfying lives?

Stages of Development

"The concept of childhood, so vital to the traditional American way of life, is threatened with extinction in the society we have created" (Elkind 1988, 3). According to Elkind, the child is the unintended victim of the stress resulting from a society characterized by rapid changes and rising expectations. He contends that children in this contemporary society are pressured to "grow up fast" and in this hurrying up process, we ignore the special needs of children (p. 6).

Addressing the special needs of children is impossible without a basic understanding of child development. Normal development entails a series of social, emotional, physical, and cognitive changes. Robert Havighurst (1972) used the term *developmental task,* referring to skills, attitudes, knowledge, or functions that children and adolescents must master at various stages of development to prepare for roles and tasks in later life. Successful mastery of these tasks, acquired in part by maturation, personal effort, and fulfillment, results in competent, well-adjusted individuals who are able to deal with challenges presented in later stages of development. In contrast, individuals who fail to achieve these tasks are often maladjusted and anxious, unable to successfully negotiate future tasks.

Two developmental theorists, Erik Erikson and Abraham Maslow, developed models applying to task completion. These models can be used to increase understanding of the types of stresses children and adolescents are likely to experience at given points in life, depending on how well their needs were met and whether tasks were accomplished at earlier stages of development.

Erikson's Model of Developmental Stages

Although Erikson's stages of ego development are somewhat similar to the Freudian oral, anal, phallic, and latency stages, he emphasized social experiences and growth of the individual. He contended that each stage presents a psychosocial "crisis" to be resolved and the outcome determines progress or regression in development (Erikson 1968). The five stages which pertain to children and adolescents are as follows:

1. *Trust Versus Mistrust* (ages birth to one). Healthy development is influenced significantly by the quality of care a child receives. If he or she is treated in a consistent, loving manner, the child is likely to develop a sense of trust. In contrast, if the caretakers are aloof, rejecting, and unreliable, the child will likely become angry and frustrated. The feeling of deprivation results in mistrust.

2. *Autonomy Versus Shame and Doubt* (ages two to three). During this period of development, the child begins to assert independence. Parents who guide their children's behavior gradually help them develop a sense of pride, self-control, and autonomy. If parents are too demanding or too permissive, their children are likely to feel shame and doubt their ability to make judgments or act independently.

3. *Initiative Versus Guilt* (ages four to five). During this stage of development, children are becoming more independent and seek contact with people outside of the family. At this age, children are curious, imaginative, and intrigued by sexual matters and adult roles. Children must not be punished for this curiosity and intrigue, which can result in guilt and inhibit independence and initiative.

4. *Industry Versus Inferiority* (ages six to twelve). At this stage, children begin to prepare for the future by acquiring new skills and learning how to complete tasks. If they do not think they're competent or if they have insufficiently resolved conflicts in previous stages, they may fail to learn and are likely to develop feelings of inferiority and inadequacy.

5. *Identity Versus Role Confusion* (ages thirteen to nineteen). During this period of confusion, adolescents are searching for an identity as they attempt to integrate social roles, emerging sexual feelings, and a sense of who they have been up to this point in their lives. Determining an occupation and developing a clear set of values and vision for the future are important during this stage.

Maslow's Motivation and Actualization Theory
Abraham Maslow (1970) postulated that humans have two basic sets of needs: (1) deficiency, or basic, needs, and (2) growth, or meta, needs. To achieve self-actualization, which is a growth need, physiological, safety, belongingness, and esteem needs must first be met. Maslow's

need hierarchy is conceptualized as follows, from the most basic to higher levels.

1. Physiological needs, such as hunger and thirst.
2. Safety needs, including the needs for security, protection, structure, limits, and freedom from fear and anxiety.
3. Belongingness and love needs. According to Maslow, all people need to feel accepted and wanted; mature love cannot exist until this basic need for belongingness is met.
4. Esteem needs, based on evaluation from others and respect for one's competence and accomplishments.
5. The need for self-actualization and cognitive understanding, including the desire to understand concepts that go beyond basic need gratification and to recognize one's unique potential. This stage usually is not accomplished during childhood or adolescence (Gumaer 1984).

Developmental Tasks of Adolescence

In her diary, Anne Frank (1968) captured a sense of adolescence in writing: "I think what is happening to me is so wonderful, and not only what can be seen on my body, but all that is taking place inside. I never discuss myself or any of these things with anybody; that is why I have to talk to myself about them" (p. 115).

Adolescence is a distinct and qualitatively different stage, because, with the exception of infancy, biological changes, including the capacity for reproduction, occur more rapidly at this time than during any other stage of development (Dusek 1991). According to Schave and Schave (1989), "quantum leaps" in cognition and moral reasoning take place, which provide the impetus for development of a distinct "self," separate from the family (p. 2).

Robert Havighurst (1972), well-known for his work in adolescent development, identified the following major tasks of adolescence that characterize this transitional period between childhood and adulthood:

1. Accepting one's physical makeup and acquiring a masculine or feminine sex role.
2. Developing appropriate relations with agemates of both sexes.
3. Becoming emotionally independent of parents and other adults.
4. Achieving the assurance that one will become economically independent.
5. Determining and preparing for a career and entering the job market.

6. Developing the cognitive skills and concepts necessary for social competence.
7. Understanding and achieving socially responsible behavior.
8. Preparing for marriage and family.
9. Acquiring values that are harmonious with an appropriate scientific world-picture.

During adolescence, social roles are unclear, which can result in shyness, increased sensitivity, or aggressiveness to mask insecurity (Ornum and Mordock 1986). Adolescents have a heightened sense of social consciousness, and they fear being rejected, ignored, or disapproved of. Many feel discontent and obsessed with their physical appearance and are bewildered by the way their bodies are changing. Sexuality adds a new dimension. Mood swings and heightened sensitivity, with a tendency to overreact, can create both internal and external conflict.

Elkind (1988) coined the term "imaginary audience" (p. 113), referring to adolescents' belief that others are as preoccupied with their behavior, appearance, thoughts, and feelings as they are. He contends that early adolescents in particular actually believe that they are the focus of attention.

Complementing the concept of the "imaginary audience" is the "personal fable" (Elkind 1988), in which the adolescent has an exaggerated sense of self-importance that makes him or her feel unique and special. The personal fable also incorporates a belief in one's own invulnerability—assuming that others can get pregnant but they can't, or that they won't get addicted to alcohol even if their friends do. The personal fable also explains why adolescents feel as if they are the only ones who can understand what they are experiencing.

Schave and Schave (1989) identified the "time warp" concept as an extension of adolescent egocentrism. The inability to link events, feelings, and situations characterizes this concept. Examples include the inability to connect being "grounded" with coming in late the night before, or failing a test with forgetting to study for it. If adolescents were to associate these events, they might be overwhelmed by guilt, shame, or anger, so the "time warp" enables them to avoid responsibility.

The Case of Clarissa

Seventeen-year-old Clarissa was referred for counseling. Although the problem at first appeared to be a rather typical relationship issue with a boyfriend. Clarissa's reactions indicated that this was more than a waning romance.

When Clarissa was twelve years old, her father died suddenly of a heart attack. Because her mother suffered from severe depression and had a drinking problem, this young girl was suddenly thrust into the role of family caregiver for her mother and two younger siblings. According to Clarissa, her mom had always gone into "rages," but they got much worse after her dad's death. During these rageful periods, the mother belittled Clarissa, calling her names and telling her how stupid, incompetent, and selfish she was. Clarissa reported that no matter how good or helpful she tried to be, her mom was still verbally abusive at unpredictable times.

Because she had so many responsibilities at home, Clarissa didn't participate in many school activities and did not spend much time with friends. She met Jay right after her sixteenth birthday. By that time, things had become even worse with her mother, and spending as much time away from home as possible was a relief. Jay provided that outlet. As the relationship developed, Clarissa became more and more dependent on his support. When she was with Jay, she had a sense of belonging and security.

At the time she came to counseling, Clarissa was extremely anxious and depressed. Jay had suggested that they not spend as much time together because this was their senior year and he didn't want to feel so tied down. Because of some issues that hadn't been resolved during earlier stages of her development, Clarissa wasn't able to weather the ups and downs of a relationship like many her age do. Instead, she hooked into the fear and abandonment she felt when her father died and was terrified that Jay would leave her, too. She likened his sudden change of behavior to her mother's erratic behavior, which had interfered with the development of her safety needs. In addition, because of her mother's belittling comments during a time when Clarissa was striving for competence, she developed feelings of inferiority and projected them onto this relationship ("He's leaving because I'm not good enough").

This case illustrates how a typical developmental problem becomes much more complex because of unmet needs or lack of task completion. It clearly shows how feelings and beliefs are influenced by past events, which in turn had an impact on a young person's development.

Given the increasing numbers of children and adolescents who are growing up in poverty, in dysfunctional families, or in violent, abusive environments one can assume that the physiological, safety, belonging, and esteem needs of many youths will not be met. Shame, guilt, and lack of trust likely will have a major impact on their lives. The impact on later development cannot be ignored.

COUNSELING WITH CHILDREN AND ADOLESCENTS

"First of all," he said, "if you can learn a simple trick, Scout, you'll get along a lot better with all kinds of folks. You never really understand a person until you consider things from his point of view...." "Sir?" "...until you climb into his skin and walk around in it" (from *To Kill a Mockingbird,* Harper Lee 1962, 113).

This quote comes to mind periodically when I sense that adults don't quite understand how difficult growing up can be, and how problems that seem minor to us can seem major to a child. I am reminded by my own insensitivity when, as a first-year teacher, I asked an eighth-grade boy to assume the part of a female in a skit. Scott was adamant about not doing this and became extremely upset when I asked a second time because I needed someone for the part. At the time, I had recently become a twenty-one-year-old widow, and I was frustrated with Scott, thinking that he was making a big deal over nothing, that his problems were nothing compared to mine. Now I wish I had looked at the situation from a developmental perspective so I might have realized why this simple request would be troublesome to an adolescent who feared ridicule and rejection by peers.

Empathy is critical in the counseling relationship. In addition, because children and adolescents are referred for counseling most often by parents or teachers, we have to consider the problem from a systems perspective and understand the developmental counseling model, which is primarily educative and preventive.

The Child in the System

"Mr. Johnson, will you please see Jeff as soon as possible? He simply doesn't pay attention in reading class, and you know how important reading is in first grade."

"Ms. Smith, my husband and I want you to see our teenage daughter. She is very defiant, and we can't get her to come in on time or tell us where she's been or who she's going with."

"Ms. Jones, the kids in my junior high science class are driving me crazy. They are so disrespectful, and they aren't learning the material. Over half of them will get D and F notices this quarter."

The message is: Counselor, fix the kid! The problem is: Maybe it's not just the kid that needs to be "fixed." In the examples just cited, consider that the science teacher may not be motivating her junior high students; the parents may be too permissive or inconsistent about consequences; or the first-grade teacher may be expecting the child to be attentive for long stretches of time.

Counselors must consider the context as they conceptualize the problem. If they do not, the interventions will likely fail and they will be addressing the symptom, not the cause. When the problem clearly has to be addressed within the educational, familial, or social system, the counselor may intervene with the child but also should consult with parents, teachers, and other significant people in the child's life to effect change at all levels.

Special Considerations

When working with a younger population, the following considerations must be taken into account:

1. Depending in part on age and ability, children may not be as verbal as adults, or able to identify or express feelings as readily.
2. Children's sense of time is more immediate. A problem today may not be a problem tomorrow, and children may be more impatient about getting the problem solved.
3. Children and adolescents are less likely to refer themselves for counseling and may resist it because they don't think they have a problem.
4. Because of their inability to understand that having a problem doesn't mean they are deficient or inept, younger clients don't want to admit that something is wrong.
5. Adolescents in particular may resent being the "identified patient" when they don't see themselves as being the source of the problem.

In working effectively with children, modification of traditional counseling approaches and interventions is critical. Counselors need to make greater use of play, art, music, concrete analogies and illustrations, bibliotherapy, self-awareness and decision-making activities, simulations, and problem-solving strategies. Counselors may have to teach children a "feeling word" vocabulary and give "homework" assignments to help reinforce concepts between sessions. Briefer counseling models should be considered.

The School Counselor's Role

The American School Counselor Association (1988) adopted the following definition of school counselors:

> School counselors are specifically credentialed professionals who work in school settings with students, parents, educators, and others within the community. They design and manage comprehensive developmental guidance programs to help students acquire skills in the social, personal, educational, and career areas necessary for living in a multicultural society. School counselors accomplish this by employing such interventions as guiding and counseling students individually or in small groups, by providing information through group guidance, by contributing to the development of effective learning environments, through student advocacy, and through consulting with others.

The 1988 Council for Accreditation of Counseling and Related Educational Programs described school counseling as follows:

> School counseling is designed to facilitate self-understanding and self-development through individual and small-group activities. Counseling denotes a professional relationship that involves a trained school counselor, a student, and significant others in the student's life. The focus of such relationships is on personal development and decision-making based on self-understanding and knowledge of the environment. Services provided by the school counseling program are comprehensive and developmental in nature. The school counselor possesses knowledge and skills that enable delivery of an effective program, which includes attention to cultural diversities and special needs. (p. 39)

The Developmental Model

The transition from childhood to adulthood is a growth process that involves a series of changes in social, emotional, and cognitive areas. Although many children and adolescents master the tasks and make the transitions quite successfully, others have varying degrees of difficulty growing up. Granted, some of this may be complicated by major stressors such as death of a parent or close family member, parental divorce, an alcoholic family, or a parent losing a job, but dealing with even the normal issues that accompany stages of development can be highly challenging. For this reason, counselors are encouraged to design counseling programs around a developmental model emphasizing prevention and education.

The developmental counseling approach assumes that all children benefit from assistance with developmental tasks and that programs should be structured to include activities and experiences that will facilitate growth. As noted in the American School Counselor position statement, the focus is on personal, educational, and career development.

Within the framework of a developmental counseling program, Vernon and Strub (1990) made several assumptions:

1. Counseling is for *all* students. The intent is to provide services that assist students in maximizing their potential.
2. The counselor is not the counseling program. Rather, the counselor works with parents, teachers, support personnel, and other school staff members to coordinate efforts to deliver components of the program and to help children in their personal, social, educational, and career development.
3. The program is primarily developmental and preventive, which implies that developmental tasks are identified and experiences are designed to educate children and adolescents about these tasks. If they learn coping strategies and have new knowledge and skills, presumably they will be better equipped to master developmental tasks and thus ward off more serious problems.
4. Given that all problems cannot be prevented because children often have little control over major situations affecting their lives, a comprehensive program includes remediation of problems through individual or small-group counseling. The frequency, intensity, and duration of the problem are assessed, and specific interventions are developed to address the issue.
5. Counseling programs are sequential in scope; experiences build on each other to ensure systematic exposure to developmental concepts.
6. Quality counseling programs are not a "fly by the seat of your pants" endeavor. They have student goals that form the basis of the program, with identified competencies for each grade level. Counselors are held accountable for coordinating and delivering a quality program.

Children and adolescents who participate in a comprehensive school counseling program have opportunities to discuss their problems with adults who listen to their feelings, clarify their misguided thinking, and assist them in their problem-solving process. In this way, a potential crisis can become a positive turning point, and a major crisis stands a better chance of being resolved.

CONCLUSION

Frequently when a child or adolescent comes for counseling, I ask, "Can you tell me more about your problem and why you are here?" Invariably the response is a shrug of the shoulders accompanied by "I don't know." This is not surprising. Ornum and Mordock (1986) stated:

> Children rarely talk directly about their worries because they rarely under-
> stand their role in their problems. Not only are they incapable of seeing that
> their present behavior is an incorrect effort to solve a problem, but they also
> are incapable of identifying the problem, the kind of help they need, or the
> kinds of relevant questions they should ask to get help. (p. 19)

Developmental counseling programs "second guess" the student by presenting information and normalizing problems. In this way, young people begin to see that they are not alone and that they won't be stigmatized or labeled as "crazy" because of a specific worry or concern. Children, and adolescents in particular, are scared of being overwhelmed by their own vulnerability.

Counseling children and adolescents is a challenge much different than counseling adults. Given the multitude of problems that children growing up in a contemporary society face, we must search for effective ways to work with this age-group. As Roger Lewin (in Ornum and Mordock 1986) stated, "Too often we give children answers to remember rather than problems to solve (p. 1)." Helping children learn to solve their problems is a way of empowering them so they can live healthy, satisfying lives.

SUMMARY

Children and adolescents today experience increased stress. In addition to the inherent developmental stressors, they face changing family structures, AIDS, substance abuse, teen pregnancy, violence, and cultural diversity. Suicide and depression are more common for this age-group. Given the multitude of problems that children growing up in a contemporary society face, it is critical that we search for effective ways to deal with this age-group.

Developmental tasks are skills, attitudes, knowledge, and functions that people must master at various stages of development in order to become well-adjusted, functional individuals. Developmental theory is illustrated in the models of Erik Erikson and Abraham Maslow. Erikson's five stages pertaining to children and adolescents are: trust versus mistrust, autonomy versus shame and doubt, initiative versus guilt, industry versus inferiority, and identity versus role confusion. Maslow's progression of human needs is: physiological needs, safety needs, belongingness and love needs, esteem needs, and, finally, the need for self-actualization and cognitive understanding (usually not reached until some time during adulthood).

Effective counseling with children and adolescents considers developmental levels in designing interventions. School counseling, which is intended to promote development through individual and small-group counseling and classroom activities, also assumes a developmental approach to facilitate growth.

REFERENCES

American School Counselor Association. 1988. Definition of school counselor. In J. Rotter (1990), Elementary school counselor preparation: Past, present, and future. *Elementary School Guidance and Counseling* 24(3):183.

Capuzzi, D. 1988. Adolescent suicide: Prevention and intervention. In J. Carlson and J. Lewis, eds., *Counseling the adolescent: Individual, family, and school interventions* (pp. 41–55). Denver: Love Publishing.

Council for Accreditation of Counseling and Related Educational Programs. 1988. In J. Rotter (1990), Elementary school counselor preparation: Past, present, and future. *Elementary School Guidance and Counseling* 24(3):180–188.

Dusek, J. B. 1991. *Adolescent development and behavior.* Englewood Cliffs, NJ: Prentice Hall.

Elkind, D. 1988. *The hurried child: Growing up too fast too soon.* New York: Addison-Wesley.

Erikson, E. 1968. *Identity: Youth and crisis.* New York: Norton.

Frank, A. 1968. *The diary of a young girl.* New York: Washington Square Press.

Gerler, E. R., J. C. Ciechalski, and L. D. Parker. 1990. *Elementary counseling in a changing world.* Ann Arbor, MI: ERIC Counseling and Personnel Services Clearinghouse.

Glosoff, H., and C. Koprowicz. 1990. *Children achieving potential: An introduction to elementary school counseling and state-level policies.* Washington, DC: National Conference of State Legislatures; and Alexandria, VA: American Counseling Association.

Gumaer, J. 1984. *Counseling and therapy for children.* New York: Free Press.

Hackbarth, S. G., H. D. Murphy, and J. P. McQuary. 1991. Identifying sexually abused children by using kinetic family drawings. *Elementary School Guidance and Counseling* 25(4): 255–260.

Havighurst, R. J. 1972. *Developmental tasks and education.* New York: David McKay.

Hayes, R. L., and N. Cryer. 1988. When adolescents give birth to children: A developmental approach to the issue of teen pregnancy. In J. Carlson and J. Lewis, eds., *Counseling the adolescent: Individual, family, and school interventions* (pp. 21–40). Denver: Love Publishing.

Hipple, J. 1990. Suicide in children and adolescents. In K. Stiles and T. Kottman, eds., Mutual storytelling: An intervention for depressed and suicidal children. *School Counselor* 37(5): 337.

Kuczen, B. 1987. *Childhood stress: How to raise a healthier, happier child.* New York: Dell Publishing.

Lachance, L. 1985. *Teen pregnancy: An ERIC/CAPS fact sheet.* Ann Arbor, MI: ERIC Clearinghouse on Counseling & Personnel Services. (ERIC Document Reproduction Service No. ED 266–340)

Lee, H. 1962. *To kill a mockingbird.* New York: Fawatt Popular Library.

Lewin, R. 1986. Crisis: Lost sense of self. In W. V. Ornum and J. B. Mordock, *Crisis counseling with children and adolescents.* New York: Continuum Publishing.

Maslow, A. H. 1970. *Motivation and personality.* 2d ed. New York: Harper and Row.

Ornum, W. V., and J. B. Mordock. 1986. *Crisis counseling with children and adolescents.* New York: Continuum Publishing.

O'Rourke, K. 1990. Recapturing hope: Elementary school support groups for children of alcoholics. *Elementary School Guidance and Counseling,* 25: 2, 107–115.

Schave, D., and B. Schave. 1989. *Early adolescence and the search for self: A developmental perspective.* New York: Praeger.

Stefanowski-Harding, S. 1990. Child suicide: A review of the literature and implications for school counselors. *The School Counselor* 37: 328–336.

Thompson, C. L., and L. B. Rudolph. 1992. *Counseling Children.* Belmont, CA: Brooks/Cole.

Vernon, A., and R. Strub. 1990. *Developmental guidance program implementation.* Cedar Falls, IA: University of Northern Iowa.

Winbush, R. A. 1988. Growing pains: Explaining adolescent violence with developmental theory. In J. Carlson and J. Lewis, eds., *Counseling the adolescent: Individual, family, and school interventions* (pp. 57–71). Denver: Love Publishing.

2 Individual Counseling: Process

Ardis Sherwood-Hawes

Women's Program
Clark College
Vancouver, Washington

The conceptualization, assessment, diagnosis, and treatment of emotional and behavioral problems in young people are still in the early stages of development. Public and professional education about the facts and issues specifically related to the mental health of children and adolescents is a fairly recent phenomenon. Currently, there are at least 230 different approaches to therapy with children and adolescents. Unfortunately, only a few of these methods have been investigated empirically.

Despite the estimation that between 12 and 17 percent of children and adolescents in the United States have emotional and behavioral problems, the literature pertaining to development and identification of effective treatments for the emotional and behavioral disorders of children and adolescents is rare (Kazdin, Bass, Ayers, and Rodgers 1990). Compounding the problem of limited research is the fact that most of the published research investigating treatment for children and adolescents is methodologically unsound (Barrnett, Docherty, and Frommelt 1991; Chess 1988; Jenkins and Smith 1991; Kazdin et al. 1990; Schneider 1989).

> There is little consistent, systematic and controlled evaluation of treatment approaches for young children with psychosocial or developmental disorders, and the past decade of research has not produced much in the way of new knowledge (McGuire and Earls 1991, 143)

Most of the investigation of the etiology and treatment of psychopathology has been conducted with adult populations and directed toward adult treatment strategies. The counseling approaches and interventions for children and adolescents traditionally have been grounded in these adult research studies. Children and adolescents often are diagnosed according to adult classification systems, and plans for treatment are based on modified versions of approaches designed for adults (Kazdin 1989; Tuma 1989). Generally, these altered models fail to address the idiosyncratic problems of children and adolescents (e.g., developmental changes, environmental factors) that can mitigate the effectiveness of the therapeutic process (Kazdin et al. 1990).

DEVELOPMENTAL CONSIDERATIONS

Interventions that are appropriate for adult populations can be ineffective and even harmful with children and adolescents (Brandell 1988). During their course of growth, young people process experiences differently because of the continuous changes in their physical, cognitive, social, and emotional skills. As examples, children who have not yet mastered language skills rarely profit from interventions predicated on verbal communication (Brandell 1988), and children who are in the preoperational phases of development may find the use of abstract rules for behavior control confusing, overwhelming, and detrimental to their self-esteem (Kendall, Lerner, and Craighead 1984).

> Whenever we ask another human being to do something they cannot possibly do due to lack of biological or emotional development, we are mirroring to them that there is something wrong with them, thereby setting off feelings of shame and rage. It is an injury to the deepest parts of the self. (Brenner 1988, 184)

Knowledge of the stages of chronological growth can facilitate understanding of the "average" child, yet many other factors (e.g., gender, family history, school experience) influence the developmental process. All children are unique individuals with distinctive backgrounds, environments, temperamental traits, cognitive skills, and social and emotional capabilities; their development is influenced by an interaction between themselves and their environments. For example, a child's response to his or her parents has a significant bearing on their reaction to the child, and the parents' feedback to the child has a direct impact on the child's developmental process (Chess 1988; Ellis 1990).

In addition, the maturation process can be disrupted by injurious experiences during critical growth stages of childhood. Children who encounter neglect, abuse, losses, or other detrimental environmental conditions (especially if disturbances occur during certain sensitive developmental periods) may be slower to attain the expected emotional and behavioral skills of their chronological agemates (Kilgore 1988; Norton 1981), or they may revert to earlier developmental levels to obtain comfort and avoid intolerable frustrations (Ellis 1990). Acute trauma, such as sexual molestation, can interfere with the child's normal development in the future, and the child may become fixated in an earlier developmental period. Therapy may involve re-creation of this period so the child can productively work through the developmental tasks of that stage (Clarkson and Fish 1988, Miller and Boe 1990).

The developmental processes of memory, language, conditional thinking, categorization abilities, and perception of rules can have a direct impact on symptoms children manifest and will determine whether therapeutic interventions will be propitious, useless, or even injurious to the mental health of children and adolescents (Kendall et al. 1984). A synopsis of criteria for professionals (Brandell 1988; Kazdin 1989; Kendall et al. 1984) suggests that they should:

1. Thoroughly understand the behaviors connected with each developmental stage.
2. Recognize which behaviors should normally ameliorate over the course of development and which will require treatment.
3. Comprehend how a multitude of interacting variables (biological, psychological, and sociocultural) can influence all developmental levels of functioning.
4. Be aware of the individual's personal and developmental history.
5. Understand the individual's unique capacity for development.
6. Be knowledgeable about the probability of future developmental events.
7. Thoroughly appreciate the effect cultural background may have on all aspects of assessment and therapy.

REFERRAL, ASSESSMENT, AND DIAGNOSIS

Some behaviors that may indicate maladjustment at one developmental stage are perfectly normal for other periods of growth (Clarkson and Fish 1988). As an extreme example, the sudden aggressive attacks, temper tantrums, and healthy negativism typical of the two-year-old would be considered inappropriate for the adolescent. During certain developmental periods, children and adolescents commonly show certain behaviors (e.g., lying, destructiveness, defiance, deviousness, hyperactivity, fighting) that can indicate maladjustment and emotional disturbance in adults. Adults often are perplexed and troubled by these seemingly aberrant behaviors and may refer children to treatment because they do not realize that, during the normal developmental cycle, these behaviors tend to abate naturally without any special intervention (Kazdin 1988).

Most children and adolescents are involuntary clients because they are referred by other individuals, such as parents or teachers. Counselors must be alert to all the factors surrounding the referral to counseling, be cautious in their diagnosis of young people, and avoid stigmatizing children and adolescents with premature labeling. "Where diagnoses are made, they often prove unreliable" (Seiffge-Krenke 1988, 460).

Children may be manifesting maladaptive symptoms because they are victims of sexual, emotional, or physical abuse, or they may be reacting to stressful situations in the home or other environments. Children who are abused or neglected often develop pernicious adjustment behaviors, and parents may attempt to conceal information about inadequate or injurious childrearing practices. Studies indicate that an adult's perception of a child's mental health is closely related to his or her own psychopathology, and children are more frequently referred to treatment by adults who are experiencing depression, marital dissension, low self-esteem, anxiety, and distressful life circumstances (Kazdin 1988, 1989). Counselors also should consider the possibility that referring adults are indirectly seeking treatment for themselves.

Because children and adolescents generally are identified by others as having emotional or behavioral problems, they usually do not acknowledge their need for assistance (Brandell 1988). Adolescents may resist the idea of counseling because they cannot discern any value or reason for it. Studies suggest that adolescents are reluctant to discuss their problems with adults, and preadolescent and early adolescent girls may be especially recalcitrant (Lane and Chazan 1988). Seiffge-Krenke (1988) found that, among younger children, more boys than girls attend counseling centers. This situation is reversed around age fifteen, when more girls are apt to seek professional assistance.

The unwillingness to disclose personal information to people who are older may arise from certain developmental processes specific to this age-group. For example, young women often are conflicted by a desire to be close to their mothers, yet fear that this closeness will result in loss of self-identity (Lane and Chazan 1988). The struggle for autonomy and the process of detachment from parental authority may account for teenagers' tendency to shift from discussing personal problems with parents or other adults and turn to peer relationships for intimate communication. Moreover, previous unpleasant interactions with parents (e.g., verbal abuse, poor communication, perceived lack of support) may influence the adolescent's attitude toward therapeutic assistance (Seiffge-Krenke 1988).

ETHICAL AND LEGAL CONSIDERATIONS OF CONFIDENTIALITY

Confidentiality is the issue of disclosure or nondisclosure of client-to-counselor communication to outside sources. In counseling children and adolescents, mental health professionals do not seem to take a standard, unified position. Some studies indicate that most counselors prefer to grant adolescents the same confidentiality rights as adults; school counselors, however, tend to believe they are responsible for giving the parents information about the counseling process. The most common approaches to issues of confidentiality for children and adolescents are:

1. *Absolute confidentiality.* Regardless of the client's age, no information is shared without the client's expressed consent.
2. *Limited confidentiality.* The client is informed at the onset of therapy that information will be shared when it is deemed to be pertinent to the therapeutical process.
3. *Informed forced consent.* The client is notified of the intent to disclose with or without the client's permission.
4. No guarantee of confidentiality. (Hendrix 1991)

A consensus exists among mental health professionals that the issues of confidentiality for children and adolescents should differ from those of adults, yet counselors are not given specific guidelines as to these differences (American Counseling Association [ACA] Governing Council 1988; American Mental Health Counselors Association [AMHCA] 1989; American Psychological Association [APA] 1981). The AMHCA (1989) and the APA (1981) do stipulate that whenever a mental health provider is working with minors or other individuals who are unable to give voluntary, informed consent for disclosure of personal material, the interests of the client must be the therapist's primary concern. "Confidentiality exists for the benefit of the client and when that benefit ceases to exist or is overridden by other factors, alternatives to absolute confidentiality must be applied" (Hendrix 1991, 332).

When selecting the optimal approach to confidentiality for their clients, counselors should consider:

1. The client's age and capability.
2. The importance of disclosures to the client's therapeutic progress.
3. The possibility that disclosures may be detrimental to the client or the therapeutic relationship.
4. The formal ethical standards of the profession.

5. Requirements of the state legal system and of the agency or institution where they work.

In many instances, counselors are required to discuss cases with supervisors, and, during practicum or internship training, group supervision sessions may entail sharing confidential material and reviewing tapes of sessions with supervisors and other members of the training class. Also, most parents expect feedback on their child's counseling experience, for a multitude of reasons ranging from a genuine desire to assist the child to fear that certain disclosures will embarrass, shame, or even incriminate them.

When deciding whether to reveal confidential information to parents, counselors must exercise good judgment and disclose only the details that benefit the client. Sometimes minor children are under court order to be evaluated or to receive counseling. When services are mandated by the judicial system, decisions regarding confidentiality may not be under the counselor's total control because the mandate usually stipulates that the client's progress and status be revealed to the court (Strein and Hershenson 1991).

Counselors must define their ethical and legal boundaries regarding the issue of confidentiality for minors, and they should make every effort to ensure that the parents and the child fully understand the process of therapy and the client's rights. Most professionals recommend that, at the onset of the therapeutic relationship, counselors use an informed consent form to notify their clients about the specific guidelines and limitations of confidentiality (Robinson 1991). The U.S. Supreme Court has granted individuals over age fourteen the same self-determined mental health care rights as adults, including the right to give voluntary, informed consent. Robinson, however, advised that when the client is under age eighteen, the parents or legal guardians sign the consent form. Counselors should clearly explain to the minor client, in language appropriate to the child's development, potential situations in which confidentiality may have to be broken, and, if possible, also attain the child's assent. In addition, when confidentiality has to be breached, minor clients should be informed of the counselor's specific intent in disclosing personal material and be involved as much as possible in the decision-making process (Corey and Corey 1987; Hendrix 1991; Robinson 1991).

All professionals, including medical professionals, teachers, mental health professionals, social workers, law enforcement officials, or child care providers, are required by law to report specific situations that are potentially harmful to children. Under certain circumstances, state and federal laws abolish clients' privileged communication rights, and counselors are legally obligated to break confidentiality when: (1) child abuse or neglect is suspected; (2) a minor client indicates an intent to harm himself or herself; and (3) a child or adolescent discloses a plan to harm another person (Robinson 1991). In addition, counselors must warn intended victims or inform children's parents when they suspect a potential for self-directed injury (Corey 1986). Failure to comply with state regulations and report one's suspicions that a child needs protection from adverse conditions is a misdemeanor in most states, punishable by a fine, imprisonment, or both. Some professionals also are subject to civil suits (Nazario 1988). For example, mental health professionals who fail to detect and report physical abuse of a minor client to the proper authorities (e.g., Child Protective Services) or who refrain from reporting an adult client's disclosure of child abuse may be sued for malpractice or negligence.[1] Clients' children often can preserve their cause of action against a counselor until the child reaches the age of majority (Guyer 1990). As state laws vary regarding legal aspects of confidentiality and child protection, counselors must thoroughly familiarize themselves with the laws of the state in which they practice.

Answers to the dilemma of confidentiality are not always clear-cut. Mental health professionals must realize the limits of their expertise. If uncertain about ethical and legal responsibilities, mental health professionals are advised to consult with colleagues or seek qualified supervision to help them determine an appropriate course of action (Corey 1986; Guyer 1990; Meier 1989).

SELECTING A COUNSELING STRATEGY

What methods work best with which clients under which conditions? Professionals often disagree. Relationship-based therapies, focusing on the development of close interpersonal relationships with clients, are the most frequently used methods of treating the behavioral and emotional problems of childhood. In applying these methods, counselors provide an accepting, predictable, safe environment in which young people can fully express their thoughts and feelings (Brenner 1988).

Counselors should avoid excessive questioning of and interpreting for children and adolescents, as these distancing interventions can damage their sense of self. Instead, counselors should reflect or mirror

---

[1]Noncompliance may occur when the therapist makes an independent determination that reporting the abuse will damage the therapeutic relationship and, thus, interrupt treatment strategies that serve the abused child's long-term interests.

children's verbalizations and symbolic gestures and tentatively label the feelings and actions presented. Counselors have to respond empathically to children's feelings (e.g., rage, grief, hatred, helplessness) and verbalizations (e.g., experience of abandonment, abuse). In doing this, they are acknowledging, respecting, and validating the children's thoughts and feelings; giving their emotions shape and form; and establishing a bond between themselves and their clients. Therapeutic progress with children and adolescents often comes merely through the release of blocked emotions that have impeded the emotional growth process (Oaklander 1988).

Other professionals maintain that interventions based on teaching interpersonal problem-solving skills might be more beneficial for children with emotional and behavioral problems. Studies demonstrate that young people who are emotionally or physically abused by significant others have more behavioral disturbances and an impaired ability to interact interpersonally with their peers. Research indicates that early disturbed peer interactions predict later maladjustment. Therefore, mental health professionals plan therapeutic treatment strategies that facilitate the development of adaptive social problem-solving skills (Haskett 1990). In research conducted with children ages seven to thirteen, Kazdin, Bass, Siegel, and Thomas (1989) found that variations of cognitive-behavioral problem-solving skills training are significantly more effective in reducing antisocial, impulsive, and aggressive behaviors and increasing prosocial behaviors than are modes of relationship therapy.

Kendall et al. (1984) cautioned that interventions that provide children with cognitive strategies for solving problems may be unsuccessful and even detrimental when used with children who are developmentally incapable or otherwise unable to process this form of therapy. When selecting a plan for treatment, counselors should match the intervention with the client's cognitive level and modify their strategies to address the unique and special problems of each individual child and adolescent.

Parents, family, and school factors all contribute to the functioning of children and adolescents, and childhood maladaptive behavior is not easily isolated from inadequate parenting practices and dysfunctional family interactions (Kazdin 1989). Should counseling interventions be directed solely toward the child or adolescent, or should therapy incorporate all domains—child, parents, family, community influences—into the counseling process?

Advantages of Individual Counseling

A combination of the many advantages of the individual counseling approach can facilitate the child's optimal therapeutic progress (Clarkson and Fish 1988). Individual therapy focuses on the child's unique personality, developmental process, personal distress, and special need for assistance. Because the counselor concentrates on nurturing the child, the child can more quickly develop a trusting relationship with a caring adult.

The therapeutic approach and strategies can be formulated to accommodate the child's explicit needs, and when counselors do not have to deal with information others, such as family members, contribute, they can more easily determine the child's intrapsychic dynamics and specifically work with the child's fears, anxieties, fantasies, and unresolved issues. When seen alone, the child has less fear of family reprisals when confiding to the therapist. In addition, when family members are forced to attend joint therapy sessions, they may blame the child for their mandatory involvement in therapy and may attempt to sabotage the counseling process (Clarkson and Fish 1988).

Many parent characteristics that place a child at risk for behavioral or emotional problems or developmental delay also contraindicate their involvement with intervention (McGuire and Earls 1991, 148). Parents who are distressed, discouraged, or depressed may resist or drop out of therapeutic services. Because inadequate parenting is correlated directly with childhood emotional and behavioral problems, directing the intervention toward the child might be more useful (McGuire and Earls 1991). Many children are not nourished by a stable and functional family atmosphere that promotes support, encouragement, and effective problem-solving and coping skills. When parents do not deal with distressing events adequately or successfully, their children may perceive their own situation as hopeless and fail to develop the necessary skills of survival (Allberg and Chu 1990). The literature suggests that child therapy can have a positive impact on the parents and other family members. When parents refer their child for therapy, they often feel more comfortable about the counseling process and are encouraged to seek additional forms of counseling (e.g., marital, family, or individual therapy) (Clarkson and Fish 1988).

Disadvantages of Individual Counseling

Therapies focusing exclusively on the child may inadequately address the overall problems and may ignore certain contextual factors, such as childrearing practices, that directly contribute to the child's symptoms (Kazdin et al. 1989). Furthermore, when the child is seen alone, the other family members may perceive the child as "owning" the blame for family problems. The child may internalize this blame and come to believe that he or she is responsible for evoking changes within the family.

As other major disadvantages, the child may feel isolated from the family, and the child may not have a strong enough ego to maintain the benefits of counseling in a dysfunctional family. The family system may have to be changed for the child's growth to endure (Clarkson and Fish 1988).

DEVELOPING THE COUNSELING RELATIONSHIP

The Initial Interview

The format and focus of the initial interview depend on the goals the counselor has predetermined. Some counselors prefer to use the first session to collect pertinent information about the client. Others elect to begin to establish the therapeutic relationship. Both approaches are appropriate. The structure of the session, however, differs according to the counselor's purpose. When the goal of the initial interview is to gather information about the client, the session is counselor-focused, and he or she predominately uses probes, accents, closed questions, and requests for clarification to obtain data about the client. In contrast, during the relationship-oriented first interview, the concentration is on the client's feelings, and counselor responses include restatement, reflection of feelings, summarization of feelings, request for clarification, and acknowledgment of nonverbal behavior (Gladding 1988).

Literature has emphasized, as a prelude to treatment, the importance of assessment/diagnosis (e.g., accumulation of subjective and objective data from various sources, such as psychological tests, school personnel, parents). Brandell (1988) warned that rigorous diagnostic procedures often ignore the child's own narrative and can harm the future counselor/child relationship. If the counselor conducting the clinical assessment becomes the person responsible for treating the child, he or she must make a critical shift from obtaining objective data to creating a nurturing environment in which the child can subjectively disclose his or her experience. During this difficult transition, the delicate therapeutic relationship may be irrevocably damaged. The counselor should keep in mind that "the outcome of any therapeutic intervention is determined by the quality of the relationship between the therapist and the troubled child" (Clarkson and Fish 1988, 131).

When counseling children, mental health practitioners may have to compromise assessment procedures to build a therapeutic alliance with the child. Atlas (1990) recommends that counselors use semistructured play to (1) obtain information necessary for assessment and diagnosis and (2) promote a sense of relatedness and connection with the child. Oaklander (1988) advocates an informal approach for the initial interview. She does not use an intake form but instead gathers data from the first (and subsequent) session. The child and one or both parents are interviewed together so the child can hear the discussion, get the statements (e.g., parent's version of the presenting problem) clarified, and contribute to the process. This also enables the counselor to observe the child's reactions, witness the dynamics between parent and child, and begin to establish a trusting relationship with the child. The interaction between the child and the therapist during the initial session can be crucial, as it can determine whether the child will trust the counselor and the counseling process.

In addition, information from other sources may impact the counselor's impression of the child. Oaklander (1988) wrote:

> Before I start working with a child, I sometimes receive stacks of papers relating to the child: test results, diagnostic reports, court proceedings, school records. They make interesting reading, but when it comes right down to it, I can deal with the child only as she presents herself to me. If I rely on the information given me about the child to form my basis of working with her, I would be dealing with what's written on a piece of paper, rather than with the child. Written on these papers are *someone else's* perceptions, findings, and often unfair judgements. So I must begin with the child, from where she is *with me*, regardless of anything else I hear, read, or even diagnose about her myself. She is making contact with someone who is willing to accept her as she is at the moment, without an overlay of preconceived biases and judgements about her. (p. 184)

As children often have limited verbal skills, they may act out behaviors and use symbolic play to communicate their distress (Brenner 1988). Moreover, a childhood trauma may be an experience that is beyond words (Miller and Boe 1990). Childrens' use of symbolic gestures and objects can give the counselor valuable knowledge about their unconscious processes. The counselor can glean a great deal of information about children by observing them as they perform certain activities. For example, through play, children may reveal a need for protection. In sand play therapy, children may build a fence or barrier around objects, bury objects, create safe places (e.g., churches, islands, castles) for play figures, or use allies to protect play figures (Campos 1988). In addition, symbolic movement can: (1) illustrate the types of problem-solving strategies children utilize (Brenner 1988); (2) indicate feelings of inadequacy and low self-esteem (e.g., when asked to draw a picture, children may approach the task tentatively and anxiously) (Oaklander 1988); and (3) reveal self-concept through the play object they choose to represent themselves (e.g., victim, aggressor) (Campos 1988).

An important component in the initial stages of every counseling relationship is the formation of a relationship in which clients can safely discuss, explore, and emotionally respond to their concerns, problems, and distressful circumstances; understand how these life situations influence their behavior; and move toward positive personal growth. Therefore, one of the first goals of a counselor is to establish and maintain an equal, productive, and encouraging relationship based on mutual trust, respect, and cooperation (Mosak 1984).

Counselor Qualities

Corey (1986) maintained that the counselor's demeanor is the crucial variable that determines the outcome of counseling. Carl Rogers (Meador and Rogers 1984) asserted that when counselors proficiently create a climate of *empathy, genuineness, and acceptance* in the therapeutic relationship, optimal client growth will follow. Counselors communicate empathy when they are able to accurately perceive the client's experience and clearly convey that understanding to the client. Counselors fulfill the condition of genuineness when they are completely open and honest with themselves and with clients and reveal themselves authentically as fallible individuals who are also experiencing spiritual and emotional growth. This means that counselors congruently demonstrate their humanness to clients and not hide behind a protecting but confusing and alienating professional facade. When counselors have a high level of self-awareness and are willing to fully share their personhood in the relationship, clients are encouraged to be more honest and open with themselves. In acceptance, counselors transmit feelings of unconditional positive regard or absolute and unrestricted caring for their clients. When clients are the recipients of empathy, genuineness, and acceptance in the counseling relationship, they usually become more willing to love and accept themselves and to take the risks necessary to achieve growth-oriented changes.

Counselors should be aware of their personal biases, philosophies, and values, thoroughly understand the impact these beliefs can have on the therapeutic process, and try not to impose their own values on clients. Because counselors' values are bound to have some influence on the counseling relationship, counselors should be willing to openly reveal and discuss their beliefs and prejudices with their clients. A vital role of the counselor is to promote client self-assurance, help clients discover their own solutions, encourage freedom of action and autonomous behavior, and enable clients to trust themselves and become more self-responsible and self-directed. Additional qualities of the therapeutic counselor include (Corey 1986):

- respect for self
- self-determination
- openness to change
- self-awareness (knowledge of strengths and weaknesses, needs, conflicts, defenses, biases, and vulnerabilities)
- courage (willingness to take risks)
- capacity to give and receive love
- ability to accept and willingly admit mistakes
- orientation toward continuous growth

Primarily, effective counselors are present for their clients, and they use specific behaviors to encourage open expression of their thoughts and feelings. The relationship is formulated as the counselor attentively listens, responds empathetically, accurately identifies and clarifies feelings and goals, conveys a positive belief in the client's capacity for change, and relates an authentic enthusiasm toward the mutual interaction (Corey 1986; Gladding 1988; Terry, Burden, and Pederson 1991).

Physical Setting

The physical setting in which counseling takes place should be comfortable and appealing to clients. As seating arrangement and physical distance between counselor and client can affect the therapeutic relationship, the counselor should be aware of individual clients' preferences regarding personal space (Gladding 1988). The comfort level is influenced by many variables, including age, gender, cultural background, and personal experiences.

Counselors should let children determine their own comfort zone and should offer choices in places to sit. Professionals who work with adolescents and children should not position themselves so close that their physical presence is threatening or dominating, and they should sit at eye level with their youthful clients. Counselors must understand and be alert to nonverbal signals that point to a violation of personal space.

Basic Attending Skills

Good attending behaviors—eye contact, body language, facial expression—encourage communication by transmitting the message to clients that counselors respect them and are interested in what they have to say. To convey involvement with clients, counselors should face the client squarely with a relaxed, nondefensive, and open posture (e.g., uncrossed arms and legs). They should lean forward slightly toward the client, maintain an eye contact that indicates attentive interest, and be facially responsive to the client's verbalizations. The counselor's vocal tone should be warm, pleasant, and caring and at the same time convey assurance and self-confidence (Gladding 1988; Terry et al. 1991).

Active Listening Skills

The ability to accurately listen to and understand a client's narrative is an essential component of effective counseling. Mental health professionals have to comprehend what clients are saying, and clients need to know the counselor has heard them correctly (Terry et al. 1991). In active listening, counselors clearly comprehend both the facts and the emotions of client messages, and they respond in ways that reveal their understanding (Gilliland and James 1988). Two techniques that communicate this recognition to clients are *restatement of content* and *reflection of feelings.*

Restating content means letting children know the counselor is listening to what they have to say by repeating their verbalizations. Restatement encourages clients to elaborate on a subject. Overuse of this technique, however, can create a sterile and superficial counseling relationship. Therefore, counselors should use it sparingly, interjecting connecting phrases such as "I hear" to strengthen the relationship between themselves and their young clients. "I hear you are afraid when you're alone" is more connecting than "You are afraid when you are alone." In reflecting feelings, counselors mirror feelings back to clients, revealing what they see (nonverbal) and hear (Gladding 1988).

Reflecting feelings and restating content can help establish rapport between counselors and clients. Children are gratified when someone hears and understands them, and this positive reinforcement increases the likelihood that they will like and identify with the listener. In addition, restatements and reflections often help young clients acknowledge and identify certain thoughts and feelings. Often, individuals are unaware of their experience until they hear someone else express it back to them. Counselors also can gain insight into their clients' inner worlds by attending to and highlighting their use of metaphors and their key words and phrases or tendencies to change the subject when certain topics are introduced.

Observation Skills

Empathetic understanding entails accurate identification and reflection of clients' unspoken cues, messages, and behaviors. Counselors should carefully observe clients' body language (movements, posture, skin color, gesture, facial expressions, breathing), understand the implications of nonverbal communication, and reflect their observation of nonverbal behavior to their clients (Gilliland and James 1988). When a client's verbal statement is incongruent with his or her nonverbal actions, the client is transmitting conflicting messages. Most professionals believe nonverbal responses more accurately reflect clients' internal processes and, after trust is established in the counseling relationship, should bring these inconsistencies to their clients' attention (Meier 1989). For example, the counselor might say, "I notice you're frowning as you tell me about the fun you had with your friends last night." Counselors should merely acknowledge and comment on clients' nonverbal behaviors and not attempt to interpret their meanings (Gladding 1988).

Communication Skills

Counselors need strategies that enable them to gather information while they simultaneously keep the therapeutic process focused on clients. Counselors should develop subtle, unobtrusive communication skills that encourage involvement, foster insight, and facilitate behavior changes. The bottom line: Counselors should generally talk less than their clients. Counselors can use a multitude of methods to convey a sense of commitment and concern, invite client participation, and inconspicuously manage the therapeutic process. Some of the most common counseling communication techniques are (Gilliland and James 1988; Gladding 1988; Meier 1989; Terry et al. 1991):

1. *Initial contact.* Counselors can facilitate trust during the early stages of the therapeutic relationship by allowing children and adolescents to determine a comfortable depth of interaction. For example, if a youthful client initiates a conversation about where he or she went yesterday, he or she has made contact with the counselor. The counselor should acknowledge this opening, expand it, and use it to make a deeper, more meaningful contact with the client.

2. *Minimal encouragers.* Minimal encouragers (e.g., nonverbal

gestures such as nodding, smiling, brief utterances such as "uh-huh") are active, yet unobtrusive, ways to invite verbalization.

3. *Accents.* Accents are words that are emphasized. Accents can be in the form of a question, repeating the client's last word or phrase (Child: "When my mother isn't home, I get real scared." Counselor: "Real scared?''). Accents also can identify metaphors and key words and phrases. Accent words can encourage further disclosure. For example, counselors may offer "and" or "and then" when they want clients to continue their narrative.

4. *Open-ended questions.* Open-ended questions invite the client to provide the ending. These queries usually begin with the words *who, what, where,* or *how* and require more than a one- or two-word response ("How do you feel when you're alone?"). They encourage clients to talk and thus participate in the therapeutic relationship. Counselors should not ask *why* to obtain information from clients because this word is often associated with disapproval, and clients tend to feel defensive when requested to explain their actions or feelings.

5. *Closed questions.* Closed questions are used to gather limited information or to focus on specific points of the client's narrative. They typically elicit a one- or two-word response and tend to discourage open discussions ("Do you feel afraid when you're alone?").

6. *Requests for clarification.* Counselors must state when they are confused or when they do not understand the client's message. Requests for clarification also can be used to slow down a frantic narrative, focus on key points, or reintroduce a topic that clients mention, then quickly avoid.

7. *Silence.* Beginning counselors often feel uncomfortable with silence in counseling sessions and tend to jump in too quickly when a client stops talking. Actually, silence is therapeutic; it permits clients to process their own thoughts and feelings. Counselors can use silence deliberately to give clients the opportunity to digest and internalize new knowledge gained in the therapeutic relationship. In addition, remaining silent while nonverbally attending to clients expresses a deep sense of empathy.

8. *Paraphrasing.* Paraphrasing means rephrasing the essence of clients' messages and reflecting personal observations of those messages to clients. Paraphrasing conveys counselor under-

standing, facilitates clients' insights into their own experiences, and enables counselors to verify their interpretation of what clients say.

9. *Summarization.* Through summarization, the counselor paraphrases a longer conversation, the high points of a session, or the cumulation of several sessions. Summarization often brings a focus to a multitude of seemingly overwhelming problems and can provide structure to the counseling process. Counselors can use summarization to concisely organize clients' thoughts and feelings, recap and connect important themes, outline progress, give direction, and plan future strategies.

Ineffective Counselor Behaviors

Advice-giving, lecturing, and excessive questioning block effective counselor/client communication and thwart the essential counseling goal of empowering clients to grow in self-chosen directions. Youthful clients often are reluctant to disclose information, and inexperienced counselors sometimes ask a series of questions to maintain the counselor/client dialogue. Clients can perceive this barrage of questions as an attack. They may become defensive and guarded and resist forming a relationship with the counselor. Gladding (1988) suggested that counselors do not ask more than two consecutive questions and instead rely on a solid repertoire of attending, listening, and communication skills to encourage client disclosures.

Interventions based on lecturing and giving advice are apt to disempower children and deny them the opportunity to identify and process their own feelings. This mode of counseling also may hamper their ability to cope and solve problems and ultimately discourage self-responsibility and healthy patterns of growth (Gladding 1988). When counselors solve problems for clients, they are teaching clients to depend on other people's wishes.

INTERVENTIONS WITH CHILDREN AND ADOLESCENTS

Children

Because of their rapid emotional and cognitive growth, children are highly vulnerable to developmental disturbances (Miller and Boe 1990). They are fundamentally dependent upon adults, and their egos are too weak to actively oppose forces in the external environment (Freud 1936). Young children have not developed an autonomous sense of self, and their cognitive development is not advanced enough for them to effectively cope with the complexities of life, yet they attempt to make sense of their world (Dibrell and Yamamoto 1988). In understanding life events, young children take an egocentric approach. They tend to believe that the external environment is organized around, created for, and centered on them. They blame themselves for the inadequacies of their parents and conclude they are mistreated because they are "bad" or abandoned because they are not lovable.

Young children often feel powerless when facing situations that are unfamiliar or frightening to them. They need a consistent attachment to adults who will protect them and provide the nurturing and structure necessary for their healthy development (Miller and Boe 1990). Children who do not bond with significant others and who have adverse childhood conditions, such as neglect, abandonment, emotional or physical abuse, often perceive themselves as completely helpless and totally unprotected from future traumatic events.

Brenner (1988) suggested that counselors devise methods to create an emotional connecting bridge between sessions, enabling children to maintain the fragile bonds of the therapeutic relationship. Sometimes an appointment card helps children to sustain the emotional link, or children may want to take home a drawing they created. When counselors are going to be away on vacation or other extended absences, they might trade photographs with minor clients and send them postcards to reaffirm the counseling relationship.

Children often are wary and defensive within the counseling relationship, and mental health professionals who are not prepared for the anger and rigid self-protective behaviors of reluctant or resistant children may ultimately blame themselves or their clients when the therapeutic process is unsuccessful. Counselors can gain greater understanding of difficult clients if they perceive the underlying factors attached to the behavior and genuinely empathize with the feelings, apprehensions, and experiences of those children (Gladding 1988).

Young clients frequently have good reason to resist forming relationships with counselors. Children who have not formed secure attachments with significant others often feel unprotected, unloved, and vulnerable, and thus fail to develop the basic trust necessary to establish nurturing, loving relationships. These children sometimes react with pervasive rage toward their surroundings, manifesting an inordinate need to control their world and thereby protect themselves. Children who have been abused (mentally or physically) by significant adults tend to have chaotic emotions and react with intense fear, anger, rage, and hatred toward these adults. These children long for love but demand it in a hateful way (Brenner 1988). Their repressed hostile and apprehensive feelings may generalize to other adults, including counselors, jeopardizing the opportunity for interpersonal relationships. If children do not learn to verbalize or act out these feelings in acceptable ways, they may become withdrawn and emotionally shut-down (Ellis 1990).

Counselors can assist these children by verbalizing their own personal feelings of rage about their clients' experiences. Verbalizing this anger invites children to communicate to themselves and to others their own feelings of hostility, and they can learn to experience love and hate as separate emotions (Brenner 1988).

The counseling goal with children who are reluctant to participate in the counseling relationship is to provide a consistent, nurturing, accepting, predictable, and highly structured method of treatment. If children refuse to do something (e.g., to draw a picture), the counselor should acknowledge and respect their resistance, yet gently prod them to complete the activity. The counselor might facilitate cooperation by first persuading children to attempt nonthreatening, small requests (e.g., wiggle fingers, hold pencil) or commit to a small goal. When children are extremely inhibited or fearful, the counselor might allow them to determine for themselves when they are ready to take a risk. An effective technique for helping children through resistance is modeling; the counselor can assist children in overcoming their fears by first performing the requested behavior (Oaklander 1988).

Traditional therapies—psychodynamically oriented therapy, relationship therapy, behavior therapy, and combinations of these strategies—are the most common individual treatment approaches with children (Tuma 1989). Whatever the approach, the relationship between counselor and client is vital to the therapeutic process. Children need to believe they are interacting with a trustworthy adult with whom they can form a secure and stable attachment before they begin to reveal their experiences, resolve conflicts, and gain mastery over overwhelming situations (Miller and Boe 1990).

Because of the intrinsic dependency of children on adults, counselors should take special precautions to develop an egalitarian relationship with minor clients. Counselors can convey their unconditional regard and acceptance to children by attending, understanding, empathizing, and attributing importance to children's communication of internal cognitions and emotions. They can empower young people by encouraging them for their efforts and reassuring them when they are frustrated or have setbacks (Dibrell and Yamamoto 1988).

Play Therapy

Play therapy (sand play, fairy tales, art, puppetry, and the like) encourages communication in children who have inadequate or immature verbalization skills, and it promotes nonverbal communication by children who verbalize excessively as a defense (Carey 1990). Children often do not know how to respond to direct questions about their feelings and may need assistance in expressing their emotions. Play therapy can (Lubetsky 1989):

- enable children to indirectly express inner thoughts, fears, anxieties, and feelings of rage and guilt
- help children accomplish developmental tasks through a protected modality in which they can learn to deal with difficulties in the here and now
- help children reduce anxiety and resolve conflict

The playroom provides a sanctuary in which children can safely work through their emotional issues (Campos 1988), and nondirective play allows them to be in control of their environment (Miller and Boe 1990). Children can safely project their burdensome thoughts and emotions through artwork, sand play, storytelling, or puppetry. Children often will say something to a puppet that they never would say directly to an adult (Oaklander 1988).

Children need to be able to distance themselves from overwhelming and unspeakable past occurrences. When they are given the opportunity to express distressful events metaphorically, they can become safely separated from the incommunicable reality of their pain, and when fantasy allows them to visualize their trauma as something external, they gain mastery over it and learn healthy, adaptive ways to cope with life situations (Lubetsky 1989; Miller and Boe 1990).

Behavior Therapy

A basic premise of behavior therapy is that behaviors are learned from the interaction between individuals and their environments and, through structured, systematic interventions, dysfunctional behaviors can be eliminated and replaced with more adaptive modes of functioning (Corey 1986; Wilson 1984). In the counseling process, behavioral therapists typically function as educators, directors, and experts; focus on current patterns of behavior; attempt to modify behavior by manipulating environmental contingencies; and evaluate treatment strategies by observing and recording overt behavior changes. The ultimate goal of behavior therapy is fulfilled when the natural environmental responses to the more adaptive behavior eventually become reinforcing enough to maintain the new pattern of functioning and the systematic artificial reinforcement schedule can be gradually reduced and eliminated.

Proponents of behavior therapy assume that dysfunctional behavior occurs when children have not acquired effective competencies necessary for coping and dealing with life contingencies and their faulty coping patterns are being sustained by environmental reinforcers (Coleman, Butcher, and Carson 1984). Counselors focus on symptoms and advocate the systematic application of interventions to change maladaptive behaviors. These interventions are most effective when children receive clear, concrete guidelines on what behavior is expected, what the reinforcers will be, and how reinforcers will be administered. Reinforcements have to be applied immediately following the desired response. Behavior therapy has been effective in counseling children with mental retardation, autism, and those who manifest behavioral problems (Corey 1986; Wilson 1984). Some of the interventions commonly used in counseling children are positive reinforcement, token economy systems, self-management, extinction, shaping, aversion therapy, and contracts (Coleman et al. 1984; Corey 1986; Gladding 1988; Wilson 1984).

1. *Positive reinforcement.* Positive reinforcement is a pleasurable consequence to one's actions. Usually, when a child is first learning a behavior, it is reinforced every time (continuous reinforcement), and when the desired behavior is established, less frequently (intermittent reinforcement) but still according to a preset schedule determined by the counselor.

2. *Token economy.* The token economy system helps children develop adaptive behaviors. When they perform desirable behaviors, they are immediately given tokens (stars, chips, points) that they can later exchange for coveted objects or privileges. In a variation of this system, a response cost intervention is combined with a token economy, and children lose tokens after inappropriate behavior. The token economy system teaches children self-control and the concept that both positive and negative consequences are attached to their behaviors.

3. *Self-management.* Self-management strategies enable children to learn productive behaviors under carefully controlled conditions. They typically do well when they are given control of their own change program and, with guidance, are allowed to choose targeted behaviors and the type of reinforcement they

want for making the change. Reinforcements are self-adminis-
tered, and children monitor their own programs.

4. *Extinction.* Behaviors tend to decline and end when they are not
   supported. One of the simplest methods to stop undesirable
   behavior is to not acknowledge it and to recognize the desired
   behavior.

5. *Shaping.* The desired behavior is broken down into minute,
   concrete units or positive movements, each of which is reinforced as it leads toward the overall behavioral goal.

6. *Aversion therapy.* Aversion therapy or punishment can be used
   to eliminate unwanted behavior by presenting negative stimuli
   or removing positive reinforcers. Punishment is considered less
   effective than positive reinforcement in changing behavior and
   may result in negative emotional reactions such as resentment,
   anger, and depression. Common forms of aversive therapy are
   timeout and overcorrection. During timeout, children are removed from sources of positive reinforcement by being isolated, sitting alone in a chair, or the like. This technique is most
   effective for short periods and is helpful with children who are
   aggressive and self-destructive. Overcorrection typically is used
   when children deliberately destroy some part of their environment. They not only are required to immediately make restitu-
   tion for their destructive behavior, but they also must design
   ways to further improve their surroundings.

7. *Contracts.* Simple contracts can be an effective way to help
   children focus on behavior to be changed. The counselor should
   identify the behavior with the child, and together specify what
   he or she will do, how, and when. The counselor and the child
   sign the contract. Progress usually is monitored each week.

Termination of Therapy

Most childhood emotional disturbances are relatively short-lived, so
counselors should be alert to signs that therapy should end. Generally,
children do not require long-term treatment programs and after a few
months may no longer benefit from therapeutic interventions. In addition, parents often become less anxious when their children enter therapy
and the atmosphere at home becomes more relaxed. This enables children to benefit more fully from the therapeutic process and make
positive behavior changes more quickly.

Children need the opportunity to pause and integrate the growth
changes of therapy with their own maturational processes. A natural

time to terminate therapy may be when children have reached a plateau in the counseling process. Some of the indicators for termination include external reports and counselor observations of positive behavior change, more involvement in outside activities, and less enthusiasm for attending counseling sessions (Oaklander 1988).

Counselors must carefully prepare children to say good-bye. If children have a history of losses, counselors should begin the termination process early and use at least five sessions to prepare children for the upcoming separation. Counselors may want to make termination gradual, perhaps seeing children on alternate weeks and using these sessions to talk about what saying good-bye feels like. Counselors might encourage children to draw pictures of these feelings. These pictures also might be part of a good-bye ritual. Counselors can tell children how and where they will hang the pictures and that they will think of the children every time they look at their drawings. Counselors also might give graduating children talismans or anchors as reminders of the relationship and therapeutic gains. Depending on the child's frame of reference, these tokens may be metaphoric or tangible.

Adolescents

Because adolescence is a time of profound changes and transitions, adolescents are subject to an onslaught of psychosocial stressors (Forehand, Neighbors, and Wierson 1991). They are faced with the sometimes distressful issues of attachment, autonomy, and establishment of peer relationships. Most teenagers adequately survive this turbulent stage of life, but when they encounter additional stressors—divorce; abuse; social pressures to use drugs or alcohol and make premature decisions about sexual intercourse, contraception, and abortion; rejection; low self-esteem; depression; world instability—adolescents may not have the experiential capabilities to deal effectively with these issues.

Many teenagers resist discussing their problems with adults. They are convinced that adults do not understand them, and they protect themselves by withholding information from parents, teachers, and counselors. Because adolescents mistrust adults' abilities to assist them, they often manifest acting-out behaviors, such as defiance, rebellion, deviousness, rage, or secretiveness, to get adults to leave them alone (Bauman and Riche 1986). Blos (1966) maintained that some acting-out behaviors may be a natural part of the developmental process for adolescents and a way for them to solve problems. These behaviors can have adaptive functions, enabling adolescents to separate from parents and establish a self-identity, relieve tensions, and work through difficulties experienced in earlier developmental stages.

Adolescents' disinclination to engage willingly in the counseling process has direct ramifications for counselors. Kazdin (1988) suggested that the active involvement of adolescents in treatment decisions can influence their motivation for treatment and increase their positive evaluation of the counseling process. Initial therapeutic strategies should include interventions that promote trust and autonomy, establish an internalized value for the counseling process, facilitate motivation for behavior change, and encourage adolescents to remain in therapy.

Because of adolescents' advanced cognitive thinking processes, many professionals advocate cognitive-behavioral therapy approaches for this age group. Adolescents, however, also enjoy and benefit from many forms of fantasy. Music lyrics, films, television shows, and video games are good examples of adolescents' uses of fantasy. Incorporating fantasy or symbolic play into the therapeutic process can facilitate conflict resolution, independence, and feelings of self-worth (Lubetsky 1989). Therapists should respect the boundaries established by adolescents and be alert to issues of countertransference or reliving their own unresolved issues of adolescence through their client's problems. Therapists also should resist judging adolescents' behaviors and avoid imposing their own standards, values, and expectations on these young people (Lane and Chazan 1988).

Cognitive-Based Therapies

Most cognitive theories are based on the assumption that both environmental conditions and internal tendencies contribute significantly to the way humans act upon and respond to external and internal stimuli (Corey 1986). People are not always able to change environmental events, but they have an inherent capacity to choose how they will cognitively and emotionally attend to certain situations. People have a predisposition toward happiness, self-preservation, satisfactory interpersonal relationships, productivity, and self-actualization, but they often choose to disturb themselves with negative self-statements, self-defeating beliefs, and faulty thinking (Ellis 1984).

Emotional and behavioral difficulties are considered to be a consequence of these maladaptive thinking processes. Thus, cognitive therapists do not direct interventions to behaviors and emotions but, rather, emphasize cognitive restructuring or modifying how adolescents view themselves and their world in order to change feelings and behaviors. Cognitive-oriented counselors typically are more active and directive and use logic, persuasion, occasional lecturing, and homework to challenge adolescents to change irrational thoughts into healthier and more adaptive ways of thinking.

Developmental Therapy

Willison and Masson (1990) generated a model for treating developmentally deprived adolescents. During the formative years, the physical and psychological needs of these young people are not all met, primarily because of traumatic occurrences, such as parental death, abandonment or divorce, or ineffective, neglectful, or abusive parenting practices. As a consequence, they are emotionally and developmentally stunted and often unable to establish meaningful relationships with other people.

> People do not move on to more mature levels of functioning until certain needs are met or developmental stages are complete. One must master the developmental tasks of trust, autonomy, initiative, and industry before grappling with the adolescent task of identity formation. (Willison and Masson 1990, 144)

When counselors determine that an adolescent client has developmental deficits, they can devise strategies to fulfill the client's needs at the developmental level in which the deprivation occurred.

Treatment for developmentally deprived adolescents is generally a two-stage process of nurture and structure, or therapeutic reparenting. Initially, counselors focus on providing clients with consistent unconditional acceptance and love. The first goal is to promote trust and encourage an emotional connectedness with another person. The second goal is to identify the client's unmet needs and facilitate developmental growth to more mature levels of functioning. Counselors can provide structure and assist clients in acquiring skills they did not learn in their family of origin (such as self-discipline; survival skills, including coping, problem-solving; setting and achieving goals; development of morals and values) by generating hope, providing encouragement, giving constructive feedback, and assuming the parental role of basic life educator. The ultimate goal is for the client to develop self-love, self-value, self-determination, and self-responsibility.

Termination of Therapy

In concluding the therapy, the counselor should facilitate a therapeutic transition to a future orientation and promote visualization of anticipated changes and how therapeutic experiences differ from real-life situations. Counselors should help adolescents explore how they plan to obtain support in the future and how they can determine if they need to come back to counseling. What signs might signify a need for assistance? How will they reconnect with a therapist? Counselors can encourage autonomous behavior by encoding future behaviors and encouraging adolescents to spot specific, concrete behaviors (sadness, sleep disturbances, avoiding friends, thoughts of suicide) that denote warning signs.

Counselors should allow adolescents to self-determine if they want to be touched or hugged as part of the good-bye process. Adolescents often feel awkward and embarrassed by uninvited overtures of physical affection. The termination process should be predicated on the ego strength and level of emotionality clients can tolerate. Typically, counselors should avoid heavy-duty emotionalism with adolescents. The process of saying good-bye is mainly for the benefit of clients. If therapists feel the need to share and vent personal feelings about the separation process, they should consult a professional or peers to process these emotions.

SUMMARY

Most counseling approaches used with children and adolescents have been geared toward the adult population. Interventions with younger clients must take into account their developmental levels, which are idiosyncratic; that is, interventions with young children are not necessarily appropriate with adolescents, and adolescents likewise require specific approaches. These developmental variables must be considered in referral, assessment, and diagnosis. Young children are also normally less verbal, so methods must consider nonverbal behaviors to gain insight into the child's problems. An additional confounding factor is that children, and adolescents in particular, tend to resist counseling for a variety of reasons.

Because this population is unique, ethical and legal issues must be understood in terms of minors, especially in regard to confidentiality. Although mental health professionals agree that confidentiality concerns are different for children and adults, no consensus has been reached on governing criteria.

Professionals often disagree on the relative merits of relationship-based therapies versus the teaching of interpersonal problem-solving skills. Advantages of individual counseling are the singular focus on one client, allowing nurturing and trust, and the sometimes adverse effects of family involvement when significant others may be contributing to the child's problems. Disadvantages are that individual counseling does not consider the total context in which the child's problems developed, the child may feel isolated from the family, and the family system may require change for the child's progress to endure.

The counselor's qualities are crucial to the therapeutic relationship. Empathy, genuineness, and acceptance are vital, along with basic attending skills, such as active listening, observation, minimal encouragers, accents, open-ended questions, silence, paraphrasing, and summarization.

Effective therapies with children include play therapies and behavior therapy. Because adolescents are more advanced in their cognitive development, cognitive-behavioral approaches may work best with this age group. In all cases, counselors must be sensitive to their young clients' needs for self-preservation and respect, and should not lecture or advise. Most interventions are short-term, so counselors must give attention to the termination of counseling and facilitate a vision for the future.

REFERENCES

Allberg, W., and L. Chu. 1990. Understanding adolescent suicide: Correlates in a developmental perspective. *School Counselor* 37(5): 343–350.

American Counseling Association Governing Council. 1988. Ethical standards for counseling and development. *Journal of Counseling and Development* 67: 4–8.

American Mental Health Counselors Association. 1989. *Code of ethics for mental health counselors.* Alexandria, VA: AMHCA.

American Psychological Association. 1981. Ethical principles of psychologists. *American Psychologist* 36: 633–638.

Barrnett, R. J., J. Docherty, and G. Frommelt. 1991. A review of child psychotherapy research since 1963. *Journal of American Academy of Child and Adolescent Psychiatry* 30(1): 1–14.

Bauman, L., and R. Riche. 1986. *The nine most troublesome teenage problems and how to solve them.* New York: Ballantine.

Blos, P. 1966. The concept of acting out in relation to the adolescent process. *Journal of the American Academy of Child Psychiatrists* 2: 118–136.

Brandell, J. 1988. Narrative and historical truth in child psychotherapy. *Psychoanalytic Psychology* 5(3): 241–257.

Brenner, A. 1988. From acting out to verbalization. *Journal of Contemporary Psychotherapy* 18(2): 179–192.

Campos, L. 1988. Empowering children II: Integrating protection into script prevention work. *Transactional Analysis Journal* 18(2): 137–140.

Carey, L. 1990. Sandplay therapy with a troubled child. *The Arts in Psychotherapy* 17: 197–209.

Chess, S. 1988. Child and adolescent psychiatry come of age: A fifty-year perspective. *Journal of the American Academy of Child and Adolescent Psychiatry* 27(1): 1–7.

Clarkson, P., and S. Fish. 1988. Systematic assessment and treatment considerations in a TA child psychotherapy. *Transactional Analysis Journal* 18(2): 123–132.

Coleman, J., J. Butcher, and R. Carson. 1984. *Abnormal psychology and modern life.* 7th ed. London: Scott, Foresman.

Corey, G. 1986. *Theory and practice of counseling and psychotherapy.* 3d ed. Pacific Grove, CA: Brooks/Cole.

Corey, M., and G. Corey. 1987. *Groups: Process and practice.* 3d ed. Pacific Grove, CA: Brooks/Cole.

Dibrell, L., and K. Yamamoto. 1988. In their own words: Concerns of young children. *Child Psychiatry and Human Development* 19(1): 14–25.

Ellis, A. 1984. Rational-emotive therapy. In R. Corsini, ed., *Current psychotherapies* (pp. 196–238). Itasca, IL: F. E. Peacock.

Ellis, M. 1990. *The special child: Strategies for treatment and management.* (ERIC Document Reproduction Service No. ED 330184) For practicum paper that this resource manual supplements see EC 300155.

Freud, A. 1936. *The ego and mechanisms of defense.* New York: International Universities Press.

Forehand, R., B. Neighbors, and M. Wierson. 1991. The transition to adolescence: The role of gender and stress in problem behavior and competence. *Journal of Child Psychology and Psychiatry* 320(6): 929–937.

Gladding, S. 1988. *Counseling. A comprehensive profession.* Columbus, OH: Merrill.

Gilliland, B., and R. James. 1988. *Crisis intervention strategies.* Pacific Grove, CA: Brooks/Cole.

Guyer, M. 1990. Child psychiatry and legal liability. Implications of recent case law. *Journal of American Academy of Child and Adolescent Psychiatry* 29(6): 958–962.

Haskett, M. 1990. Social problem-solving skills of young physically abused children. *Child Psychiatry and Human Development* 21(2): 109–118.

Hendrix, D. 1991. Ethics and intrafamily confidentiality in counseling with children. *Journal of Mental Health Counseling* 13(3): 323–333.

Jenkins, J., and M. Smith. 1991. Marital disharmony and children's behavior problems: Aspects of a poor marriage that affect children adversely. *Journal of Child Psychology and Psychiatry* 32(5): 793–810.

Kazdin, A. 1988. *Child psychotherapy. Developing and identifying effective treatments.* New York: Pergamon.

Kazdin, A. 1989. Developmental psychopathology. Current research, issues and directions. *American Psychologist* 44(2): 180–187.

Kazdin, A., D. Bass, W. Ayers, and A. Rogers. 1990. Empirical and clinical focus of child and adolescent psychotherapy research. *Journal of Consulting and Clinical Psychology* 58(6): 729–740.

Kazdin, A., D. Bass, T. Siegel, and C. Thomas. 1989. Cognitive-behavioral therapy and relationship therapy in the treatment of children referred for antisocial behavior. *Journal of Consulting and Clinical Psychology* 57(4): 522–535.

Kendall, P., R. Lerner, and W. E. Craighead. 1984. Human development and interventions in childhood psychopathology. *Child Development* 55: 71–82.

Kilgore, L. 1988. Effect of early childhood sexual abuse on self and ego development. *Social Casework*, April, 224–230.

Lane, R., and S. Chazan. 1988. Psychoanalytic perspectives on the treatment of early adolescent girls. *Journal of Contemporary Psychotherapy* 18(1): 5–15.

Lubetsky, M. 1989. The magic of fairy tales: Psychodynamic and developmental perspectives. *Child Psychiatry and Human Development* 19(4): 245–255.

McGuire, J., and F. Earls. 1991. Prevention of psychiatric disorders in early childhood. *Journal of Child Psychology and Psychiatry* 32(1), 129–154.

Meador, B., and C. Rogers. 1984. Person-centered therapy. In R. Corsini, ed., *Current psychotherapies* (pp. 142–195). Itasca, IL: F. E. Peacock.

Meier, S. 1989. *The elements of counseling*. Pacific Grove, CA: Brooks/Cole.

Miller, C., and J. Boe. 1990. Tears into diamonds: Transformation of child psychic trauma through sandplay and storytelling. *The Arts in Psychotherapy* 17: 247–257.

Mosak, H. 1984. Adlerian psychotherapy. In R. Corsini, ed., *Current psychotherapies* (pp. 56–107). Itasca, IL: F. E. Peacock.

Nazario, T. 1988. *In defense of children: Understanding the rights, needs, and interests of the child*. New York: Charles Scribner's Sons.

Norton, F. 1981. Foster care and the helping professions. *Personnel and Guidance Journal* 60(1): 156–159.

Oaklander, V. 1988. *Windows to our children. A gestalt therapy approach to children and adolescents*. Highland, NY: Center for Gestalt Development.

Robinson, S. 1991. Ethical and legal issues related to counseling or it's not as easy as it looks. In D. Capuzzi and D. Gross, eds., *Introduction to counseling. Perspectives for the 1990s* (pp. 447–468). Boston: Allyn and Bacon.

Schneider, W. 1989. Problems of longitudinal studies with children: Practical, conceptual and methodological issues. In M. Brambring, F. Lösel, and H. Skowronek, eds., *Children at risk: Assessment, longitudinal research, and intervention* (pp. 313–335). New York: Walter de Gruyter.

Seiffge-Krenke, I. 1988. Problem intensity and the disposition of adolescents to take therapeutic advice. In M. Brambring, F. Lösel, and H. Skowronek, eds., *Children at risk: Assessment, longitudinal research, and intervention* (pp. 457–477). New York: Walter de Gruyter.

Strein, W., and D. Hershenson. 1991. Confidentiality in nondyadic counseling situations. *Journal of Counseling and Development* 69(4): 312–316.

Terry, A., C. Burden, and M. Pederson. 1991. The helping relationship. In D. Capuzzi and D. Gross, eds., *Introduction to counseling. Perspectives for the 1990s*. Boston: Allyn and Bacon.

Tuma, J. 1989. Mental health services for children. The state of the art. *American Psychologist* 44(2): 188–199.

Willison, B., and R. Masson. 1990. Therapeutic reparenting for the developmentally deprived student. *School Counselor* 38: 143–151.

Wilson, G. T. 1984. Behavior therapy. In R. Corsini, ed., *Current psychotherapies* (pp. 239–278). Itasca, IL: F. E. Peacock.

3 Counseling for Typical Developmental Problems

Susan E. Reynolds

Counseling Director
Indian Creek High School
Trafalgar, Indiana

Some people may have had an easy time growing up. Others have painful, poignant memories—being rejected by peers, teased about their looks, wetting their pants in class, or feeling humiliated when the teacher announced their failing grade to the entire group. Although these negative experiences don't maim a person for life, they are significant at that point in time and they do matter. Someone to talk to helps people get through the tough times.

Years ago school counselors were not routinely available to help elementary school students with typical developmental problems, and secondary counselors were too busy with scheduling and paper shuffling. As a result, students had a hard time meeting their educational potential as they struggled with developmental concerns. Now, thanks to the developmental counseling impetus, counselors at all levels are aware that growing up has its ups and downs and that mastering developmental tasks is easier for some students than for others. Counselors help all students master developmental tasks through classroom guidance, individual planning, consultation, group counseling, and individual counseling. These preventive and responsive interventions enable students to more nearly meet their full educational potential.

As discussed in chapter 9, classroom guidance programs are designed to be preventive. The topics anticipate the tasks to be mastered at each developmental level, providing students with tools for achieving the tasks. Naturally, not all students are able to master every developmental task. Small-group (chapter 8) and individual counseling experiences also address students' developmental problems.

The discussion in this chapter identifies typical developmental issues of children and adolescents that interfere with their educational progress as well as interventions to address these concerns in individual counseling settings.

DEVELOPMENTAL COUNSELING CONCEPTS

Developmental Tasks

A developmental task is a thought pattern, feeling, or behavior that must be mastered in order to become a successfully functioning adult. A developmental task may center on physical growth, psychological growth, or social growth. For example, being able to separate from significant adults for brief periods is a task that must be mastered before a child can successfully participate in school. Learning assertiveness skills is a task that helps the student relate successfully to peers and teachers. As students master these and other developmental tasks, they progress toward becoming successfully functioning adults.

Developmental Goals

Developmental tasks can be grouped into general goals. Organizing developmental tasks into goals provides a structure that simplifies the discussion of developmental counseling while promoting growth in several different areas. In its publication, *Counseling Paints a Bright Future,* the American School Counselor Association (1990) listed eight developmental goals for social/personal growth:

1. Gaining self-awareness.
2. Developing positive attitudes.
3. Making healthy choices.
4. Respecting others.
5. Gaining responsibility.
6. Developing relationship skills.
7. Resolving conflicts.
8. Making effective decisions .

Developmental Levels

Developmental tasks correspond to child and adolescent developmental levels. In other words, developmental tasks are age appropriate. Certain tasks are appropriate for younger children, and others are appropriate for adolescents or young adults. Within each of the goals listed above, students master tasks corresponding to their developmental level. For example, the goal "Resolving Conflicts" would involve different tasks for a kindergartener and a sophomore. A kindergarten task may involve sharing and cooperation, while a sophomore task may center on communication skills required to resolve a rivalry over a boyfriend or girlfriend. In another example, the goal "Gaining Self-Awareness" for a first grader may entail a concept of physical size and uniqueness, whereas for an adolescent, awareness of changing bodies and sexuality might be a more appropriate task. In the area of "Relationship Skills," elementary school children may learn "tease tolerance" and high school students may develop tasks required to relate to the opposite sex. Chapter 1 provides a background on developmental tasks of children and adolescents.

Sequential Nature of Developmental Tasks

Developmental tasks are sequential in nature, and successfully mastering tasks at one developmental level influences the mastery of tasks at later levels. For example, if an elementary student never mastered the task of separating from significant adults for a period of time, it is unlikely that the student would later develop a healthy sense of personal identity or independence. Or if an elementary student never broadened his or her social world to include peers, it is unlikely that the student would later develop healthy intimate relationships during adolescence. In *Thinking, Feeling, Behaving* (Vernon 1989a, 1989b) identified developmentally sequenced tasks. For instance, tasks leading to the goal "Making Effective Decisions" may involve, for a third or fourth grader, learning to evaluate the effectiveness of possible solutions (Vernon 1989a, 137–138) or, for ninth and tenth graders, distinguishing between acting and reality in problematic situations (Vernon 1989b, 445).

Developmental Stressors

As children and adolescents pass through the developmental levels, they undergo behavioral and emotional changes that may induce stress. Youngs (1985) identified the most likely developmental challenges of children and adolescents as they progress through school, some of which are, by grade level:

K–5: Uncertainty and fear of abandonment by a significant adult

Fear of riding the bus

Ridicule by class peers and older students in the school setting

Frequently missing the presence of a particular parent

Being chosen last on *any* team

6–8: Fear of the unknown concerning sexuality

Fear of being unpopular

Fear of being selected first (and having to lead a team or group) and fear of being picked last (interpreted as being disliked or unpopular)

Fear of not being able to complete homework/schoolwork/project Extreme concern and worry about emotional happiness and unhappiness (emotional fitness)

9–12: Fear of coming to terms with sexuality (based on lack of information concerning sex)

Fear that another peer will vie for the person they are dating

Fear of being "not okay"/ridiculed in class when asked to speak or demonstrate

Fear that other adults will interpret roles for them (they seek to define themselves in relation to peers and their own values and goals)

Fear of inadequate vocational or academic training

These developmental issues often result in behaviors and attitudes that lead to referral to counselors. Manifestations of developmental problems include alcoholism, anxiety, apathy, depression, drug abuse, lack of self-control, anorexia, detachment, irresponsibility, violence, absenteeism, reduced productivity, and even suicide (Youngs 1985). Armed with a knowledge of developmental tasks and associated developmental concerns, counselors can design appropriate interventions.

INTERVENTION DESIGN

Successful interventions address problems in a manner that the young client understands. When designing interventions, school counselors should consider the change process, the student's learning style, and brief counseling.

Change Process

The counselor and the student must have some sense of purpose and direction provided through a defined change process. The major stages in this process are planning, implementation, and evaluation.

Planning Stage

In this stage, the counselor and student explore and define concerns and needs. The counselor must use counseling skills that encourage the student to feel "safe," such as those discussed in chapter 2. When students develop a sense of trust with the counselor, they can examine their problems more thoroughly and accurately. The planning stage has six substages:

1. *Current situation.* How does the student describe his or her current life? What are the demographics: family situation, school achievement, support system? What is positive? What are the problems? During this stage, the counselor gains background information and helps the student define the presenting problem.

2. *Vision.* How does the student picture his or her dream-self and dream-life? In this step, the student is a magician, able to create a picture of his or her ideal life. Later interventions will be designed to enable the student to realize this vision.

3. *Analysis.* What internal or external factors enable or inhibit that vision? The student and counselor might discuss factors that will help or hinder the student in realizing his or her vision.

4. *Objective.* What specifically would the student like to change? The counselor helps the student focus on the part of the whole vision that will become the priority. That part of the vision is stated as a measurable objective, such as "earning a grade of "B" in science class," "talking positively about myself for two minutes," or "listing three career choices that match my interests and abilities."

5. *Exploration.* What interventions may help the student achieve the objectives? What interventions has the student already tried? What interventions have other counselors used with their clients in similar situations? What research or publications are available to help in designing an intervention?

6. *Intervention Design.* Contrary to the traditional medical model paradigm of counselor as "fixer," the counselor and student decide upon an intervention by consensus. Either the counselor or the student may propose the intervention, or they may design it together. This consensus-building lessens student resistance (Searight and Openlander 1984). The student and counselor also agree on a plan of action or in other words, "Who will do what by when?"

Implementation Stage

The intervention then is implemented. It may be conducted on a trial basis, may be a stepped implementation, or can be fully implemented. In a *trial implementation* the strategy is in place for a short time, followed by evaluation and a possible adjustment. This is especially helpful when a student hesitates to try an intervention or has some doubt concerning its potential effectiveness. A trial implementation allows for early feedback and adjustment.

Stepped implementation allows the student to keep a large objective in focus while working on smaller aspects of it. For example, an adolescent who feels awkward with the opposite sex may set, as the larger objective, asking for a date, but begin with a smaller step, such as saying "hi" to girls in the halls.

The third possibility is *full implementation* of the intervention. Advantages of this strategy include a greater sense of success from realizing the vision; the disadvantage is that it has a "sink or swim" quality that may be discouraging or threatening to the student.

Evaluation Stage

As the intervention is implemented, the counselor and the student check the results. If the results are positive, they may want to take on a more challenging objective or work on another part of the vision. If not, they may adjust the intervention. Either way, the process starts over with a new planning stage, dependent on the evaluation of the current intervention. In this way, evaluation is continuous and "in-flight" adjustments can be made. Evaluation of a measurable objective holds the counselor accountable to students as well as to his or her supervisor, principal, or school board.

Learning Style

When designing an intervention, a student's learning style also must be considered. Traditionally, counseling has been primarily verbal. Myrick (1987) noted that some students "may feel hopelessly inundated with words when being 'counseled.' They may feel overwhelmed, insecure, or lost in the intellectual efforts that seem to form the basis of most school counseling and guidance" (p. 131). This verbal orientation is limiting to students who have different learning styles (Nickerson and O'Laughlin 1982). Griggs (1983) cited several environmental factors as influencers of learning and the counseling process:

- environmental stimulus (light, sound, temperature, design)
- emotional stimulus (structure, persistence, motivation, responsibility)
- sociological stimulus (pairs, peers, adults, self, group, varied)
- physical stimulus (perceptual strengths, mobility, intake, time of day)

● psychological stimulus (global analytic, impulsive/reflective, cerebral dominance)

Griggs (1985) advocated using counseling interventions that address differing learning styles to facilitate the counseling process. These interventions include art therapy, imagery, bibliotherapy, psychodrama, and mime. Myrick (1987) suggested puppets, music and movement, games, and high-technology interventions.

Brief Counseling

School counseling interventions often are restricted by time constraints unique to the school setting. These limitations result from high student/counselor ratios, administrative and clerical tasks, and availability of students. Therefore, the school counselor has to design interventions that rely primarily on short-term or brief counseling (Myrick 1987).

Brief counseling does not imply that counselors provide "scaled down versions of traditional long-term intervention models (i.e., 'less of something')" (Searight and Openlander 1984, 387). Rather, brief counseling is *a developed, complete, optimal, and effective treatment of short duration*. The focus of brief counseling is problem-solving. With this approach, the student's problems are taken at face value rather than as a symptom of some deep and fundamental deficit in the student or the student's family (Amatea and Sherrard 1991).

Many students have problems simply from the mishandling of developmental difficulties by themselves or others (Amatea and Lochausen 1988; Amatea and Sherrard 1991). Brief counseling interventions attempt to interrupt old responses and provide new ways of responding to developmental difficulties. These interventions can be designed according to the change process described earlier. By using brief counseling, school counselors can help students within the time constraints of the school counseling setting.

Considering developmental tasks and stressors, the change process, learning style, and time constraints, counselors design interventions that are beneficial to positive developmental growth. Concerns that are typical at various developmental levels are discussed next, along with suggested interventions and case studies.

COMMON DEVELOPMENTAL CONCERNS

Elementary-Age Developmental Concerns
Grades K–5

Elementary students face challenges that center on peer relationships as their contacts broaden to include school and neighborhood friends, not just family members. Because children spend more time with peers and less time with parents (Hill and Stafford 1980), elementary school children have to develop the skills needed for participation in social relationships (Cole and Cole 1989). Because elementary school students function at lower cognitive levels than those at higher grade levels (Piaget 1976), interventions often involve games, art, music, and other techniques that do not rely solely on didactic exchanges. The following are examples of typical developmental concerns of elementary school children.

Bossiness

Goal:	Respecting others
Developmental problem:	Fear of peer disapproval
Student outcome:	The student will explore his or her social interactions
Interventions:	Clay figures
	Mutual storytelling

Bossiness is a common behavior of elementary school children. In the extreme, bossiness can cause students to be shunned by their peers, resulting in isolation. Peer approval is important to elementary children, who are broadening their social interactions, and isolation from peers can be distressing. Two effective counseling interventions utilize clay figures and mutual storytelling.

Clay Figures. The counselor invites the students to make up a story, using clay figures, about anything the child chooses. This and other forms of art help children share their behaviors, thoughts, and feelings. Rubin (1988) pointed out that "art, like talk, is simply a way of getting to know each other, another mode of communication" (p. 181).

Mutual Storytelling. Mutual storytelling facilitates expression of thoughts and feelings and enables the counselor to make creative and efficient use of the student's ability to communicate and learn metaphorically (Gardner 1992). After listening to the student's story, the counselor responds with a similar story but changes parts that represent unhealthy or inappropriate behaviors, thoughts, and feelings. The counselor may suggest different endings or ask the student to complete the sentence: "The lesson of this story is...." Using the student's own metaphors, the counselor communicates new ways of feeling, thinking, and behaving.

Chris's mother called the school counselor one morning because she was worried that Chris, a third grader, had no friends. The mother told the counselor, "Chris comes home every day saying that no one will play with him and everyone hates him. I'm afraid he's beginning to hate school." He also had frequent arguments in Cub Scouts because he was too bossy.

During their first meeting, the counselor asked Chris if he'd like to make clay figures and tell a story with them. Chris made a dragon and a mouse. In his story, the dragon and the mouse decided to go to the playground.

Dragon:　Let's go to the playground.

Mouse:　Okay.

Dragon:　Let's play on the swing set. We'll be fighter jets. I'll push you up high.

Mouse:　Okay.

Dragon:　Now I want to play on the slide. I'll go first.

Mouse:　Okay.

Dragon:　Now let's play tag.

Mouse:　Okay.

As the story went on, the counselor noticed that the dragon continued to be bossy toward the mouse. She interjected:

Counselor:　It sounds like the mouse just does whatever the dragon tells it to do.

Chris:　That's because the mouse loves the dragon.

Counselor:　Could I tell you a story about the dragon and the mouse?

Chris:　Sure.

Dragon:　Hi, Mouse! I'd like to go to the playground. Would you like to go with me?

Mouse:　I'd love to go with you Dragon. I love you very, very much. But I don't like it when we do what you want to do all the time. It makes me angry, and then I don't want to play with you anymore. I'd like to take turns deciding what we're going to do.

Chris:　What did the dragon say?

Counselor:　The dragon said, "You're right. You should get to do what you want some of the time. And I know you love me even when we don't do what I want to do.

Chris:　Then what?

Counselor: Then they went to the playground and took turns deciding which things to play on, and they both felt loved.

Using clay figures and mutual storytelling, the counselor helped
Chris see how his friends might react to his bossy behavior. In later
meetings, Chris and his counselor worked on other behaviors that may
be viewed as bossy, as well as on self-image, and respecting others.

Fear of Being Abandoned

Goal:	Gaining self-awareness
Developmental problem:	Uncertainty and fear of abandonment by a significant adult
Student outcome:	The student will feel confident that he or she will not be abandoned by significant adults
Intervention:	Masks

Fear of being abandoned is a common developmental concern of
lower elementary school students. They sometimes cry and cling to a
parent or other significant adult who drops them off at school, and long
to be home during the day. This fear may be extreme and result in fearful
daydreams and nightmares. In the case cited next, a kindergartner was
afraid that "bad guys" would kidnap his parents. The counselor used
masks to empower the student.

The use of masks enables the child to become someone or something different from his or her self-perception. When wearing a mask,
the student can become brave, popular, funny, or whatever characteristic
he or she would like to portray. In many cases, just making the mask can
produce a change in attitude that influences behaviors.

In this intervention, the counselor provides the student with paper
and crayons and invites the student to make a "brave mask," or "test-
taker mask," or "patience mask," or other mask. As the student makes
the mask, discussion can center on how someone would feel and act if
he or she were wearing the mask. After the mask is finished, the student
can first wear it while role-playing various situations and later imagine
wearing it as he or she deals with real life.

Timmy's kindergarten teacher referred him to the school counselor because he was always falling asleep in class. The counselor
gained little insight from Timmy, who acknowledged sleeping in class

but couldn't offer any information that would explain his behavior. The counselor then called Timmy's home and talked with Timmy's mother, who was also tired!

For the past several months Timmy had refused to go to sleep because of nightmares in which he lost his parents. Most of his disturbing dreams Involved "bad guys" who took away his parents as he screamed for help. He thought that if he didn't go to sleep, the bad guys wouldn't take away his parents.

In their next appointment, Timmy talked about seeing bad guys one night on top of his neighbor's house. He was convinced that they would come to his house, look in his windows, an take away his parents.

"What do these bad guys look like?" asked the counselor.

Timmy replied, "They're ugly. They have scars."

The counselor questioned, "Do you think they'd be scared away by someone who is even uglier than they are?"

"I don't know...," Timmy replied. "Maybe."

The counselor offered Timmy paper and crayons and suggested that he make a mask to wear so he could scare off the bad guys. Timmy's mask featured large scars, red eyes, and huge green teeth. The counselor suggested that Timmy sleep with the mask under his pillow and put it in front of his face if the bad guys looked in his window or tried to come in. He also informed Timmy's parents, who supported the idea.

After the first night, Timmy's mother called to report that Timmy had gone to bed with the mask under his pillow. He had gone straight to sleep and had slept through the night.

Teasing by Peers

Goal:	Developing a positive attitude
Developmental problem:	Ridiculed by class peers and older students in the school setting
Student outcome:	The student will model a method for maintaining a positive attitude when teased by peers
Intervention:	Silly songs

Teasing by peers can be a horrendous experience for elementary school children. Many students turn inward and say they do not want to go to school (Youngs 1985). Others come home each day in tears and think they must be among the most undesirable people on earth. Counselors can help students learn "tease tolerance" through interventions that promote a positive attitude and self-image.

One intervention that can be effectively used for this problem is "silly songs." "Silly songs" interrupt the expression of an undesirable emotion. By singing silly songs with original silly lyrics, the student often ends up replacing undesirable feelings with giggles, empowering the student to handle undesirable feelings in a more appropriate manner or at a more appropriate time. The counselor simply suggests that the student compose a "silly song" and sing or hum it when feeling angry, sad, and so on. In many cases, the end result is a sincere smile and a more positive outlook.

Rita came to the counselor sobbing because her first-grade friends had called her names. When asked what her friends were saying about her, she replied that they kept calling her a "whale."

"Are you a whale?" asked the counselor.

"No..., but they shouldn't call me names."

"Well, let's suppose you can't change that, but you can make up a silly song to sing to yourself so you can laugh instead of feeling upset when they call you a whale."

The counselor sang a silly song in a silly voice. They both laughed. She then invited Rita to write silly words to the tune of "Twinkle, Twinkle, Little Star." Rita wrote the following: "I like swimming with the whales. They may bite me with their tails!" Rita and the counselor laughed, and Rita agreed to sing the song to herself when she was being teased. Rita learned that silly songs could prove to be a powerful coping tool when she was being teased.

Being Picked Last

Goal:	Gaining self-awareness
Developmental problem:	Being selected last on a team
Student outcome:	The student will be able to identify his or her unique abilities and skills
Intervention:	Super Star/Super Self

When selected last as a team member by peers, students often feel ashamed, humiliated, or discouraged. Often students generalize the failure, feeling that they are failures in life rather than failures at one activity. These feelings may result in "verbal expression of not wanting to play 'this stupid game'; being absent ('sick') on a given day" (Youngs 1985, 57).

"Super Star/Super Self" enables the student to recognize his or her unique set of skills and abilities. The counselor draws several large stars on a piece of paper upon which the title "Super Star/Super Self" has been written at the top and "I am good! I am valuable! I am lovable!" at the bottom. The student is invited to write one special skill or ability in each star. This is a difficult task for many students who tend to think their skills and abilities are limited to "headline" successes such as being a cheerleader or a varsity basketball player.

Counselors should encourage students to take a broader view of their skills and abilities. Perhaps a student is good at keeping secrets or supporting a needy friend. Each student has unique skills that make him or her a valuable member of the school.

Jerry's fifth-grade classroom teacher referred him to the counselor because Jerry had not been participating in gym class. Jerry often volunteered to keep score or hung back so he did not take a turn. For the past several weeks, he told his classroom teacher that he felt too sick to attend gym class.

The counselor observed Jerry's gym class and noted that when forming teams for competition sports, the teacher selected captains, who took turns picking team members. On that day Jerry was picked last, and several boys groaned as he was placed on their team.

Later, when the counselor talked alone with Jerry, her suspicions were confirmed. Jerry felt ashamed and humiliated when he was the last to be picked for team sports, and he dreaded going to gym class. They talked about Jerry's ability to "shine" in other areas, and the counselor suggested that he list those situations on a Super Star/Super Self sheet. With the counselor's encouragement, Jerry identified several of his skills and abilities, including dependability, courtesy, and spelling.

"Playing kickball well is a skill some people have," said the counselor, "and being dependable is a skill other people have."

Jerry replied, "And I'm dependable. It doesn't matter that I get picked last for sports. When it comes to being dependable, I'm the best!"

"Right," the counselor smiled.

Middle School Developmental Concerns
Grades 6–8

Students have to make many developmental adjustments during their middle school years. Biological maturation results in new desires and emotions, and a new form of social relationship emerges. In addition to same-sex relationships, intimate relationships with members of the opposite sex may occur (Havighurst 1972). Friendship becomes more important; young people seek friends as sources of advice and self-confirmation. Attaining social status and being included in the top cliques has great influence in the lives of many adolescents (Coleman 1962). Erickson (1958) contended that adolescents also must rework earlier parts of their development as a new personal identity takes form. This author noted the need for establishing trust with a larger social world, establishing independence in decision-making from parents, taking the initiative for one's future, and assuming responsibility for goals and the qualities of one's works. As young people struggle to adjust to sexual maturity, social relationships, and a new personal identity, personal concerns often arise. Cole and Cole (1989) suggested that the shift that defines transition to adulthood is influenced by a partial failure of our social system to change at the same rate and manner as the adolescent.

During adolescence, students view friends as people with whom they can share feelings, solve personal problems, and share their deepest secrets. Providing emotional support, standing up for one another, and mutual acceptance are important to adolescent friendships, as are the qualities of being nonjudgmental, open, honest, and spontaneous (Smollar and Youniss 1982). Friendships are important to adolescents as they shift their source of self-confirmation from parents to peers. The interventions introduced in this section touch upon peer-related developmental problems and problems that arise as students are expected to accept substantial responsibility and develop self-discipline.

Bullying

Goal:	Developing relationship skills
Developmental problem:	Fear of being unpopular
Student outcome:	The student will recognize situations in which he or she is bullied, understand why he or she has been chosen as the victim, and respond verbally in ways that discourage bullying.

Interventions: Bully card
Role-play
Anti-bully tactics

Middle or junior high school counselors often see students who don't succeed in making friends. Many of these students are victims of bullies who tease or attack them daily to relieve their own feelings of inadequacy (Hoover and Hazler 1991). These students may conclude that school is not a safe place to be and, as a result, may not achieve as well academically (Anderson 1982). Students who are victimized frequently respond to bullying by sulking, crying, blushing, and don't "fight back." This allows the bully to control the victim without danger of retaliation. Hoover and Hazler (1991) noted, "Many times the offering of some straightforward verbal tactics to a young person gives them both the tools and the permission they did not know existed" (p. 217).

Marie, a clean-cut, polite seventh grader was well-liked by her teachers and received good grades. She was referred to the counselor by a teacher who discovered her crying one day after class. Marie explained to the counselor that her classmates had started an "I Hate Marie" club, complete with requirements for initiation and membership cards. Between sobs, Marie explained that to be in the club the students had to hold their breath around her and call her names.

To elicit further information, the counselor invited Marie to fill out a Bully Card during the next week. A Bully Card is simply a piece of paper with the numbers 1–100 on it. Every time the student is bullied, he or she writes the bully's initials over the number representing that episode. At the end of the designated time, the counselor meets with the student to evaluate the card. The student and counselor then can establish the extent of the problem and with whom it exists (family, peers, teachers, and so on).

After filling out the card for a week, Marie met with her counselor. The card indicated that Marie was put down several times a day, but by only two students, Linda and Jack. Marie and the counselor then used a role-play to further explore the problem.

The counselor first asked Marie to role-play Linda while the counselor played Marie. This role-play revealed how Marie perceived the bully's behavior. Playing Linda, Marie stood upright and looked down at the counselor.

"You stupid jerk," she said, "Get out of my sight. Go take your ugly, fat body to another school." Then she sneered and laughed, "Go on! Get out of here, you filthy pig!"

"How should I play you?" asked the counselor.

Marie replied, "Just ignore me."

The counselor sat quietly as Marie continued, "You smell! Everyone hold your breath! Ugh! You stink! Let's call her Barbara because she's such a barbarian. Ha, ha, ha!"

"Okay," said the counselor, "let's change roles now. I'll be Linda and you be yourself. Let's see what you do when Linda bullies you."

The counselor repeated the scene that Marie had enacted earlier, "You stupid jerk! Get out of my sight!" She watched Marie for behaviors that might make her a desirable victim, such as showing some reaction to the bullying (for example, sulking, crying, turning red, whining, tattling), and not "fighting back" or standing up for herself.

Marie didn't say anything. She sat quietly and turned her head away from the counselor. She appeared uncomfortable, as if she didn't know what to say or do. After several moments, the counselor talked quietly with Marie.

They discussed how bullies are most likely relieving their own feelings of inadequacy and that Marie's passive behavior made her a "safe" target. Marie relaxed and nodded her head. The counselor offered to teach Marie verbal tools to use when she was feeling bullied or teased. Marie enthusiastically agreed.

During their third meeting, the counselor taught Marie three "anti-bully tactics" designed to put Marie in control of the dialogue while being polite and nonaggressive. These tactics also removed the bully's "pay-off"—being able to control Marie. With no pay-off, the bullies would soon lose interest in picking on Marie. The counselor explained the anti-bully tactics to Marie as follows:

1. *Agree and exaggerate.* The student simply agrees with any put down and exaggerates its intensity while smiling. For example, a student who is called a slob smiles and says, "Why, yes! I *am* a slob! As a matter of fact, I am such a slob that I almost didn't make it to school this morning because I couldn't find the door to my bedroom. It was hidden by all my junk!"

2. *Unending questions.* The student tirelessly asks questions about the bullying, again with a smile. As an illustration, if a student is called a "dog," the student might respond by asking with a smile, "Now let's see...Just what kind of dog am I? A cocker

spaniel? An Irish setter? Do I have black hair? Am I spotted? Am I an outside dog or an inside dog?" The student continues to ask questions with a smile until the bully tires of answering.

3. *Put-down coach.* The student compliments the bully on his or her aggressive behavior and makes suggestions for improvement. For instance, if a student is continually ridiculed by a gang of bullies who encourage the student to fight, the student might respond, "You know, you guys would look much tougher if you'd pump up your shoulders more when you talk, or maybe you could bulge out the veins in your forehead."

Marie laughed. After hearing the three tactics, she role-played each technique and agreed to practice at home and then try the tactics with Linda and Jack. Marie agreed to schedule another appointment after using the tactics with Linda and Jack.

Within two weeks, Marie scheduled an appointment. As she sat down with a smile on her face, she said, "I really don't need this appointment. It works!"

Accepting Responsibility

Goal:	Accepting responsibility
Developmental problem:	Fear of not being able to complete home-work/schoolwork/project assignment
Student outcome:	The student, with assistance from parents (guardian) and school, will make concrete plans for improving schoolwork
Intervention:	Roundtable consultation

Another developmental adjustment that students must make upon entering middle school derives from teachers' greater expectations of student responsibility. Students are no longer allowed to stay in at recess to make up work that is not completed during the morning. Unlike elementary school, homework that is not turned in at this level may result in a failing grade. Many students have difficulty handling these adjustments and receive poor grades

Roundtable consultations can help students develop responsibility. The purpose of consultation is for the counselor to assist the consultee in helping the client. In the school setting, the client is usually the student, and the consultee(s) may be parents, teachers, administrators, or other concerned individuals. The counselor acts as a third party and generally is not responsible for long-term implementation of the intervention

(Kurpius and Rozecki 1992). Typically, the student's teachers or parents comprise a support team, assisted by the counselor. This seems to be an efficient intervention, as students are aided by people with whom they have daily contact.

Using a roundtable approach, the student and the student's parents, teachers, coaches, and other significant adults get together to discuss areas of concern. The roundtable meeting allows participants to plan appropriate actions or programs for the student, coordinate the delivery of services, increase communication, and share ideas and techniques (Mathias 1992). By involving parents, the counselor is able to establish parent roles and seek their support in clarifying the frequency and nature of the child's misbehavior (Gaushell and Lawson 1989).

Referral to the roundtable meeting may be by the student, counselor, parent, teacher, or administrator. The referral may incorporate family information, medical information, educational history, an objective description of the presenting problem, and previous interventions.

Roundtable meetings are often limited to twenty to thirty minutes and should be held at a time when all interested persons may attend. The meeting has five parts:

1. Individuals are invited to share their concerns about the student's academic achievement.
2. Group members are invited to visualize the student being successful and share their visualization with the group (Campbell 1991).
3. Group members share a history of previously attempted interventions, noting results.
4. The group discusses what future interventions will enable the student to actualize the vision.
5. The group comes to consensus on interventions to implement.

Although the tendency is to determine changes for the student to make, possible changes should be considered for the parents, teachers, school system, and community as well (Kurpius and Rozecki 1992). Decisions concerning behavior changes should be made by consensus, and a behavior contract, which reflects each person's responsibilities, positive rewards, and negative consequences, can be drawn up.

In an urban school, John's eighth-grade math teacher consulted with John's counselor because he considered John to be poorly motivated in school. The teacher thought John was bright but didn't use his time wisely. In the teachers' lunchroom, the math teacher learned that John's other teachers were having similar experiences with him. The counselor suggested that the teacher refer John for a roundtable meeting.

During the roundtable meeting, the math teacher expressed his concerns about John's lack of motivation. John reported that he, too, was frustrated but just couldn't seem to "get it together" and felt "stupid" when he asked questions in class. His parents reported that they were both busy with professional careers and had little time to monitor John's academic progress. The teachers reported that John usually "dilly-dallied" when given unstructured time in class.

The group then visualized the desired outcomes. John's teachers and parents envisioned John using his time wisely and asking questions when he didn't understand something. John envisioned his parents taking more time to check his homework and compliment him when his homework was complete.

Then the group discussed several interventions they had tried previously. John's parents reported that they had "grounded" John from the telephone and had several long talks with him about his classwork. Both consequences had little effect. A teacher noted that John seemed motivated by positive comments concerning his use of class time.

The roundtable group then brainstormed several possible interventions, followed by a discussion and consensus on the following plan of action: John would get directly to work during unstructured time and would ask questions when he didn't understand. His teachers would observe John's use of time and provide positive feedback. His parents would check to see that his homework was completed each evening, and compliment him. They also would reward him with a ticket to an upcoming rock concert if he would raise his grade in four of seven classes by the end of one month. The group agreed to meet again in four weeks to monitor John's progress.

Failure to Complete Homework

Goal:	Accepting responsibility
Developmental problem:	Fear of not being able to complete home-work/schoolwork/project assignments

Student outcome: The student will turn in an increased per-
centage of homework assignments

Intervention: Homework assignment sheet

As with roundtable consultation, this intervention promotes the
student's responsibility. Homework assignment sheets are helpful for
students who struggle to complete and turn in their assignments. In this
process, the counselor consults with the student, teachers, and parents to
make sure homework assignments are completed and turned in on time.

The Form: Many formats are workable (Fairchild 1983; Gaushell
and Lawson 1989), but they typically include a space for the student to
record the daily homework assignment in each class, a space for the
teacher to indicate whether the assignment was or was not recorded
correctly, and a space for the teacher to note whether the previous
assignment was or was not turned in on time. Assignment sheets may
pertain to one day or one week.

Student Responsibility: The student is responsible for obtaining the
homework sheet from his or her counselor. He or she writes down the
assignment from each class and presents the assignment sheet to each of
the teachers at the end of class and to his or her parents each evening.
The student is responsible for taking home the appropriate study materials and completing all assignments on time.

Teacher Responsibility: The teacher is responsible for checking the
recorded assignment, initialing its correctness, and indicating whether
the previous assignment was or was not turned in on time.

Parent Responsibility: The parents are responsible for supporting
completion of homework during the evening and checking to make sure
all assignments are finished. Parents also may offer a system of negative
consequences and positive rewards.

As the student begins to accept responsibility for completing assignments on time, he or she is "weaned" from the assignment sheet
and given the opportunity to accept responsibility without being monitored.

Josh's mother called the school's counseling center because Josh's
grades (several Ds) were not acceptable to her. She was frustrated and
felt hopeless. In tears, she explained that Josh, a sixth grader, never
brought home a book and always said he got his homework done at
school. She had tried punishments and rewards, but Josh still never
seemed to know what his homework assignments were. The counselor

checked with Josh's teachers, and their gradebooks substantiated the mother's claims. Josh had turned in only a handful of assignments.

Josh's mother and counselor agreed to require that Josh use assignment sheets for four weeks. After that time, they would check Josh's progress and determine whether to continue the assignment sheets. For those four weeks, Josh would be grounded from all intramural sports and electronic games. At the end of four weeks, if he had turned in 75 percent of his assignments, he would be allowed to rejoin his intramural team and his mother would purchase an additional electronic game of Josh's choosing.

During the next four weeks, Josh completed assignment sheets, which his teachers and his mother checked. Occasionally he forgot to take the assignment sheet to class, but overall he accepted responsibility for his homework. At the end of four weeks, a check by Josh's counselor showed that he had turned in 90 percent of his assignments. Josh rejoined his intramural team, and his mother followed through on her promise to buy him an electronic game. It was agreed that as long as Josh kept his grades above the D level, he would no longer be required to fill out assignment sheets.

High School Developmental Concerns
Grades 9–12

During the high school years, students continue to develop their relationship skills, sense of identity, and independence. Friendships are increasingly sincere, consistent, and longlasting. During this period of development, time spent with family decreases and time with peers increases. Although acceptance by peers, and particularly those of the opposite sex, is very important, high school students want to be recognized as unique individuals within their peer group (Karns and Myers-Walls 1987).

Two important goals of high school students are independence and identity (Karns and Myers-Walls 1987). As students become independent, they need better decision-making skills. Students make significant decisions concerning a myriad of issues: educational and career goals, sexuality, drug use, gang involvement, and dating. High school students struggle to keep up with the time and energy demands of schoolwork, athletic schedules, extracurricular activities, job responsibilities, church involvement, social schedules, family expectations, and post-secondary planning. As a result, they often have physical and emotional stress.

Counseling interventions for high school students may be more didactic, as adolescents function at a higher cognitive level than elementary and middle school children (Piaget 1976). Although didactic interventions may be appropriate, the counselor should still consider the student's learning style. Many students benefit more from interventions that are visual or "hands-on." Interventions for high school students are provided here for the developmental areas of relationships with adults, post-secondary planning, and stress.

Passivity Toward Adult Authority

Goal:	Developing relationship skills
Developmental problem:	Fear that adults will interpret their roles for them
Student outcome:	The student will learn and model assertiveness skills
Interventions:	Assertiveness training

As high school students work on developing independence and identity, many become more sensitive to adult authority. As a result, some students become hostile or defensive toward adults, especially teachers and school administrators who maintain authority in the school setting. Other students respond passively toward adults and may be frustrated as adults manipulate their behaviors.

Hutchinson and Reagan (1989) reported that seniors consider counseling for conflicts with teachers more than any other social/personal concern. Assertiveness skills can help students interact with teachers and other adults in authority. As defined by Robbins (cited in Votey 1989), "Assertive behaviors are the expression of one's rights, honest opinions, needs, and feelings in such a way as not to infringe on another's rights, opinions, needs, and feelings." Votey drew a distinction between assertiveness and passiveness (expressing versus not expressing) and assertiveness and aggressiveness (expressing without infringing versus expressing with infringing). Assertiveness skills enable students to stand up for themselves in a nonthreatening way that portrays respect for others.

Being assertive requires students to:

- state their needs and opinions
- explain how they feel
- tell what behaviors they are likely to elicit
- make requests of others, if appropriate

While being assertive, the student takes care not to make others feel defensive by attacking, criticizing, or blaming.

The counselor might demonstrate assertive skills by role-playing with the student. Role-playing (McFall and Marston 1970) combined with modeling and coaching, for the purpose of behavior rehearsal, is effective in helping students employ assertiveness techniques (McFall and Lillesand 1971).

April referred herself to her counselor because she thought her teacher showed preference to the boys in her senior-level physics class. She reported that the teacher spent more time helping the boys with their assignments and called on them more often in class. April felt left out and unimportant. She had thought about talking with the teacher but didn't think that was a good option.

"It won't do any good to talk to him. He won't listen. He only listens to his pets. He'll just get mad."

The counselor responded, "How about if I teach you a way to talk to adults so they might listen without getting mad"

"Like what?" asked April.

"Well, here's a couple of ways to be sure teachers *don't* hear what you have to say. Here's the first way."...

The counselor sat quietly for several minutes without saying a thing.

After a while April said slowly, "So...if I don't say anything, the teacher won't know what I want?"

"Right," the counselor responded. "Now here's the second way to make sure teachers don't hear what you want to say." The counselor shouted, "You stupid teacher! Don't you know you're being a chauvinist! Girls can learn science, too! You're the worst teacher I've ever had. I'm going to get the school board to fire you!"

April laughed at the counselor's exaggerated aggression. The counselor then explained the steps in assertive communication and modeled a possible discussion for April:

"Mr. Johnson, I'm having a problem in class that I thought you might be able to help me with. It's hard for me when you spend a lot of time with the boys. I feel left out and unimportant. It makes me feel like just giving up, not trying. I would really like it if you could spend time helping me with assignments and calling on me more in class."

April slowly nodded her head, "I can do that."

The counselor then played the role of the teacher while April practiced the new assertive behavior. They agreed that April would make an appointment with her physics teacher and then make another appointment with the counselor.

Hostility Toward Confrontive Adults

Goal:	Developing relationship skills
Developmental problem:	Fear that other adults will interpret roles for them
Student outcome:	The student will learn that others' behaviors are not indicative of their worth, and practice a method for remaining nonhostile in confrontive situations
Intervention:	Self-talk

As noted in the previous case study, high school students sometimes react with hostility when they are treated rudely or confronted by an authoritative adult. The students, wanting to define their own identity and independence, may work to "save face" by challenging or ignoring this type of adult behavior.

For example, a teacher bluntly accused one of his students of talking in class. The teacher shouted, "Josh! You stupid little brat! I told you to stop talking!"

The student snapped, "I wasn't talking!"

Upon hearing the student's words and his tone of voice, the teacher told the student to shape up or get kicked out of class. The student responded by storming out of the room and slamming the door.

In this example, the teacher and the student were each backed into a comer and the result was a lose-lose situation. The teacher failed to earn the student's respect, and the student was viewed as belligerent and most likely would be punished. The student can, however, turn this into a "win" situation.

Even though students have no control over rude or confrontive adults, they can control how the confrontation affects their own behavior and self-image. "Self-talk" enables students to feel good about themselves by stressing that another's rude or confrontive behavior does not necessarily indicate the student is "bad."

When using self-talk, the student simply repeats thoughts of "I'm okay. I don't agree with the way _____ is treating me, but that's his/

her problem. I'm okay." Students focus on their "okay-ness" rather than on the behavior of the teacher or other adult. This enables them to feel less victimized, enhances their self-image, and lessens their need to save face by being hostile.

The counselor may wish to emphasize the student's okay-ness by reflecting the student's thoughts and feelings while being careful not to enter into the criticism of a colleague. The counselor may reflect, "I can see you think Mr. Smith is acting unprofessionally when he calls you stupid in front of the class. In your opinion, Mr. Smith has the problem and you're okay."

The school counselor received an urgent message requesting his presence in a classroom where a small crisis was taking place. One of his junior counselees, Katie, had just called her substitute teacher a rude name, and the substitute had fled from the room in tears.

The counselor invited Katie to go for a walk with him, whereupon Katie vented her frustrations about the substitute. She seemed angry and defensive. Katie recounted that the substitute made uncomplimentary comments about her intelligence and appearance, calling her a "dumb blond" after a disagreement concerning a homework assignment. As they talked further, it became clear that in situations where Katie felt criticized by adults, she typically reacted with hostility.

The counselor introduced Katie to self-talk, suggesting that Katie repeat to herself, "I'm okay. I don't respect the way _____ is acting, but I'm okay." As the counselor gave Katie permission to disown the problem, she became quieter and calmer. Katie role-played the new behavior, reported feeling confident and calm, and said she intended to use self-talk in her next confrontation with a teacher.

The next day Katie returned to the counselor's office, "I just finished talking to the principal," she exclaimed. "He's a jerk! He gave me three 'Saturday Schools,' but I stayed calm. I just kept saying to myself, 'He's a jerk, I'm okay. He's a jerk, I'm okay.' It's a good thing I kept my mouth shut, too, because I think he was getting ready to suspend me!"

By using self-talk, Katie was able to stay calm and nonconfrontive. She affirmed her self-worth and also avoided being suspended from school.

Post-Secondary Planning

Goal:	Making effective decisions
Developmental problem:	Fear of inadequate vocational or academic training
Student outcome:	The student will employ a decision-making model in making high school course selections
Intervention:	Decision-making model

Making high school course selections can be nerve-wracking when students are undecided concerning their post-secondary plans. They often are afraid of being unprepared to enter college, technical school, or the career of their choice. A decision-making model can help students clarify their educational and career goals and plan their high school courses accordingly. One such model involves six steps:

1. *What is the problem?* In this step, the student defines the problem he or she would like to address.
2. *What is the student's vision?* The student pictures his or her life with the problem solved. What is he or she doing, how is he or she feeling, what are others doing, and so on?
3. *What has the student already tried?* The student recounts the interventions or solutions already tried and evaluates the effectiveness of each.
4. *What possible solutions could be tried next?* The student generates as many solutions as possible.
5. *What effect would each possible solution have on the vision?* The student considers each possible solution and analyzes its potential for leading to the desired vision.
6. *Which solution will be implemented?* Based on the analysis in step five, the student selects and implements the solution that is most apt to lead to the defined vision.

Paul, a tenth grader, was having trouble deciding which classes to take during his junior year and came to his counselor for assistance. The counselor discovered that Paul's difficulty was related to an unclear picture of his post-secondary plans. He agonized in deciding whether to take college preparatory or courses that would prepare him for a technical school (tech prep).

The counselor suggested a decision-making tool, introduced the model just outlined, and worked through the process with Paul. Because Paul had indicated earlier that he learned and organized best through visual expression, the counselor asked Paul to write down each of the steps. As the counselor looked on, Paul wrote the following:

1. Problem:	What courses should I take next year?
2. Vision:	Nice house / two cars / TV, CD player, etc. / able to pay bills / married / children / friends / vacations / parties / outdoor job / mechanical skills / work with people / college / apprenticeship ???
3. Already Tried:	College prep courses: hard / too much work / requires good grades / currently maintaining a 3.2 GPA / admissable to college
4. Possible Solutions:	a. All college prep courses b. All tech prep courses c. Combination of college prep and tech prep courses
5. Analysis:	a. All college prep— not ready for technical career / too hard / too much work / admissable to college / good income / promotions b. All tech prep— can't get into college / less income / easier classes / less work c. Combination— keeps all options open / still able to attend college or technical school
6. Selected Solution:	Combination of college prep and tech prep courses

Based on his problem-solving procedure, Paul decided to take a combination of college prep and tech prep courses. Although he didn't like the hard work involved with college prep courses, he recognized that college would most likely lead to the lifestyle he desired. With this in mind, he decided to keep all his options open. Paul signed up for Advanced Algebra, English, U.S. History, Chemistry, Spanish III, Construction Planning, and Technology II.

Stress

Goal:	Making healthy choices
Developmental problem:	Physical and emotional stress caused by one or more developmental problems

Student outcome: The student will learn and model a simple stress-reduction activity
Intervention: Diaphragmatic breathing

Growing up is stressful. Striving to master developmental tasks and their associated challenges causes the stress that most students experience. Many students add to this stress by overcommitting themselves to academics, sports, hobbies, clubs, jobs, and social activities. Some students leave for school almost every day at 6:30 am. for preschool activities and return home at 10:00 p.m. after sports practices and club meetings. The pressure of these commitments coupled with normal developmental stressors may tax students' physical and emotional capabilities. Counselors can provide an outlet for students to vent their concerns and can help them learn simple stress-reduction techniques.

Youngs (1985) discussed several simple stress-reduction techniques including diaphragmatic breathing, progressive muscle relaxation, autogenic training, visualization, and imagery. In diaphragmatic breathing, the student sits comfortably, eyes closed, and inhales while counting slowly to four. Next, the student slowly exhales while counting to six. The student continues this breathing pattern, placing the hands on the stomach. The counselor also may suggest that the student imagine his or her concerns being tossed away with each exhale and being filled with calmness with each breath. Diaphragmatic breathing may be used anywhere without bringing attention to the student.

Judy, a freshman, was referred to the counselor by her algebra teacher because she was failing most tests. The teacher was convinced that Judy knew the material covered in class but when tested, Judy almost always failed. As an experiment, the teacher included on a quiz several questions that had been assigned previously as classwork. Judy failed the test, missing the same questions she had gotten correct on the class assignment.

The counselor met with Judy, who reported that she felt terrified when facing a test. She clenched her teeth during the test and did her best, but she never could seem to remember how to do the problems. The counselor recommended diaphragmatic breathing, explained the technique, and modeled the behavior. Together, the counselor and Judy inhaled and exhaled while the counselor directed Judy to concentrate on her stomach, inhaling calmness and exhaling tension. Judy agreed to try the technique with her next test, and they agreed to meet again.

Before the counselor's next meeting with Judy, her algebra teacher stopped in the counselor's office to report that Judy passed that week's quiz and seemed to be relaxed during the test. Later, Judy reported that she had used diaphragmatic breathing and it had helped considerably.

SUMMARY

As they mature, students master developmental tasks, which may center on physical, psychological, or social growth. The American School Counselor Association groups these tasks into goals, which include: respecting others, developing positive attitudes, developing relationship skills, gaining self-awareness, gaining responsibility, resolving conflicts, making effective decisions, and making healthy choices.

Developmental tasks are age-appropriate and sequential, building upon each other. Students may have trouble mastering developmental tasks, making later tasks difficult and resulting in stress. Some stressors are common among different age groups.

School counselors can help struggling students by providing individual counseling experiences. During individual counseling, interventions are used to help students master difficult developmental tasks. While interventions are different for elementary-aged children, middle school students, and high schoolers, the same process is utilized in designing interventions for each developmental level.

An effective change process used in designing interventions includes three major stages: planning, implementation, and evaluation. In the planning stage, the counselor and student together define and explore the student's concerns and needs. The resulting plan may be implemented as a trial implementation, a stepped implementation, or full implementation, depending upon the student's needs. Other considerations in intervention design include the student's learning style and time constraints unique to the school counseling setting, which may be addressed through a brief counseling model.

Growing up has its ups and downs as students struggle to master developmental tasks. School counselors empower students to master these tasks through well-planned interventions used in individual counseling. Students are enabled to lead healthy, rich, and complete lives as they successfully travel the developmental pathway.

REFERENCES

Amatea, E. S., and L. Lochausen. 1988. Brief strategic intervention: A new approach to school counseling practice. *Elementary School Guidance and Counseling* 23(1): 39–47.

Amatea, E. S., and P. A. D. Sherrard. 1991. When students cannot or will not change their behavior: Using brief strategic intervention in the school. *Journal of Counseling and Development* 69(4): 341–343.

American School Counselor Association. 1990. *Counseling paints a bright future.* Alexandria, VA: ASCA.

Anderson, C. S. 1982. The search for school climate: A review of the research. *Review of Educational Research* 52: 368–420.

Bowman, R. P. 1987. Approaches for counseling children through music. *Elementary School Guidance and Counseling* 21: 284–291.

Campbell, C. A. 1991. Group guidance for academically undermotivated children. *Elementary School Guidance and Counseling* 25: 302–307.

Cole, M., and S. R. Cole. 1989. *The development of children.* New York: W. H. Freeman and Co.

Coleman, J. S. 1962. *The adolescent society.* Glencoe, IL: Free Press.

Erickson, E. H. 1958. *Young man, Luther.* New York: Norton.

Fairchild, T. N. 1983. Effects of a daily report card system on an eighth grader exhibiting behavioral and motivational problems. *School Counselor* 31: 83–86.

Gardner, R. 1992. *The psychotherapeutic techniques of Richard A. Gardner.* Creskill, NJ: Creative Therapeutics.

Gaushell, W. H., and D. M. Lawson. 1989. Using a checksheet with misbehaviors in school: Parent involvement. *School Counselor* 36: 208–214.

Gladding, S. T. 1985. Counseling and the creative arts. *Counseling and Human Development* 18: 1–12.

Griggs, S. A. 1983. Counseling high school students for their individual learning styles. *Clearing House* 56: 293–296.

Griggs, S. A. 1985. Counseling for individual learning styles. *Journal of Counseling and Development* 64: 202–205.

Havighurst, R. 1972. *Developmental tasks and education.* New York: David McKay.

Hill, C. R., and F. P. Stafford. 1980. Parental care of children: Time diary estimates of quantity, predictability, and variety. *Journal of Human Resources* 15: 219–239.

Hoover, J., and R. J. Hazler. 1991. Bullies and victims. *Elementary School Guidance and Counseling* 25: 212–219.

Hutchinson, R. L., and C. A. Reagan. 1989. Problems for which seniors would seek help from school counselors. *School Counselor* 36: 271–279.

Karns, J., and J. A. Myers-Walls. 1987. *Ages and stages of child and youth development: A guide for 4-H leaders.* West Lafayette, IN: Purdue University, Department of Child Development and Family Studies.

Kurpius, D. J., and T. Rozecki. 1992. Outreach, advocacy, and consultation: A framework for prevention and intervention. *Elementary School Guidance and Counseling* 26: 176–189.

Mathias, C. E. 1992. Touching the lives of children: Consultative interventions that work. *Elementary School Guidance and Counseling* 26: 190–210.

McFall, R. M., and D. Lillesand. 1971. Behavior rehearsal with modeling and coaching in assertion training. *Journal of Abnormal Psychology* 3: 313–323.

McFall, R. M., and A. R. Marston. 1970. An experimental investigation of behavior rehearsal in assertive training. *Journal of Abnormal Psychology* 76: 295–303.

Myrick, R. 1987. *Developmental guidance and counseling: A practical approach.* Minneapolis: Educational Media Corp.

Nickerson, E. T., and K. O'Laughlin, eds. 1982. *Helping through action: Action oriented therapies.* Amherst, MA: Human Resource Development Press.

Piaget, J. 1976. *Piaget sampler: An introduction to Jean Piaget through his own words.* New York: Wiley.

Robbins, J., ed. 1979. *The gentle art of saying no: Principles of assertiveness* [Filmstrip]. Pleasantville, NY: Sunburst Communications.

Rubin, J. A. 1988. Art counseling: An alternative. *Elementary School Guidance Counseling* 22: 180–185.

Searight, R. S., and P. Openlander. 1984. Systemic therapy: A new brief intervention model. *Personnel and Guidance Journal* 62(7): 387–391.

Smollar, J., and J. Youniss. 1982. Social development through friendship. In K. Rubin and H. Ross, eds., *Peer relationships and social skills in childhood.* New York: Springer Verlag, pp. 279–298.

Vernon, A. 1989a. *Thinking, feeling, behaving: An emotional education curriculum for children* (Vol. 1, pp. 137–138). Champaign, IL: Research Press.

Vernon, A. 1989b. *Thinking, feeling, behaving: An emotional education curriculum for children* (Vol. 2, p. 445). Champaign, IL: Research Press.

Votey, S. 1989. Helping teens to say "no": An assertiveness training program for sophomores. *School Counselor* 36: 198–202.

Youngs, B. B. 1985. *Stress in children.* New York: Avon Books.

Individual Counseling:
Creative
4 Interventions

Loretta J. Bradley

L. J. Gould

Department of Educational Psychology
Texas Tech University
Lubbock, Texas

The theoretical orientation of the counselor, psychologist, social worker, or other mental health professional is a consideration in any discussion of techniques and interventions because how the mental health professional chooses an intervention, or if one is used at all, will depend on her/his theoretical base. Although most theories can be adapted for use with children, four—psychoanalytic, humanistic, behavioral, and developmental—appear to be the most widely used (O'Connor 1991).

When working with children, recognition of developmental stages is important because, to be effective, counseling must be appropriate for the developmental level. Regardless of the counseling approach, counselors often encounter problems when working with children because developmentally children experience difficulty with the verbal expression necessary for most counseling approaches. Children have seldom reached the level of cognitive development that allows for spontaneous introspection. Furthermore, children's limited attention spans cause them to be easily bored.

Counselors should be exposed to a variety of interventions. To depend on one theory or one approach restricts the counseling process, as does dependence on one counseling technique. In contrast, familiarity with a variety of interventions enhances the likelihood that the technique is selected because of the client's need, not because of counselor preference. Knowledge of several interventions also helps to prevent counselors from becoming overly reliant on a single technique. In addition, it is the counselor's responsibility to use techniques that are both interesting and developmentally appropriate for children.

Although the theoretical orientation of the counselor will affect her/his counseling style, there are certain necessary conditions that all counselors working with children must maintain. Researchers have described the following as essential (Axline 1947, 1979; Caster 1984; Guerney 1983a; Gumaer 1984; Hellendoorn 1988; Landreth 1987; Murphy

1975; O'Connor 1991; Thompson and Rudolph 1988; Waterland 1975):

1. The counselor should show genuineness, empathy, and unconditional positive regard for the child.
2. The counselor should have the ability to establish a therapeutic relationship with the child.
3. The counselor should attempt to understand the child's world. The counselor should not have any preconceived expectations or standards of behavior for the child.
4. The counselor should know himself or herself well enough to be able to remain objective and serve the child's needs without becoming overly emotionally involved.
5. The counselor should have a sense of humor and be able to enjoy play.
6. The counselor should be flexible in thinking about his or her hypotheses and goals and be able to adjust them according to the child's discovery process.
7. The counselor should have good active listening and observation skills in order to determine the child's problem areas and to aid the child's working process.
8. The counselor should use reflection to help the child gain insight into his or her problems but should be cautious in the use of interpretation so that the child is not overwhelmed.
9. The counselor should make the counseling area a safe place for the child to show actions or behaviors, even those not acceptable in the outside world.
10. The counselor should be directive in structuring the sessions according to location, date, time, and length, and set those limits necessary to keep the child safe.

PLAY THERAPY

One of the most popular techniques used with children is play therapy. Before conducting play therapy, however, counselors and other mental health professionals must understand play. Play is a pleasurable, spontaneous, and voluntary process in which a child is actively involved (Garvey 1977). It is noninstrumental and has no goal, purpose, or task orientation (Bettelheim 1972; O'Connor 1991; Plant 1979). Play is an activity in which a child feels comfortable. It is the natural way for a child to communicate, act out sensitive material, gain security, and attain self-confidence. Through play, children can express their emotions and try out new ways of thinking and behaving (Barlow, Strother, and Landreth 1985; Esman 1983; Gumaer 1984; Klein 1979). Kransor and Pepler (1980) described four components of play: nonliterality, positive affect (pleasure) intrinsic motivation, and flexibility. Smilansky (1968) offered a progression of four stages of play:

1. *Functional play.* The child manipulates objects and attempts to repeat actions while exploring his or her environment.
2. *Constructive play.* An extension of functional play, it occurs when the child sets and reaches goals and begins to create rather than simply manipulate objects.
3. *Dramatic play.* The child learns about relationships between play and reality, begins to use objects, actions, and language as realistic props, and understands how to begin to socially and verbally interact with other players.
4. *Games with rules.* When children have become comfortable interacting with each other, they begin to negotiate to make rules and learn to accept and adjust to prearranged rules.

Implementing play in counseling children has several advantages:

1. The child is given the freedom to choose whatever type of play he or she wants (Allen 1979; Axline 1979).
2. Play easily brings out fantasies and unconscious feelings (Allen 1979; Axline, 1979; Hellendoorn 1988).
3. Play offers the child familiar tools to be used in relating to his or her feelings outside of counseling and in relating to the counselor (Allen 1979).
4. The only limits imposed on the child are to prevent harm to himself or herself and others (Axline 1979; Thompson and Rudolph 1988).
5. Play therapy allows the child a safe place in which to act out his or her feelings, gain understanding about himself or herself, and change (Axline 1947; Barlow et al. 1985).

Materials and Setting

Although a permanent area in which to conduct play therapy is best, it is not a requirement (Axline 1947). Cassell (1979) described a portable playroom used in hospital counseling in which all materials are carried in two suitcases and a portable doll house. If a permanent area is available, it should have adequate available light and be easily cleaned. Furnishings and equipment should include a child-sized table and chairs, a chalkboard, storage for toys and art materials, and a sink with cold water.

Play materials should meet the following criteria (Thompson and Rudolph 1988):

1. Facilitate the relationship between the counselor and child.
2. Encourage the child's expression of thoughts and feelings.
3. Aid the counselor in gaining insight into the child's world.
4. Provide the child with an opportunity to test reality.
5. Provide the child with an acceptable means for expressing unacceptable thoughts and feelings.

Careful attention should be given to the choice of materials; the rule should be selection, not accumulation (Landreth 1987; Lebo 1979). Barlow et al. (1985) suggested three categories of play media: real-life toys, acting-out and aggressive-release toys, and creative expression and emotional-release toys. Using the three categories, the following toys are suggested for use in play therapy:

Real-life toys:	doll house and furniture, dolls, doll clothes, doll buggy, bendable doll family, rag doll, household items (iron, ironing board, play kitchen, dishes), telephone, cars, farm animals and buildings, medical kit, school kit, play money, plastic fruit, purse, jewelry.
Acting-out and aggressive-release toys:	handcuffs, balls, dart gun and suction darts, dart board, suction throwing darts, pounding bench and hammer, drum, blocks, toy soldiers and military equipment, rubber knife, toy gun, masks, inflatable punching toy.
Creative expression and emotional-release toys:	colored chalk and eraser, sandbox and sand pencils, paints and brushes, felt-tip pens, white and colored paper, easel, crayons, tape, paste, blunt scissors, Play-Doh®, clay or plasticine, pipe cleaners, hats and costumes, rags or old towels, hand puppets (family, doctor, nurse, police officer, postal worker, firefighter, witch, monsters, dog).

Play Therapy Process

Writing on the progression of play therapy, Gumaer (1984) stated:

Children express self in play and the counselor responds to their feelings and behaviors in such a way as to convey the necessary conditions of a child-centered relationship. As children experience this relationship, they tend to express conscious feelings openly and to explore and to create situations in play which allow for the expression of unconscious emotions. The counselor is then able to assist in the understanding of feelings and behaviors and their relationship to life. (p. 65)

According to Gumaer (1984), the process of play therapy is counselor-controlled and related to the following five factors:

1. The counselor's ability to establish a therapeutic relationship with the child.
2. The goals of counseling, including the counselor's ability to identify the child's problem.
3. The counselor's planning skills and his or her use of play media.
4. The counselor's facilitative responding skills.
5. The time available to be spent with the child.

These factors are considered in relation to three progressive stages.

Stage One

The first stage is characterized by an open, permissive atmosphere in which the counselor attempts to create the conditions necessary for a child-centered relationship. The counselor initially focuses on the feelings generated by the child's play behavior and responds to those feelings. The counselor may clarify or ask open-ended questions that encourage the child to verbalize about play, but he or she should refrain from giving advice, making judgments, or teaching. In this stage the counselor should develop hypotheses regarding the nature of the child's problems or needs.

Stage Two

The second stage is characterized by an established therapeutic relationship in which the counselor can be more assertive in directing the child's play without harming the relationship. In this stage, the counselor reviews his or her hypotheses and selects the one that appears to be most immediate or crucial to the child's welfare and encourages the child to play with specific toys that are most likely to elicit feelings and behaviors related to the hypothesis. As the child plays, the counselor may initiate additional exploration of feelings and behavior the child demonstrates. If the counselor decides the hypothesis is faulty, he or she should redirect play to another area.

Stage Three

Because the counselor is now more certain about the problem, he or she takes a more active role. The counselor engages the child in systematically structured play sequences that encourage the child to face the conflict area. The counselor may use a desensitization process that takes the child from relatively nonthreatening to highly threatening stimuli related to the problem.

For example, if the counselor is working with a child who is afraid of dogs, he or she might bring a puppy into the room while the child is playing with a particularly enjoyable toy. The puppy would be brought only inside the door at first. Then, as the child becomes accustomed to the puppy's presence, it would be brought closer to the child over a period of several sessions. The presence of the pleasurable stimuli (the toy) lessens the threatening nature of the aversive stimuli (the puppy). The child begins to identify the aversive stimuli with the pleasurable stimuli, thus reprogramming his or her anxiety.

In all stages, the counselor responds to feelings, clarifies behavior, and uses open-ended questions to encourage the child to verbalize during the play process. After the relationship between the child and the counselor has been established, the counselor may move from nondirective to more directive play. Some researchers (Axline 1979; Carter 1987; Guerney 1983a) concluded that children will move to the problem area on their own without the counselor's direction. Hambridge (1979) and Hellendoorn (1988) stated that directive play should be used as a stimulus when the child resists or is stuck.

TECHNIQUES

Among the techniques of child therapy are those for art therapy, bibliotherapy, dance and movement therapy, emotional release, fantasy and guided imagery, games, magic, music therapy, nondirective play, puppets, role-playing and drama therapy, sand play, self-esteem building, storytelling, and writing therapy.

Art Therapy

Art is relaxing and soothing to a nervous child, and manipulation can be a lubricant for the verbal communication of thoughts and feelings (Rubin 1988). Children should be allowed to choose the medium they want to use; counselors' suggestions should be limited to technical areas. Children may create masks of clay or construction paper to facilitate hiding games; make sculptures of people they know (possibly targets of anger and hostility); or draw their dreams or fears (Rubin 1984). Regardless of the medium the children choose for their art, the counselor should leave time at the end of the session for them to discuss their work (Nader and Pynoos 1991).

Some children may be concerned that their art products will not be good enough, so the counselor must stress that the process, rather than the product, skill, or aesthetic quality, is the most important thing (Dalley 1990).

Color Your Life

Prerequisite: The child must be of average intelligence and have the cognitive ability to name colors and recognize affective states.

Materials: Any type of coloring instruments (paint, crayons, chalk, pencils), plain white paper. Available colors must include: yellow, green, blue, black, red, purple, brown, and gray.

Procedure:

1. Ask the child to pair an emotion or feeling with a color. If the child seems to be having trouble, the counselor may prompt him or her with questions such as, "What feeling might go with the color red?"

2. Have the child continue to pair emotions with color. The most common associations are red/anger, purple/rage, blue/sad, black/very sad, green/jealousy, brown/bored, gray/lonesome, and yellow/happy; the child might also pair orange/excitement, pink/feminine, and blue-green/masculine. Combinations are limited only by the child's knowledge of feelings and colors, imagination, and ingenuity. Usually, however, limiting the associations to eight or nine pairs is wise.

3. Once the pairs are established, give the child the white paper. Tell him or her to fill the paper with colors to show the feelings he or she has had during his or her life. The counselor might ask, "How much of your life have you been happy?" Color that much of your paper (yellow)."

4. Explain to the child that he or she is to color the paper in whatever designs he or she wishes until it is completely covered in colors. Encourage the child to verbalize as he or she colors. (O'Connor 1983)

Directed Art Counseling

Materials: pencil, white paper

Procedure:

1. Ask the child to focus on one image or some aspect of a drawing that seems symbolic.

2. At the beginning of the next session, ask the child to amplify the image and draw it again. When discussing the drawing, talk directly to the symbol or image because it contains and reflects the child's emotions and experience.

3. As the child draws the image over several sessions, watch for symbols of pain (hurt, wounds, damage) or growth (new trees, flowers, babies). Early sessions more likely will focus on pain, and later sessions are more apt to show growth images, indicating progress.
(Allan and Clark 1984)

Finger Painting

Materials: paints, paper (14" x 17", thicker than regular), water
Procedure:

1. Invite the child to make a picture using finger paints. Avoid giving any suggestion of theme or colors. Younger children are likely to use several colors; older children may use only one.

2. Observe the child's behavior and choice of colors for indication of mood.

3. When the painting is complete, ask the child if it tells a story.
(Arlow and Kadis 1979)

Fold-Over Game

Materials: pencils, paper
Procedure: (This game is for two players—counselor and child or two children):

1. Have each player draw a person's head and neck at the top of a sheet of paper. Then fold the paper forward to leave the base of the neck showing.

2. Exchange the papers, and have each player draw the body from neck to waist. Again fold and exchange the papers.

3. Ask each player to draw the body from the waist (clue marks indicate where to start) to the feet.

The game's purpose is to bypass blocks, find hidden resources, induce conversation, and encourage cooperation.
(Nickerson 1983)

Psycho-Iconography

Materials: paper, felt-tip pen
Procedure:

1. Draw a dot on the paper with a felt-tip pen, and give it to the child.

2. Ask the child to draw anything that comes to mind from a doodle to a picture.
3. Ask the child to tell about the significance of the drawing. (Nickerson 1983)

Serial Drawing Technique

Based on Jung's belief that drawings should be viewed in a series over time, this technique may be nondirective, partially directive, or directive, depending on the child's ability to control his or her own process.
Materials: 8-1/2" x 11" white paper, pencil without eraser
Procedure:
1. Give the child paper and pencil and ask him or her to draw a picture (nondirective). If the child seems unable to call on his or her own initiative, suggest a subject based on your assessment of the child's problem. The House-Tree-Person test (Buck 1948) may prove useful (directive).
2. If the child has demonstrated that a certain symbol has special relevance, ask the child to redraw it every four to six sessions, allowing enough time to elapse for processing changes in attitude or relationships (partially directive).
3. After the child has completed his or her drawing, ask if it tells a story. Also ask about any observations he or she made during the drawing.
(Allan 1988)

Squiggle Drawing Game

Materials: pencil or felt-tip pen, paper
Procedure:
1. Draw a squiggle on a piece of paper and give it to the child.
2. Ask the child to make the squiggle into a picture.
3. Ask the child to tell a story about the drawing.

This technique is often used with resistant or reluctant children.
(Nickerson 1983)

A discussion of art therapy would not be complete without mention of computer graphics. Most graphics programs have both free-drawings (using a mouse or stylus) and symbol representations that may be overlain with line graphics or colors. Johnson (1987) suggests Koala Pad (1983), for use with the Apple II computer, which has special features that allow drawing lines, circles, rectangles, and using colors.

Bibliotherapy

Bibliotherapy may be divided into two parts: (1) surface theory, which refers to what the reader can report as a response to the reading, and (2) depth theory, which refers to hypothesizing about what happens unconsciously during fiction reading (McKinney 1977). According to McKinney, depth theory leads to the reader's catharsis by recalling past events and discussing those events with the counselor.

Bibliotherapy allows children to identify with a character, gain insight into their own behavior, feel anxiety about the story's situation, and have an emotional release. Watson (1980) set forth the goals of bibliotherapy as:

1. Teaching constructive and positive thinking.
2. Encouraging free expression of problems.
3. Assisting the child in analyzing his or her attitudes and behaviors.
4. Fostering the search for alternative solutions to problems.
5. Allowing the child to discover that his or her problem is similar to others' problems.

Just as children may accept themselves as they accept fictional characters, the reverse is also true. The fiction might produce anxiety so profound that children will condemn and reject the characters.

Bibliotherapy is not limited to books and stories. Filmstrips, films, videotapes, and movies also may be used. For an extensive bibliocounseling book list, see Thompson and Rudolph (1988).

Basic Technique

Materials: Assorted books and stories, related to the child's problem area

Procedure:

1. Allow the child to select from a prepared list or have the books available for the child to look through.
2. Give the child time to read the selection of his or her choice, or read the book aloud to the child.
3. Focus on the literature. Ask the child to tell the story and focus on the characters and action.
4. Ask the child about his or her perceptions of the characters' behavior and feelings. Help the child to identify alternatives and consequences of the story.
5. Focus on the child's reality. Be sure the child is ready to accept and define the problem as it exists for him or her. Encourage the

child to personalize and relate to the themes in the story in view of his or her personal experience.

6. Evaluate, with the child, the effectiveness of the characters' behaviors. Aid the child in determining how he or she could apply those behaviors to his or her own life.
   (Gumaer 1984)

Dance and Movement Therapy

Dance and movement therapy are vehicles for reducing anxiety and working out anger and frustration. Children may be invited to express themselves by marching, skipping, hopping, clapping hands, snapping their fingers, stomping their feet, or dancing. Self-expression is the object of the play. Dance and movement therapy may be used with or without background music as an accompaniment. Most techniques are focused toward group work (Gumaer 1984; Payne 1988).

Emotional Release

Children often have trouble finding acceptable ways to express their emotions. The following are helpful techniques:

Aggression/Anger

1. Give children something they can tear up. Old telephone books, magazines, or newspapers work very well.
2. Give children several Nerf® balls to throw across the room. If these balls are not available, obtain objects that are small and will not do damage (small plastic figures, rubber balls, bean-bags).
3. Give children a punching bag or pillow for hitting, punching, or kicking.
4. If children are unable to display their anger, introduce the parallel with animals. Ask, "How does a dog act when it is angry?" Growl and bark like a dog, and ask the child to join in. Other animals you might refer to are bears, tigers, lions, and cats.

Feelings

1. For young children: Write a feeling word on each of several 3" x 5" cards, perhaps printing positive feelings in red and negative feelings in black. Give the cards to the child and ask him or her to select several feelings from both groups. Then give the child a stack of blank cards and ask him or her to "Show me how

much you feel happy (sad, safe, afraid, love, hate, etc.)." Have the child take a card with a feeling word and place it on top of as many of the blank cards as he or she believes expresses the amount of his or her feeling.

2. For older children: Give the child blank cards and ask him or her to write how he or she feels, one feeling per card. Then sort the cards into positive and negative emotions. Ask which feeling the child would like to work on. Then discuss with the child the problem that evokes that feeling. When the child believes he or she has managed the problem, give him or her the card to tear up.

3. Board games can help a child clarify and express feelings. Using a game board with colored spaces (red, yellow, green, blue), assign feelings to the colors: red/anger, blue/sadness, yellow/happiness, green/worry. Have the child roll a die and move a marker along the board, then describe a time when he or she may have felt like that color.

Other Techniques

1. *Thought-stopping* (a behavioral technique). Ask the child to signal the counselor when he or she has an inappropriate thought. Shout "Stop!" which startles the child. As counseling progresses, teach the child to subvocalize "Stop!" when he or she begins thinking inappropriately. As a variation of this technique, have the child make a "stop" sign to put inside his or her notebook, pocket, or desk as a reminder to stop negative thoughts or behaviors

2. *Reframing*. When a child says, "I hate my mom because she won't let me do the things I like," ask the child to reframe the statement into an "I love" statement such as, "I love my mom because she cares enough to set limits." This technique also can be applied with self-concept statements such as, "I'm too lazy to get my homework done," reframed to, "I get so involved in interesting things that I choose to do that I sometimes forget my homework."

3. *Paradoxical interventions*. Consider this technique with a child who worries a lot. Ask the child to exaggerate a thought or behavior that is disrupting. Ask the child to set aside a specific time each day to worry about everything. Ask a child who fears speaking out in class to sit in the back of the room and say nothing at all. By exaggerating the behavior, the child is con-

fronted with how he or she reacts in certain situations, and the consequences of that behavior. Paradoxical intentions should be limited timewise, possibly from one counseling session to the next.

Fantasy and Guided Imagery

Guided imagery and fantasy techniques can be applied to a variety of situations including emotional problems and blocks, reducing anxiety and fear, behavior change, and enhancing self-concept. The counselor evokes three types of images: (1) *spontaneous images*, without conscious direction of content, including daydreams, fantasies, creative thinking, and contemplation; (2) *directed images*, in which the child is given a specific image on which to concentrate or react; and (3) *guided imagery*, which combines both spontaneous and directed images by giving the child a starting point and allowing him or her to fill in the actions or ambiguous situations (Witmer and Young 1985). Imagery may be used in problem-solving to help a child reexperience and resolve past situations or fantasize about future possibilities (Witmer and Young 1987).

Basic Technique

1. Make sure the room is quiet and has comfortable chairs or a carpeted floor on which to lie. Keep a calm and soothing voice at all times. Emphasize that the child is in control of the process.
2. Start by helping the child to relax, perhaps suggesting that the child close his or her eyes and breathe slowly and deeply. Say, "Concentrate on your breathing ...in...out...in...out.... Feel the tension flow out of your body." If the child seems to have trouble relaxing, try some tense/relax exercises to help.
3. When the child has relaxed, begin the fantasy/guided imagery. Keep the exercise simple at first. Suggest that the child allow his or her mind to become blank, like an empty TV or movie screen.
4. Ask the child to imagine a single object, something familiar, such as an orange. Lead the child in experiencing the orange— how it looks, how it feels, how it smells, how the juice runs out when it is cut. Be sure to use something that is not threatening to the child.
5. Ask the child to allow his or her mind to go blank again. Then tell the child to open his or her eyes. Ask the child how he or she felt during the exercise.

Body Trip

1. Ask the child to imagine shrinking to the size of a small pea.
2. Have the child imagine entering his or her own body through the mouth. As the child travels from one part of the body to another, instruct him or her to explore each part and think about how feelings are expressed there (butterflies in the stomach, tension in the shoulders).
3. After the child completes his or her journey and exits the body, ask about the experience and how he or she felt during the exercise.

Concentration Box

1. Help the child relax, then count backward from ten to one. Ask the child to close his or her eyes on the count of one.
2. Ask the child to imagine an empty box of any shape, size, and color. Ask the child to examine the box completely—top, sides, and bottom.
3. Instruct the child to maintain the image of the box and not allow other thoughts to enter his or her mind.
4. Ask the child to imagine a door with a lock appearing on the box.
5. Instruct the child to open the door and allow another image to enter. (Any concrete image will work—a witch, favorite food, animal, or favorite character from a book.)
6. After the image enters the box, instruct the child to lock the door.
7. Ask the child to examine the image, to notice colors, textures, and details that make the image unique.
8. Instruct the child to concentrate on the actions of the image, to control the actions of the image.
9. Periodically remind the child to keep other thoughts out of the box even if they are knocking on the door.
10. Bring the child slowly out of the fantasy by instructing the child to open the door and allow the image to fly away while counting from one to ten.
    (Brackett 1979)

Relaxation

Ask the child to sit back and relax, to focus on his or her breathing, and to listen to soft music. Instruct the child to allow his or her thoughts to become pictures that flow through his or her mind with the music. After

five to ten minutes, ask the child to open his or her eyes. This exercise often aids children in attention and concentration.
(Anderson 1980)

Wise Person Imagery

1. Instruct the child to relax and let go of any tension and worry.
2. Instruct the child to allow the face of a wise, loving person (may be parent, friend, stranger) to appear.
3. Tell the child that he or she may ask the wise person any questions he or she wishes, to listen, and to be receptive to whatever response comes. The child may have a conversation with the wise person, or the wise person may have a special message for him or her if the child is willing to receive it.
4. Tell the child that the wise person can return at any time to help him or her find strength or guidance.
5. Ask the child to say goodbye for now and open his or her eyes.
   (Witmer and Young 1987)

Imagery is not suitable for all children. It should not be used with children who are psychotic or have serious emotional problems as they are already too involved in fantasy. Further, the child and the parents should be informed about imagery before it is used in counseling. The counselor should emphasize that the child is in control of the process. If the question of hypnosis arises, the counselor should explain that imagery is simply focused attention and imagination, not hypnosis (Anderson 1980).

Games

Games have a variety of functions in counseling. They serve to establish rapport with a child because they are familiar and nonthreatening. They often have diagnostic value in that the counselor may observe a variety of behaviors, thoughts, and feelings. The child receives positive feedback, gains a sense of mastery, and indulges in a pleasurable experience, all of which strengthen the ego. Games allow feelings to be safely expressed or rechanneled. They permit the child to test reality by playing out different solutions in a safe environment. Finally, games allow the child to come to terms with objects and people, and learn to work within a system of rules and limits (Frey 1986; Nickerson and O'Laughlin 1983). Most children, even the most reluctant and negative, will consent to play a game with the counselor. Many board games are noncompetitive, which places the focus on the game's content rather than on the goal of winning. The child's family also tends to be open to playing games. Frey (1986) suggested three categories of games: (1) interpersonal communication games, (2) games for specialized populations, and (3) games with specific theoretical orientations.

Although board games are popular and used most often, they are not the only types of games played in counseling. When selecting games for use in counseling, according to Nickerson and O'Laughlin (1983):

1. The game should be familiar or easy to learn.
2. The game should be appropriate for the child's age and developmental level.
3. The game should have clear, inherent properties related to the therapeutic goals of counseling.

Games are suggested for use with resistant children, verbally deficient children, children in denial, anxious children, and inhibited children (Frey 1986).

Interpersonal Communication Games

Imagine. (Burks 1978) (For ages six to adult) The focus is on understanding emotions, attitudes, needs; enhancing creativity; and self-expression. The game is noncompetitive. Self-disclosure and expression are encouraged through the use of mythological symbols that hold conscious and unconscious meanings. Play is untimed.

Reunion. (Zakich and Monroe 1979) (For ages eight to adult; two to six players) This noncompetitive game focuses on childhood relations, feelings, visual imagery and perceptions, and empathic understanding. Play is untimed.

Social Security. (Burten 1976) (For ages six to adult) The game is noncompetitive and focuses on six areas—ownership of problems, exploration of feelings, problem-solving, adaptation to change, conflict management, and exploration of values. Play is untimed.

Talking, Feeling, Doing Game. (Gardner 1986) (For ages seven to twelve; ages four to six may play if the cards are read to them) This game is aimed at the counseling setting. The object is to accumulate chips by responding to cards that cover cognitive, affective, and behavioral aspects of the child.

Talking/Listening Game. (Shadle and Graham 1981) (For ages six to twelve; two to six players) The main focus is on improving interpersonal communication through enhanced listening and confronting skills, problem-solving, positive feedback, problem ownership, and environmental change. The game is noncompetitive and may be played by individuals, partners, or teams. Play is untimed.

Tiskit, Taskit (Kritzberg 1975) and *Board of Objects Game* (Gardner 1975) These are competitive games in which players tell a story about a common object or word. They receive chips for participating by telling a story, either factual or made-up, about the selected object or word. The objective is to collect the most chips (from telling the most stories) in the allotted time limit.

The Ungame. (Zakich 1975) (For ages five to adult; two to six players) This noncompetitive game encourages exploration of attitudes, feelings, motives, and values. Decks of colored cards contain questions and statements from areas such as lighthearted fun, other children, family communications, deeper understanding, psychologists and counselors, and ministers. Blank cards are included so the children or counselors can write their own questions. "Tell it like it is" spaces on the board encourage self-disclosure and communication with others. Play is untimed.

Specialized Games

Changing Family Game. (Berg 1986) (For ages approximately seven to adult; two to six players) The game uses cognitive restructuring and behavioral rehearsal to aid children in adjustment to divorce, visitation, and single-parent and blended families. The game covers six stages of the divorce cycle—family troubles, told of separation, parent moves out, life with mother, life with father, and life with different families—and eight major areas—peer ridicule and avoidance, paternal blame, maternal blame, self-blame, fear of abandonment, hopes for reunification, single parenting, and visitation. The game is competitive.

Family Contract Game. (Blechman and Olson 1976) The players (family members) negotiate with each other to move around the board. The counselor assists the family members in making a behavioral contract that is mutually satisfying and relevant to stated problems. The emphasis is on family interdependence. The game is noncompetitive and is structured with a low threat level.

Picture That. (Behrens 1986) The game uses cards (with drawings of children displaying affective responses and body postures) to depict how a child might feel in response to a "situation" card. The game helps children learn about interactions and gain awareness of the messages conveyed through body language and facial expression.

Problem-Solving Game. (Behrens 1986) A stack of cards reflects common problems for children, including shyness, aggression, fear, confusion, anger, difficulties with adults, divorce, and others. Players receive chips by giving solutions to the problems. The game is competitive but nonthreatening, because the child is helping someone else rather than himself or herself.

Self-Esteem Game. (Creative Health Services 1983) (For ages approximately eight to twelve; two to four players) The game is competitive but also cooperative in that all players must reach the "well-being" area for the game to end. The focus is on enhancing self-esteem by attending to individual behavior and interpersonal behavior with family, friends, and others. The game also presents coping options to help children learn to deal with both intra- and interpersonal setbacks.

Games with Specific Theoretical Orientations

Instant Replay Game (Bedford 1986) (For ages six to adult; can be played with children as young as 2 years by adjusting the vocabulary). The game is based on cognitive restructuring, within rational emotive therapy's (RETs) ABCDE framework. The child is asked to recall an event and describe what he or she was thinking before and during the event, and what the consequences were. The child then is asked to speculate on other possible options. The counselor points out the part that thinking played in the behavioral and emotional reactions to the event.

Rational Emotive Game (Frey 1986) (For ages six to eleven; two to six players). The objective is to learn to differentiate rational and emotional thinking. Game cards present stories demonstrating that beliefs are the underlying cause of emotions and actions. The game is competitive; a player wins by thinking rationally and advancing across the board.

Transactional Awareness Game (Oden 1976) (For adolescents to adult; one to six players). The game centers on improving self-understanding and relationships through feedback. The essential aspects of human transactions—power, warmth, acquiescence and resistance—are incorporated into the game play as players identify life scripts. The game is competitive.

Magic

Magic tricks may get the child's attention in counseling and can be used as rewards or reinforcements for the child's progress. Magic also can help the counselor build rapport with the child. The counselor can help build the child's self-esteem and self-confidence by teaching the child some magic tricks to use in his or her relationships with other children.

If the counselor is going to use magic, he or she should practice first, to become comfortable with the tricks (Bowman 1986).

Bag Trick

Illusion: throwing an "invisible rock" into the air and catching it in a
   paper bag, which jerks and makes a popping sound
Materials: one small paper bag
Procedure:
   1. Determine which finger is used with the thumb to make the best snapping sound.
   2. Grab the bag at the top with the thumb on the outside and the "snap" finger on the inside.
   3. Practice snapping finger and thumb until it produces the loudest possible sound. Notice that as fingers are snapped, the bag twitches slightly. Practice making the bag jerk more obviously as fingers are snapped.
   4. Once the snap and jerk are mastered, practice throwing "rocks" into the bag. Timing is important to make it look and sound real.
   5. Be creative in throwing rocks—over the shoulder, under the knee, behind the back, with eyes closed, and so on.
   6. Later, find rocks hidden behind ears, in belts, pockets, mouths, and so on.

Pin Through Balloon Trick

Illusion: thrusting a safety pin or needle through an inflated balloon
   without popping it
Materials: 1"-long safety pin or needle
   Balloon
   Piece of transparent tape
Procedure:
   1. Blow up balloon to 3/4 full of air; secure with a knot.
   2. Secretly place a 1"-long piece of transparent tape on the side of the balloon a few inches from the knot. The tape will keep the balloon from tearing.
   3. Hold the balloon so the tape is on top, facing away from the other person. Slowly thrust the pin through the tape and into the balloon.
      (Note: A commercial kit for this trick from Loftus is available at most magic shops.)

Other Magic Techniques

Bowman (1986) suggests that the following magic tricks work well with children in the counseling process. They are commercially available at most magic shops.

Magic Coloring Book. Show the child each page of a coloring book. The first time through, the pages have outlines of pictures just like a normal coloring book. The next time through, all of the pages are filled in with bright colors. The third time through, all of the pages are blank. When the book is opened the fourth time, the outlines are back.

Mouth Coil Trick. Take a tissue, tear it up, and wad it into a ball, then place it in his/her mouth. The magician grabs the tissue and pulls out a stream of multicolored paper 50 feet long.

Multiplying Sponge Balls. Place one large ball in your hand. Close your hand. When you open your hand, three or four balls jump into the air.

Separating Fan Trick. Show the child a fan that works properly until you say the magic word. The fan then seems to fall apart. Say another magic word, and the fan works properly again.

Music Therapy

Music therapy may be introduced to reduce anxiety, develop rapport, motivate, stimulate, or calm. For example, a child might beat a drum to work out frustration or anger. Music therapy often is applied in conjunction with other techniques to elicit memories, fantasies, and visual imagery. The counselor may use songs to teach children about their feelings, help them cope with their fears, or aid in self-understanding. Most techniques in music therapy are designed for group work (Bowman 1987; Gumaer 1984).

Nondirective Play

Materials: toys (chosen according to child's age)
Procedure:
1. Invite the child into the playroom and allow him or her to explore the area and the toys available.
2. Give the child time to become comfortable in the area.
3. When the child makes his or her toy choice and begins to play, observe quietly, accepting the child's feelings and behaviors.
4. Reflect on the child's behavior or respond to the child's verbalizations about play.

5. At the end of the session, ask the child to tell a story about the play.
   (Barlow et al. 1985)

Puppets

Puppets provide an opportunity for the child to play out feelings, reenact anxiety-causing events, and try out new behaviors (Axline 1947). The child may ask the counselor to take part in puppet play or to take a turn playing with the puppets (Hawkey 1979). Counselors who plan to use puppets themselves have to be skilled in their use. This includes developing a voice consistent with the puppet's personality, learning to keep the puppet constantly animated to hold the child's attention, and knowing when to talk to the child and when to talk to the puppet (James and Myer 1987).

Materials: 15–20 puppets, enough to stimulate the child's interest and offer a real choice. (Puppets may be bought or handmade.); puppet stage

Categories: realistic family (father, mother, sister, brother—black and white), royalty (king, queen, knight, lady, prince, princess), occupations (police officer, firefighter, cowboy, mail carrier), animals (tame and wild), monsters (devil, witch, ogre, skeleton)

Procedure:

1. Introduction: Ask the child if he or she would like to tell a story using puppets as the characters. Stress that the child can choose whether to play or not to play, and that the story may be on any subject the child desires.

2. Selection: Invite the child to choose the puppets with which he or she wishes to play. Observe the process for insights into the child's coping skills in facing new experiences, attitudes, interests, actions, and spontaneous verbalizations.

3. Warm-up: Invite the child to take the puppets he or she has chosen and go behind the stage and introduce the "characters" for the show. This helps the child prepare for the story. If the child seems to be having trouble getting started, ask open-ended questions about the character, such as "And this is..." or "This seems to be a cowboy; could you tell me about him?"

4. Play: After the introductions, say, "And now, the story." Most children will be intrigued enough to begin on their own. Observe the plot and action. If the child seems to be stuck at some point, comment on the "5 Ws" of construction (who, where, when, what, why).

5. Post-play interview with the characters: Speak directly to the puppets. This helps to clarify the plot and themes of the story—what did/did not happen, meanings, and motivations. The focus on the puppets extends the make-believe.

6. Post-play interview with the child: Invite the child to talk directly about the experience. Ask what stimulated his or her choice of puppets or story and if anything similar has happened in real life. This gives the counselor an opportunity to assess the child's capacity for self-observation, defenses, strengths and weaknesses, and coping mechanisms.
   (Irwin 1991)

Role-Playing/Drama Therapy

Drama therapy is spontaneous dramatic play involving a highly personalized kind of improvisation. The role the child plays may represent himself or herself, others in his or her life, or symbolic character types. The counselor gains information from the way in which the child plays the role. Drama therapy encourages safe expression of strong feelings, both positive and negative, and allows the child to learn from externalizing an experience. Drama play may be used in combination with other media, such as puppets or dolls (Irwin 1987). Costumes may be used with older children to facilitate dramatic play (Marcus 1979). Costumes may aid the child in switching roles (passive to aggressive, strong to weak, good to bad).

Smilansky (1968) suggested that children perform four different representations during role play.

1. The child may pretend by imitating the actions or words of familiar people and objects; the child is capable of enacting the role simply by declaring that he or she is someone or something.

2. The child may elaborate on his or her portrayals by using actions or words to represent real objects (for example, the child pretends to be a knight and uses an imaginary sword).

3. The child verbally creates actions and situations that demonstrate his or her ability to use representational thought (for example, the child creates a world in which he or she is the ruler and controls all of the action and people in his or her world).

4. The child develops play themes that relate to imaginary situations and preferred roles that are increasingly realistic; the child practices real life situations in play.

Gestalt Techniques

Gestalt therapy has added many techniques to the counselor's repertoire. Gestalt techniques often elicit a strong emotional reaction from clients. With some modification, most Gestalt techniques can be used with children. One that is especially valuable in conflict situations is the *empty-chair technique*.

Materials: 2 chairs
Procedure:

1. Invite the child to sit in one chair and play his or her role in the conflict, if the conflict is with another person, or play one side of the conflict if it is within himself or herself.
2. Ask the child to move to the other chair and play the other side of the conflict.
3. Have the child dialogue back and forth between the two sides of the conflict.

Variations of the empty-chair technique include

1. *Topdog/underdog*, in which the child confronts "I should" statements with "I want" statements.
2. *Dialoguing*, in which the child speaks to the empty chair as if it is someone in his or her life (parent, sibling, friend, teacher) (Okun 1987; Thompson and Rudolph 1988).
3. If the child is unable to talk to a chair, suggest a tape recorder or a dictaphone (Durfee 1979).

Sand Play

Sand play seldom requires active interpretation to the child. It seems to be a self-healing process in which the child engages with the counselor as a witness. The child demonstrates three stages in sand play: (1) chaos, which reflects and objectifies his or her emotional turmoil; (2) struggle, representing destructive impulses; and (3) resolution, as life begins to be more balanced (Allan and Berry 1987).

Materials: two 20" x 30" x 3" waterproof trays with sand (one for dry sand and one for wet sand); miniature toys and objects from which the child may choose (people, buildings, animals, vehicles, vegetation, structures, natural objects, and symbolic objects)
Procedure:

1. Invite the child to play in the sand, choosing from any of the objects available to create a landscape or sculpture or just play. Observe the child's actions and behaviors during play.

2. When the child indicates that he or she has completed the creation, ask him or her to tell a story about it. If the child has trouble verbalizing, gently ask questions or make comments that associate the sand play with real life.
3. Take a photograph of each completed work to maintain a record of the child's progress.
(Allan and Berry 1987; Vinturella and James 1987)

Techniques to Build Self-Esteem

Magic Box

Place a mirror in any type of box so it will reflect the face of anyone who looks inside. Say to the child, "I have a magic box that will show anyone who looks inside the most important person in the world." Ask the child who he or she thinks is the most important person in the world, and then invite him or her to look inside the box. After the child looks into the box, comment on the child's reaction and ask what he or she thought when seeing himself or herself. Explain that the box is valuable because it allows the child to see himself or herself as a special person.

Mirror, Mirror

Have a full-length mirror in the counseling room. Ask the child to stand in front of the mirror and say what he or she sees. Facilitate the process by statements such as: As you look at yourself in the mirror, tell what you like best. If the mirror could talk to you, what do you think it would say? What doesn't the mirror know about you? Often the child has difficulty saying anything positive about himself or herself. Encourage positive expressions by pointing out things you see in the child.

Positive Mantra

Ask the child to close his or her eyes and repeat with you, "No matter what you say or do to me, I'm still a worthwhile person." Although this seems simple, it can have a profound impact when done repeatedly. Ask the child, each time he or she begins the sentence, to imagine the face of someone who has put down him or her in the past. Have the child stick out his or her chin and repeat the sentence in a strong and convincing voice. After the child has become used to the sentence, interject statements such as, "You're stupid, ugly, lazy" (whatever the child says was directed to him/her) and let the child respond with, "No matter what you say or do to me, I'm still a worthwhile person."

Pride Line

Ask the child to make a statement about a specific area of behavior. Say, for instance, "I'd like you to tell me something about your free time that you're proud of." The child is instructed to say, "I am proud that I..." Specific behavior areas that might be used include: things done for parents or friends, school work, religion, something recently bought, habits, something shared, something worked hard for, and something owned.

What If

Ask the child, "Did you ever think of things like 'What if my bike could talk?' What do you think it would say about you?" The item could be a toothbrush, bed, dog, television, school desk, coat, or anything the child comes up with. This allows the child to become aware of his or her feelings about himself or herself by the use of projection. An alternative is to use, instead of objects, people in the child's life. This, however, depends on how trusting and open the child is and on the therapeutic relationship.

Wishing

Ask the child to imagine that he or she has been given three wishes. What would he or she wish for himself or herself, his or her parents, or a special friend? Ask what the child would wish for if he or she could relive the previous day. What would change or stay the same? Another variation is to ask if the child wishes he or she could be someone else. Who is this, and why does the child wish to be the other person? Also ask the child if he or she thinks anyone would wish to be him or her and, if so, why.

(Canfield and Wells 1976)

Storytelling

Mutual Storytelling Technique

Most children are intrigued by this activity, and willing to participate. If the child is not, substitute another form of play.

Materials: tape recorder
Procedure:

1. Ask the child if he or she would like to make a tape of a make-believe TV or radio show in which the child is guest of honor. Show the child other tapes that children have made, if available.
2. Turn on the tape recorder and make a few brief statements.

Asking children their name, address, age, school, and grade usually puts them at ease.

3. Ask the child to tell a story. Most children start immediately, but some may need time to think, or help to get started. If the child needs help, ask him or her about interests, hobbies, family, and the like.

4. While the child tells his or her story, take notes on the story's content and possible meaning.

5. When the child ends the story, ask if it might have a moral or lesson to be learned. Also ask for more details or information about specific items.

6. Make some comment about the child's story, such as how good (exciting, interesting, unusual) it was.

7. Turn off the tape recorder and prepare the child's story. Have him or her determine which figures represent the child and significant others in the child's life, what symbols the child used, and the overall "feel" of the setting and atmosphere of the story. Take into account the emotional reactions the child showed while telling his or her story. Use the child's moral or lesson in selecting the story's theme. Consider healthier resolutions or adaptations to problems than the child's story.

8. Turn on the tape recorder and tell your story, which involves the same characters, settings, and initial situation as the child's story but has a better resolution of conflict. In the story, provide the child with more alternatives to problems he or she encountered, and tell the child he or she may change his or her behavior. This story should attempt to emphasize healthier adaptations.

9. Turn off the tape recorder and ask the child if he or she would like to hear the completed program.
(Gardner 1979)

Child as Consultant

The counselor should be comfortable with this approach and the manipulation involved in this technique. Some counselors feel more comfortable using a "suppose" situation rather than leading the child to believe he or she is helping with a real client. Statements such as "a problem like yours" and "going through something like you are" should be avoided. The child and the imaginary child should be clearly differentiated while maintaining the dynamics of the situation (Thompson, Davis, and Madden 1986).

Procedure:
1. Review the relevant information about the child and his or her current situation obtained from the child and others. Then develop a situation analogous to the child's that incorporates the relevant dynamics.
2. Ask the child if he or she will be a "consultant" to help you with another problem.
3. If the child agrees, share the analogous situation with the child.
4. Ask the child to speculate, guess, or think about what the "other" child might be thinking or feeling. Then ask what advice or help might be given to the child in that situation.
5. Interpret the information and feed it back to the child in a story, or reframe the situation into a metaphor.

Writing Therapy

Writing may prove valuable when working with older children. It often goes deeper than cognitive functioning by tapping emotions and images. For example, it enhances children's awareness by helping organize their thoughts and feelings, providing cathartic emotional release and contributing to personal integration and self-validation. Some useful writing activities include:

- correspondence, which may be used when the child is unable or unwilling to sustain a verbal dialogue with another person.
- journal-keeping, which may be a stream of consciousness or structured in some manner.
- creative writing, prose, or poetry, which may be used to clarify projections, explore problems and solutions, or fantasize.
- structured writing, including making lists, instructions, and questions and answers, used in deliberate and conscious ways to organize specific concerns.

In any writing technique the child should be told that grammar, style, spelling, punctuation, and neatness are not important. The following techniques are suggested by Brand (1987) and Gumaer (1984).

Autobiography

Ask the child to write his or her autobiography. For children who are skilled in written expression, this can be an effective way to encourage self-disclosure and interaction with the counselor.

Brag Day

Ask the child to identify good things that have happened to him or her, or good things he or she has done, or talents that he or she has. This technique is for self-validation.

Lifeline

Draw a long line on a sheet of paper with a baby with a zero over his or her head at one end. Explain that the baby indicates the child's birth. Then ask the child to place a symbol on the line to indicate his or her age when he or she was the happiest or saddest and when the best and worst things happened in his or her life. As the child adds each event, encourage brief discussion.

Outer/Inner Exercise

Draw a line down the middle of a sheet of paper to make two columns. Label them "outer" and "inner." The "outer" column is for the events that took place at the time, and the "inner" column is for the child's feelings in relation to the events. Ask the child to focus on a specific, memorable time in his or her life.

Uninterrupted, Sustained, Silent Writing

Have the child write down everything that comes to mind until you tell him or her to stop, usually three to five minutes.

What's in a Name

Ask the child to focus on his or her own name and write about the kind of person who owns that name, what he or she looks like, how he or she acts, thinks, and feels. This technique is for self-exploration.

SUMMARY

Familiarity with a variety of interventions allows the counselor to select those that most closely match the child's developmental level and his or her needs. However, the counselor's preference must be secondary to the child's needs. The counselor should be genuine and empathetic in establishing a therapeutic relationship with a child during the counseling process. Additionally, he or she should attempt to understand the child's world, be objective, have a sense of humor, enjoy play, be flexible and willing to make adjustments as needed, and make the child feel safe. The counselor must have good listening and observation skills and be directive if necessary.

Play therapy is one of the most popular techniques employed when working with a child. The child feels comfortable playing because it is a natural pastime. In play therapy the child can communicate more naturally, act out sensitive material, gain security, and attain self-confidence. By observing play, the counselor can learn about the child's problems from his or her perspective.

This chapter has included techniques and interventions in the areas of art therapy, bibliotherapy, dance and movement therapy, emotional release, fantasy and guided imagery, games, magic, music therapy, nondirective play therapy, puppets, role-playing and drama therapy, sand play, self-esteem building, storytelling, and writing therapy. Although these techniques and interventions focus on children in individual counseling, most may be adapted for use with older clients and groups.

The information in this chapter is not limited to the counselor's office but may be used in many settings with clients experiencing a variety of problems. Many of these techniques and interventions have been used successfully in the following areas: abuse victims (Fagot and Kavanagh 1991; Mann and McDermott 1983; Sager 1990; Watson 1980); aggression and acting-out (Confer 1984; Swanson 1986; Trostle 1984; Willock 1983); crisis or trauma (Allan and Anderson 1986; Carter 1987; Nader and Pynoos 1991; Segal 1984; Terr 1983); developmental disorders and mental retardation (Jernberg 1979; Leland 1983); divorce (Epstein 1986; Mendell 1983); family therapy (Griff 1983; Ross 1991; Rubin 1984; Smith 1991; Stollak, Crandell, and Pirsch 1991); children with a disability (Rubin 1984; Solomon 1983); ill children (Cassell 1979; Golden 1983); psychiatric diagnosis and illness (Behar and Rapoport 1983; Ekstein 1983); and school guidance (Canfield and Wells 1976; Guerney 1983b; Landreth 1983, 1987).

REFERENCES

Allan, J. 1988. Serial drawing: A Jungian approach with children. In C. E. Schaefer, ed., *Innovative interventions in child and adolescent therapy* (pp. 98–132). New York: John Wiley & Sons.

Allan, J., and E. Anderson. 1986. Children and crises: A classroom guidance approach. *Elementary School Guidance and Counseling* 21: 143–149.

Allan, J., and P. Berry. 1987. Sandplay. *Elementary School Guidance and Counseling* 21: 300–306.

Allan, J., and M. Clark. 1984. Directed art counseling. *Elementary School Guidance and Counseling* 19: 116–124.

Allen, F. H. 1979. Therapeutic work with children. In C. Schaefer, ed., *The therapeutic use of child's play* (pp. 227–238). New York: Jason Aronson.

Anderson, R. F. 1980. Using guided fantasy with children. *Elementary School Guidance and Counseling* 15: 39–47.

Arlow, J. A., and A. Kadis. 1979. Finger painting in the psychotherapy of children. In C. Schaefer, ed., *The therapeutic use of child's play* (pp. 329–343). New York: Jason Aronson.

Axline, V. 1947. *Play therapy*. Boston: Houghton Mifflin.

Axline, V. 1979. Play therapy procedures and results. In C. Schaefer, ed., *The therapeutic use of child's play* (pp. 209–218). New York: Jason Aronson.

Barlow, K., J. Strother, and G. Landreth. 1985. Child-centered play therapy: Nancy from baldness to curls. *School Counselor* 32: 347–356.

Bedford, S. 1986. The "instant replay" game to improve rational problem solving. In C. E. Schaefer and S. E. Reid, eds., *Game play. Therapeutic use of childhood games* (pp. 147–157). New York: John Wiley & Sons.

Behar, D., and J. L. Rapoport. 1983. Play observation and psychiatric diagnosis. In C. E. Schaefer and K. J. O'Connor, eds., *Handbook of play therapy* (pp.193–199). New York: John Wiley & Sons.

Behrens, C. 1986. Therapeutic games for children. In C. E. Schaefer and S. E. Reid, eds., *Game play: Therapeutic use of childhood games* (pp. 187–194). New York: John Wiley & Sons.

Berg, B. 1986. The changing family game: Cognitive-behavioral intervention for children of divorce. In C E. Schaefer and S. E. Reid, eds., *Game play: Therapeutic use of childhood games* (pp. 111–128). New York: John Wiley & Sons.

Bettelheim, B. 1972. Play and education. *School Review* 81, 1–13.

Blechman, E. A., and D. H. L. Olson. 1976. The family contract game: Description and effectiveness. In D. H. L. Olson, ed., *Treating relationships* (pp. 133–150). Lake Mills, IA: Graphic.

Bowman, R. P. 1986. The magic counselor: Using magic tricks as tools to teach children guidance lessons. *Elementary School Guidance and Counseling* 21: 128–138.

Bowman, R. P. 1987. Approaches for counseling children through music. *Elementary School Guidance and Counseling* 21: 284–291.

Brackett, S. 1979. The concentration box. *Elementary School Guidance and Counseling* 14: 134.

Brand, A. G. 1987. Writing as counseling. *Elementary School Guidance and Counseling* 21: 266–275.

Buck, J. N. 1948. The H-T-P test. *Journal of Clinical Psychology* 4: 151–159.

Burks, H. 1978. *Imagine*. Huntington Beach, CA: Arden.

Burten, R. 1976. *Social security*. Anaheim, CA: The Ungame Company.

Canfield, J., and H. C. Wells. 1976. *100 ways to enhance self-concept in the classroom: A handbook for teachers and parents*. Boston: Allyn and Bacon.

Carter, S. R. 1987. Use of puppets to treat traumatic grief: A case study. *Elementary School Guidance and Counseling* 21: 210–215.

Cassell, S. 1979. The suitcase playroom. In C. Schaefer, ed., *The therapeutic use of child's play* (pp. 413–416). New York: Jason Aronson.

Caster, T. R. 1984. The young child's play and social and emotional development. In T. D. Yawkey and A. D. Pellegrini, eds., *Child's play and play therapy* (pp. 17–29). Lancaster, PA: Technomic.

Confer, C. 1984. Alleviating aggressive behaviors using therapy and play objects in the psychoanalytic mainstream. In T. D. Yawkey and A. D. Pellegrini, eds., *Child's play and play therapy* (pp. 105–115). Lancaster, PA: Technomic

Creative Health Services. 1983. *The self-esteem game*. South Bend, IN: Creative Health Services.

Dalley, T. 1990. Images and integration: Art therapy in a multi-cultural school. In C. Case and T. Dalley, eds., *Working with children in art therapy* (pp. 161–198). London: Tavistock/Routledge.

Durfee, M. B. 1979. Use of ordinary office equipment. In C. Schaefer, ed., *The therapeutic use of child's play* (pp. 401–411). New York: Jason Aronson.

Ekstein, R. 1983. Play therapy for borderline children. In C. E. Schaefer and K. J. O'Connor, eds., *Handbook of play therapy* (pp. 412–418). New York: John Wiley & Sons.

Epstein, Y. M. 1986. Feedback and could this happen: Two therapeutic games for children of divorce. In C. E. Schaefer and S. E. Reid, eds., *Game play: Therapeutic use of childhood games* (pp. 159–185). New York: John Wiley & Sons.

Esman, A. H. 1983. Psychoanalytic play therapy. In C. E. Schaefer and K. J. O'Connor, eds., *Handbook of play therapy* (pp. 11–20). New York: John Wiley & Sons.

Fagot, B. I., and K. Kavanagh. 1991. Play as a diagnostic tool with physically abusive parents and their children. In C. E. Schaefer, K. Gitlin, and A. Sandgrund, eds., *Play diagnosis and assessment* (pp. 203–218). New York: John Wiley & Sons.

Frey, D. E. 1986. Communication boardgames with children. In C. E. Schaefer and S. E. Reid, eds., *Game play: Therapeutic use of childhood games* (pp. 21–39). New York: John Wiley & Sons.

Gardner, R. A. 1975. *Psychotherapeutic approaches to the resistant child*. New York: Jason Aronson.

Gardner, R. A. 1979. Mutual storytelling technique. In C. Schaefer, ed., *The therapeutic use of child's play* (pp. 313–321). New York: Jason Aronson.

Gardner, R. A. 1986. The talking, feeling, and doing game. In C. E. Schaefer and S. E. Reid, eds., *Game play: Therapeutic use of childhood games* (pp. 41–72). New York: John Wiley & Sons.

Garvey, C. 1977. Play. Cambridge, MA: Harvard University Press.

Golden, D. B. 1983. Play therapy for hospitalized children. In C. E. Schaefer and K. J. O'Connor, eds., *Handbook of play therapy* (pp. 213–233). New York: John Wiley & Sons.

Griff, M. D. 1983. Family play therapy. In C. E. Schaefer and K. J. O'Connor, eds., *Handbook of play therapy* (pp. 65–75). New York: John Wiley & Sons.

Guerney, L. F. 1983a. Client-centered (nondirective) play therapy. In C. E. Schaefer and K. J. O'Connor, eds., *Handbook of play therapy* (pp. 21–64). New York:

John Wiley & Sons.

Guerney, L. F. 1983b. Play therapy with learning disabled children. In C. E. Schaefer and K. J. O'Connor, eds ., *Handbook of play therapy* (pp. 419–435). New York: John Wiley & Sons.

Gumaer, J. 1984. *Counseling and therapy for children*. New York: Free Press.

Hambridge, G., Jr. 1979. Structured play therapy. In C. Schaefer, ed., *The therapeutic use of child's play* (pp. 187–205). New York: Jason Aronson.

Hawkey, L. 1979. Puppets in child psychotherapy. In C. Schaefer, ed., *The therapeutic use of child's play* (pp. 359–372). New York: Jason Aronson.

Hellendoorn, J. 1988. Imaginative play techniques in psychotherapy with children. In C. E. Schaefer, ed., *Innovative interventions in child and adolescent therapy* (pp. 43–67). New York: John Wiley & Sons.

Irwin, E. C. 1987. Drama: The play's the thing. *Elementary School Guidance and Counseling* 21: 276–283.

Irwin, E. C. 1991. The use of a puppet interview to understand children. In C. E. Schaefer, K. Gitlin, and A. Sandgrund, eds., *Play diagnosis and assessment* (pp. 617–642). New York: John Wiley & Sons.

James, R. K., and R. Myer. 1987. Puppets: The elementary school counselor's right or left arm. *Elementary School Guidance and Counseling* 21: 292–299

Jernberg, A. M. 1979. Theraplay technique. In C. Schaefer, ed., *The therapeutic use of child's play* (pp. 345–349). New York: Jason Aronson.

Johnson, R. G. 1987. Using computer art in counseling children. *Elementary School Guidance and Counseling*; 21: 262–265.

Klein, M. 1979. The psychoanalytic play technique. In C. Schaefer, ed., *The therapeutic use of child's play* (pp. 125–140). New York: Jason Aronson.

Koala Pad. 1983. [Computer Program]. Santa Clara, CA: Koala Technologies.

Kransor, L. R, and D. J. Pepler. 1980. The study of children's play. *New Directions in Child Development* 9: 85–96.

Kritzberg, N. 1975. *The structured therapeutic game method of child analytic psychotherapy*. Hicksville, NY: Exposition.

Landreth, G. L. 1983. Play therapy in elementary school setting. In C. E. Schaefer and K. J. O'Connor, eds., *Handbook of play therapy* (pp. 200–212). New York: John Wiley & Sons.

Landreth, G. L. 1987. Play therapy: Facilitative use of child's play in elementary school. *Elementary School Guidance and Counseling* 21: 253–261.

Lebo, D. 1979. Toys for nondirective play therapy. In C. Schaefer, ed., *The therapeutic use of child's play* (pp. 435–447). New York: Jason Aronson.

Leland, H. 1983. Play therapy for the mentally retarded and developmentally disabled child. In C. E. Schaefer and K. J. O'Connor, eds., *Handbook of play therapy* (pp. 436–454). New York: John Wiley & Sons.

Mann, E., and J. F. McDermott, Jr. 1983. Play therapy for victims of child abuse and neglect. In C. E. Schaefer and K. J. O'Connor, eds., *Handbook of play therapy* (pp. 283–307). New York: John Wiley & Sons.

Marcus, I. M. 1979. Costume play therapy. In C. Schaefer, ed., *The therapeutic use of child's play* (pp 373–382). New York; Jason Aronson.

McKinney, F. 1977. Exploration in bibliotherapy. *Personnel and Guidance Jour-*

nal 55: 550–552.

Mendell, A. E. 1983. Play therapy with children of divorced parents. In C. E. Schaefer and K. J. O'Connor, eds., *Handbook of play therapy* (pp. 320–354). New York: John Wiley & Sons.

Murphy, G. W. 1975. Play as a counselor's tool. In W. M. Walsh, ed., *Counseling children and adolescents: An anthology of contemporary techniques* (pp. 300–306). Berkeley, CA: McCutchan.

Nader, K., and R. S. Pynoos. 1991. Play and drawing techniques as tools for interviewing traumatized children. In C. E. Schaefer, K. Gitlin, and A. Sandgrund, eds., *Play diagnosis and assessment* (pp. 375–389). New York: John Wiley & Sons.

Nickerson, E. T. 1983. Art as a play therapeutic medium. In C. E. Schaefer and K. J. O'Connor, eds., *Handbook of play therapy* (pp. 234–250). New York: John Wiley & Sons.

Nickerson, E. T., and K. S. O'Laughlin. 1983. The therapeutic use of games. In C. E. Schaefer and K. J. O'Connor, eds., *Handbook of play therapy* (pp. 174–187). New York: John Wiley & Sons.

O'Connor, K. J. 1983. The color-your-life technique. In C. E. Schaefer and K. J. O'Connor, eds., *Handbook of play therapy* (pp. 251–258) New York: John Wiley & Sons.

O'Connor, K. J. 1991. *The play therapy primer: An integration of theories and techniques.* New York: John Wiley & Sons.

Oden, T. 1976. *The transactional analysis game.* New York: Harper & Row.

Okun, B. F. 1987. *Effective helping: Interviewing and counseling techniques.* 3d ed. Pacific Grove, CA: Brooks/Cole.

Payne, H. 1988. The use of dance movement therapy with troubled youth. In C. E. Schaefer, ed., *Innovative interventions in child and adolescent therapy* (pp. 68–97). New York: John Wiley & Sons.

Plant, E. 1979. Play and adaptation. *Psychoanalytic Study of the Child* 34: 217–232.

Ross, P. 1991. The family puppet technique: For assessing parent-child and family intervention patterns. In C. E. Schaefer, K. Gitlin, and A. Sandgrund, eds., *Play diagnosis and assessment* (pp. 609–616). New York: John Wiley & Sons.

Rubin, J. A. 1984. *Child art therapy: Understanding and helping children grow through art.* 2d ed. New York: Van Nostrand Reinhold.

Rubin, J. A. 1988. Art counseling: An alternative. *Elementary School Guidance and Counseling* 22: 180–185.

Sager, C. 1990. Working with cases of child sexual abuse. In C. Case and T. Dalley, eds., *Working with children in art therapy* (pp. 89–114). London: Tavistock/ Routledge.

Segal, R. M. 1984. Helping children express grief through symbolic communication. *Social Casework: Journal of Contemporary Social Work* 65: 590–599.

Shadle, C., and J. Graham. 1981. *The talking/listening game.* San Luis Obispo, CA: Dandy Lion Press.

Smilansky, S. 1968. *The effect of sociodramatic play on disadvantaged preschool children.* New York: John Wiley & Sons.

Smith, G. 1991. Assessing family interaction by the collaborative drawing technique. In C. E. Schaefer, K. Gitlin, and A. Sandgrund, eds., *Play diagnosis and assessment* (pp. 599–607). New York: John Wiley & Sons.

Solomon, M. K. 1983. Play therapy with the physically handicapped. In C. E. Schaefer and K. J. O'Connor, eds., *Handbook of play therapy* (pp. 455–469). New York: John Wiley & Sons.

Stollak, G. E., L. E. Crandell, and L. A. Pirsch. 1991. Assessment of the family in the playroom. In C. E. Schaefer, K. Gitlin, and A. Sandgrund, eds., *Play diagnosis and assessment* (pp. 527–548). New York: John Wiley & Sons.

Swanson, A. J. 1986. Using games to improve self-control deficits in children. In C. E. Schaefer and S. E. Reid, eds., *Game play: Therapeutic use of childhood games* (pp. 233–242). New York: John Wiley & Sons.

Terr, L. C. 1983. Play therapy and psychic trauma: A preliminary report. In C. E. Schaefer and K. J. O'Connor, eds., *Handbook of play therapy* (pp. 308–319). New York: John Wiley & Sons.

Thompson, C. L., J. M. Davis, and B. Madden. 1986. Children as consultants and bibliocounseling. *Elementary School Guidance and Counseling* 21: 89–95.

Thompson, C. L., and L. B. Rudolph. 1988. *Counseling children.* 2d ed. Pacific Grove, CA: Brooks/Cole.

Trostle, S. L. 1984. Play therapy and the disruptive child. In T. D. Yawkey and A. D. Pellegrini, eds., *Child's play and play therapy* (pp. 157–169). Lancaster, PA: Technomic.

Vinturella, L., and R. James. 1987. Sand play: A therapeutic medium with children. *Elementary School Guidance and Counseling* 21: 229–238.

Waterland, J. C. 1975. Actions instead of words: Play therapy for the young child. In W. M. Walsh, ed., *Counseling children and adolescents: An anthology of contemporary techniques* (pp. 307–315). Berkeley, CA: McCutchan.

Watson, J. J. 1980. Bibliotherapy for abused children. *School Counselor* 27: 204–208.

Willock, B. 1983. Play therapy with the aggressive, acting-out child. In C. E. Schaefer and K. J. O'Connor, eds., *Handbook of play therapy* (pp. 386–411). New York: John Wiley & Sons.

Witmer, J. M., and M. E. Young. 1985. The silent partner: Uses of imagery in counseling. *Journal of Counseling and Development* 64: 187–190.

Witmer, J. M., and M. E. Young. 1987. Imagery in counseling. *Elementary School Guidance and Counseling* 22: 5–16.

Zakich, R. 1975. *The ungame.* Anaheim, CA: The Ungame Company.

Zakich, R., and S. Monroe. 1979. *Reunion.* Placentia, CA: The Ungame Company.

5 Counseling with Exceptional Children

Thomas V. Trotter

School Psychology and
Counselor Education Program
University of Idaho, Moscow

W orking with children whose exceptionalities place them significantly outside the average range of functioning has not been a counseling priority. Many counselors have avoided professional interaction with this population, which includes individuals with physical, behavioral, emotional, and mental disabilities, as well as the highly able, or gifted. Perhaps a lack of understanding and appreciation, a limited repertoire of techniques, and apprehension and values conflicts are at fault. In avoiding these cases, counselors have denied exceptional children the benefit of their expertise, and themselves the enrichment that comes from working with a challenging, deserving, and responsive clientele.

As we gravitate toward more comprehensive forms of intervention and become more sensitive to individual differences, the value of counseling as an adjunct to working with young exceptional clients will become more widely recognized. In this chapter, the term "exceptional" applies to children with disabilities, as well as those who are highly able. The first section focuses on working with young clients with disabilities, and the last section, counseling gifted and talented children.

WORKING WITH CHILDREN WITH DISABILITIES

Although some educational programs for children with disabilities were in place prior to passage of the Education for All Handicapped Children Act, Public Law 94-14, which formally guaranteed access to free and appropriate educational programs and related services, few professions responded with as little vigor as the counseling profession. Counselors have been too willing to defer to special education teachers and other staff members in responding to the personal/social, career development, and educational needs of clients with disabilities. As a precautionary note, generalizing across handicapping conditions puts children with disabilities at risk. Individuals who comprise the exceptional client population vary just as much as any client group does. For the sake of brevity, however, working with these young clients will be treated generically in this chapter. Readers are encouraged to do more in-depth research on specific disabilities.

Developmental Experiences

Some of the more typical life experiences of individuals with disabilities are as follows (Mishne 1986):

1. Throughout their school years, many exceptional children and youth are subjected to a multitude of roadblocks. They encounter a great deal of nonacceptance. Peers and instructors avoid them. Discrimination and stereotypical thinking are common. These factors tend to limit their potential to accomplish in many arenas.

2. As noted in the Virginia Department of Education (1985) guide, these children experience more than the normal share of frustration and difficulty in attempting to resolve the problems that come with day-to-day living. As a result, they may have low tolerance for frustration and overreact in stressful situations.

3. Chronic hopelessness is very common for this population, due to the frequency with which they experience distress, anxiety, and depression.

4. Children with disabilities have access and performance problems in school, evidenced by limited placement options or long-term tracking in special programs.

5. This population shows delayed development of self-concept, which can result in grossly underestimated ability and a pervasive sense of being dumb, damaged, weak, and vulnerable. This mindset tends to crystallize in early adolescence, and without intervention will remain throughout life.

Although this is not an exhaustive list of developmental issues that affect young exceptional clients, these issues are significant and may determine the scope and direction of interventions.

Barriers to Effective Counseling

For professionals working with exceptional children and adolescents, a variety of factors tend to get in the way of effective intervention. These include, but are not limited to, poor preparation, an orientation toward internal loss of control, reluctance to become involved, resistant parents or caregivers, problems with networking, and feelings of being overwhelmed. Proactive counselors take steps to ensure that these impediments don't surface as roadblocks and short-circuit an otherwise productive encounter.

Graduates of counselor education programs frequently receive inadequate preparation and training in regard to exceptional children. Many in the counseling field dismiss exceptional individuals as the province of other professionals who specialize in working with children with disabilities. Compounding this problem, appropriate forms of intervention are not always readily available.

We also often take the traditional approach that assumes that problems are located within individuals and, therefore, should be resolved internally. This same approach suggests that such problems are more responsive to talk than to action. In reality, children with disabilities may benefit more from a hands-on approach to problem resolution in which they assume ownership for taking action.

In addition, counselors may be apprehensive about working with disabled clientele, particularly those who are more severely challenged. Counseling professionals should be cognizant of their limits and biases, research the availability of referral resources, and not hesitate to refer if they think that continued involvement with the client would be nonproductive.

A compounding problem is that caregivers who have a vested interest in maintaining the status quo may present a significant obstacle to progress in counseling. Legal options are available, such as the Coalition of Advocates for the Handicapped, through which a parental/guardian stance can be challenged if it is deemed counterproductive and not in the young person's best interests.

Lack of cooperation among service providers and helping professionals may also be detrimental to the child with disabilities who could benefit greatly from a collaborative, more holistic approach to intervention. The service providers in the community who have a mandate or specialization or who already are professionally involved with the client should be encouraged to take an interagency approach to intervention.

Finally, counselors, particularly those in the schools, are frequently so overburdened with a variety of assignments that they cannot spend enough quality time with children and youth who need most of the attention. These young clients need a disproportionate amount of time. More efficient forms of programming, such as developmental school counseling, should be explored. This approach calls for more collaborative working relationships with other professionals and shedding time-consuming responsibilities that are nonschool counseling in nature.

Considerations for Intervention

The following considerations are important in designing interventions for young clients with disabilites.

1. The most significant psychosocial issue affecting children with disabilities is that they see themselves as failures, a perception which can sabotage opportunities for success. To many individuals with disabilities, negative thoughts about self become all too familiar and "second nature." Therefore, emphasizing the development, restoration, or maintenance of self-esteem in working with young clients is essential. This issue should be addressed through career planning, development of personal/social skills, and skills for educational success.

2. Because of their intellectual or physical limitations, young people with disabilities may be confused about their sexual identity and need help in understanding the fundamentals of sexuality.

3. As a result of the lack of opportunity, disabled children may need encouragement in developing lifetime recreational and leisure skills. This potentially can improve stress management skills, enhance their self-esteem, and contribute to wellness.

4. Career development and life planning work is essential in effectively transitioning young clients with disabilities from secondary schools to the world of work. Collaborative intervention with local vocational rehabilitation specialists with diagnostic, vocational planning and placement expertise is necessary.

5. It is not uncommon for young disabled clients to be dependent on their parents or for parents to encourage this dependency. Teaching independent living skills and working with parents to "let go" is important.

6. Depending on the age at which they first become handicapped and how parents/guardians treat this condition, some children have difficulty adjusting to their disability and experience significant feelings of loss. Children will need help in working through the stages of grief.

7. Disabled clients may see themselves as their disability, not recognizing that they have other areas of strength or expertise. Helping them identify uniqueness and accept the disability as one aspect of self is critical.

8. The home, school, and workplace can be stressful environments. Learning to cope with stress and anxiety through relaxation exercises, stress inoculation, cognitive change procedures,

and other interventions that facilitate coping skills are salient interventions.

9. Children with disabilities need to learn goal-setting skills and how to develop workable action plans to accomplish goals. Because this population often is characterized as impulsive and not always reflective, teaching young clients more effective ways to solve problems and make decisions should be emphasized.

10. Children with disabilities may need help in improving their receptive and expressive communication skills. They may not be as adept at "reading" nonverbal messages as their mainstream counterparts and can benefit from instruction in this area.

11. Because they sometimes are taken advantage of, these children may need help in becoming more assertive. They should be made aware of their basic human rights and how to assert themselves through identification of target behaviors, modeling, and behavior rehearsal in the safety of the counseling relationship. Skills learned in this context will eventually generalize to the real world.

12. Young disabled clients need to become aware of their overt behavioral responses to situations and how to monitor their own internal self-talk so that they don't overreact to negative circumstances.

13. Disabled clients may have counterproductive behaviors that negatively affect their relationships with peers. Group work or individual interventions need to address this dimension.

The following issues, applicable to the population with handicapping conditions, originated, in part, from Price's (1988) helpful suggestions on working with students with learning disabilities.

1. Be sensitive to timing. Although regularly scheduled sessions provide more consistency and allow better use of counselors' time, more flexibility may be needed to work with students in crisis. This enables counselors to help the client work through presenting problems while they are occurring rather than after the problem situations have passed.

2. Focus on one behavior at a time. Encourage these young people to direct their energy, concentrate on one issue at a time, and fully process it before moving on to other issues.

3. Summarize each session. Toward the end of the session, verbally clarify what has transpired, and invite the client to share

his or her perceptions of what occurred during counseling and what will be accomplished as homework between sessions.

4. Encourage self-monitoring. In becoming more independent, exceptional children must assume responsibility for constructively dealing with any self-defeating behavior by learning how to monitor it through daily logs and similar tools.

5. Blend approaches. Relaxation activities may be helpful in working with young clients who are overburdened with frustration, stress, and anxiety, or who tend to respond impulsively. Being in a relaxed state enables them to channel their attention and energy into selected goal(s) for action.

6. Network with other professionals. Young clients with disabilities often require the assistance of several specialized professionals and other service providers. Recognize your own limitations to provide comprehensive intervention and refer clients for extended or supportive services by other professionals, as warranted.

Specific Strategies

From a prevention perspective, discrimination can be tempered by promoting and implementing classroom-based awareness activities designed to short-circuit stereotypical thinking and negative attitudes. Ball (1974), for example, created an exemplary classroom-based program entitled *Innerchange*, an upward extension of the *Magic Circle* program, which is applicable in part to special populations. Some specific strategies to employ in prevention programs follow.

1. Place limits on client behaviors, and do not be overly permissive out of sympathy. Require young clients to accept responsibility for their actions. Discuss your expectations for appropriate behavior, and spell out consequences for inappropriate behaviors.

2. When serving as consultants to other professionals with programming responsibilities for children with disabilities, help them adapt strategies, materials, and equipment to meet the needs of individuals with disabilities.

3. Implement concrete, hands-on, activity-oriented approaches with young disabled clients. This can help them internalize positive images of themselves by learning to master their own situations.

4. Consider group counseling as an option. Group membership should be homogeneous with regard to background, age, pre-

senting issues, and abilities, and heterogeneous with regard to personalities. A structured, goal-directed program is more effective than an open or nondirected group process with this population.

5. Deploy trained peer helpers. Through the Natural Helpers (Roberts, Fitzmahan, and Associates 1989) program, students in secondary schools select peers who subsequently receive intensive training in communication skills, problem-solving, and referral skills that enhance their ability to interact more constructively with fellow students who approach them for advice and assistance. Natural helpers have been utilized successfully in assisting exceptional students to adjust to school situations.

6. Involve the entire family as a prospective resource by helping them understand the dynamics of the child's handicapping condition within the context of the institution. Parents can play a major role in encouraging their children to apply themselves to the fullest.

7. Introduce media, including bibliotherapy and audiovisual resources, to demonstrate appropriate behaviors in certain situations. These are especially effective if models or central characters have disabilities which expedite client identification with message conveyed.

8. Seek to fully understand the disabled child's world by learning about the handicapping condition that characterizes him or her (Thompson and Rudolph 1988). Know his or her prevailing needs, and be aware of important behavioral characteristics that frequently are evident in children with disabilities.

9. Form a working relationship with the child through which his or her limits and responsibilities are defined and he or she feels free to share any fears, doubts, and insecurities. Building this relationship necessarily entails certain core counselor attitudes of empathy, genuineness, and positive regard. Expertise, attractiveness, trust, listening, and nonverbal responses are additional relationship enhancers in building a productive working relationship.

10. Consider informal methods of assessment such as observations, interviews, and self-reports, looking for patterns in performance and appearance of influential variables in the process. Help children assess and conceptualize the presenting problem, and remember that more standardized forms of diagnostic work

can perpetuate their doubts and fears by sending messages that
something is wrong with them.

11. Most important, take a systematic and structured approach. A
developmental strategy is recommended through which the counselor first studies the presenting disability, then works at building rapport with the child, assesses and conceptualizes the focus
of concern, chooses an appropriate form of intervention, and
evaluates therapeutic accomplishments through counseling.

12. Select and implement strategies that involve the children and
their significant others and that are composed of varied and
combined forms of intervention. Consider support services,
referral to professionals who can provide supplemental help in
specialized areas, environmental intervention, and the like. Specific strategies include the following:

    a. *A problem-solving approach.* Help the child clarify the pre-
    senting problem, explore alternative courses of action and
    the likely outcomes of each, and develop an action plan to
    follow the chosen path to solution.

    b. *Behavioral rehearsal.* Identify and model appropriate be-
    haviors, have the child practice these in counseling, then
    gradually try them out in the "real world."

    c. *Cognitive change procedures.* Involve the child in identify-
    ing and replacing irrational beliefs, negative self-statements,
    and thoughts by identifying the troublesome thoughts, intro-
    ducing and practicing coping thoughts, shifting from self
    defeating thoughts to coping thoughts, and applying self-
    reinforcement to coping thoughts.

    d. *Relaxation training.* Help the child learn to distinguish be-
    tween tensed and relaxed muscles, and then to monitor and
    respond to the signals of tension the body sends.

13. Evaluate progress in counseling to determine the extent to which
counseling has helped. Strategies for evaluation are many, including observations by teachers, parents, other students, and
school staff. Another useful evaluative exercise is role-play, an
activity through which children are challenged to demonstrate
mastery of skills. Self-monitoring of applied skills in the real
world by keeping log entries can be informative. Standardized
pre- and post-test measures as well as other data gathering
devices can yield useful evaluative information.

WORKING WITH GIFTED AND TALENTED CHILDREN

Children who are gifted and talented are considered exceptional because they face unique challenges related to their advanced aptitudes. Although interest in special accommodations for the highly able has ebbed and flowed over the years, it is critical for counselors to be sensitive to the unique needs of this group of children.

During the same time the nation was enacting the Education for All Handicapped Act of 1975, the National Association of State Boards of Education identified intervention on behalf of the gifted and talented as the fourth out of forty priority issues during its 1976 session. Following closely on the heels of this event, the federal government issued the Gifted and Talented Children's Act of 1978, which legitimized their special programming needs. In addition, the government defined this exceptionality and advocated for special services, including counseling.

Because gifted children are perceived as outstanding and as natural problem-solvers, we often fail to recognize that they may need help in coping with personal-social, educational, and career development issues. Even though gifted and talented children have knowledge and skills beyond their years, they may lack the emotional strength and coping skills commensurate with this level. The pressures highly able children impose on themselves and pressures imposed by others may be overwhelming.

Healthy emotions and positive self-concept are essential to productive growth. Good communication skills, adequate coping strategies, and appreciation and acceptance of others also play a vital role in the maturation process. If these attributes are not developed, the creative, intellectual, and leadership potential of gifted and talented children may never be fully realized. Counselors should take the lead in communicating the necessity of building a strong affective basis for the cognitive pursuits of gifted and talented children and youth (Blackburn and Erickson in Radford 1987).

Developmental Issues and Other Characteristics

Blackburn and Erickson (in Radford 1987) identified a series of developmental dilemmas that most gifted children experience. Each of these trouble spots presents the counselor with an opportunity for helping highly able children make successful transitions throughout their school years.

1. Gifted children, primarily males, may show signs of developmental immaturity at the outset of their school experience, attributable to developmental lags and a supersensitivity to sensory stimulation. The highly charged and energetic child typically is punished for this "immature" behavior and seeming unwillingness to comply with classroom standards of behavior.
2. Highly able children may become underachievers or nonachievers as learned reactions to an inadequate and unchallenging school curriculum and attendant debilitating insistence on conformity.
3. The irrational mood swings, inconsistent behavior patterns, and tension accompanying biological changes that occur naturally during adolescence may confuse gifted children who may have been adept at reasoning and rational problem-solving before the onset of these physiological and psychological changes.
4. Making personal, educational, and occupational choices can be overwhelming to gifted children, who typically have multiple interests and abilities. This "overchoice" can lead to stress that adversely affects the child's self-esteem and subsequent performance in many arenas.
5. Having mastered earlier crises and succeeded at every endeavor, gifted children may be devastated in the face of stronger competition and more challenging goals as they come to interact with their intellectual peers. This may result in paralyzing perfectionism in which they become unwilling to pursue any new experience unless assured of success. Gifted children are in need of special support, particularly because they are accustomed to knowing the answers and haven't learned how to ask for help when they need it (Mallis and Heinemann 1979).

The degree to which gifted students overcome the obstacles they face may be predicated on the quality of support provided and skills they learn. Herein is our challenge for helping the highly able reach their potential.

Roth (in Radford 1987) identified three interpersonal patterns that characterize gifted children with social problems: feelings of disapproval, entitlement, and unmet expectations. These characteristics occurred with considerable frequency in the studies from which he drew.

Feelings of peer disapproval and subsequent social isolation stem from other children's feeling jealous or threatened, which may tempt gifted children to behave in an unacceptable or self-deprecatory manner out of eagerness to belong. Because gifted children are different from the average and are aware of these differences, they easily recognize that being different from the norm is "not okay." Gifted children sometimes are confused by being in dual norm groups of chronological and intellectual peers. Strong pressures to conform often result in compromised development or, its opposite, various degrees of rejection and isolation.

Overindulgent parents tend to idealize their gifted children, which causes some highly able children to routinely act in an egotistic or arrogant manner and have difficulty moving beyond self-centeredness. This egocentric outlook alienates exceptional children from their peers, sometimes to the point of being virtually unapproachable.

Highly able children also may become convinced that they can never live up to others' high expectations. This may lead to two types of self-punishing behavior: (1) distancing from meaningful involvement with peers or school work, or both, and (2) pushing them to accomplish unrealistic goals. This latter response to pressure to perform can produce the perfectionistic tendencies prevalent in gifted children. These self-imposed demands lead to frustration, self-criticism, and discouragement (Kerr 1989; Radford 1987). Highly able children need the freedom to be children and not be treated like miniature adults.

Gifted children with social adjustment problems have unique characteristics that distinguish their interpersonal difficulties from those of others (Roth in Radford 1987). Kerr (1989) explains that while gifted children experience the same societal expectations as others, their advanced intellectual development can create special problems in relationships. Counseling strategies for this population should be based on their specific interpersonal patterns.

Relative to their chronological age counterparts, gifted children become aware of human problems and develop values early (Gowan and Bruch 1971). They also are inclined to question and search for meaningfulness earlier on. These earlier levels of awareness, coupled with what Mallis and Heinemann (1979) identified as heightened perceptivity and sensitivity, make them especially sensitive to the emotional responses of others and to their own personal reactions. The expanded developmental range and sensitivity suggest a need for accessibility to supportive counseling.

If independence of action and decision-making are discouraged in school, gifted children may find school practices drill-bound and dull. Resistance to conformity may take several forms including withdrawal, tuning out the teacher, refusing to work, antagonizing others, and performing at a perfunctory level to avoid consequences but still not achieving at a level commensurate with ability.

From her work with gifted children, Galbraith (in Radford 1987) identified "eight great gripes." This list summarizes issues that can precipitate personal-social, educational, and career development problems and helps us to understand, from the perspective of the highly able child, how growing up gifted can be burdensome.

1. No one explains what being gifted is all about. It's kept a big secret.
2. School is too easy and too boring.
3. Parents, teachers, and friends expect us to be perfect all the time.
4. Friends who really understand us are few and far between.
5. Kids often tease us about being smart.
6. We feel overwhelmed by the number of things we can do in life.
7. We feel different, alienated.
8. We worry about world problems and feel helpless to do anything about them.

Considerations for Intervention

In working with the young gifted and talented population, counselors should be permissive, interceptive, client-centered, and nonauthoritarian (Gowan and Bruch 1971). Although these children can respond to counseling, they present a challenge because they are perceptive enough to recognize insensitivity or inconsistency in others, are more independent, and tend to want to solve their own problems. These children can successfully disguise their concerns or compensate in an attempt to cope with presenting problems.

Radford (1987) advised that, before working with this population, counselors ask themselves whether they believe highly able children have the potential for advanced development and if they are comfortable working with these children. In addition to professional training in the field of counseling and education of the gifted and talented, qualifications and qualities that are important in helping highly able students cope with perplexing life experiences include commitment to meeting the needs of these exceptional children and a genuine and nonauthoritarian approach that conveys unconditional positive regard, empathy, and respect (Mallis and Heinemann 1979). Counselors of gifted and talented children should be sensitive to the specific issues that characterize the highly able and be open to intelligent and stimulating ways of solving problems. Finally, these helping professionals should keep abreast of legislation and official guidelines which affect highly able children.

Prior to designing counseling programs for gifted and talented children, counselors should assess student needs and determine the availability of system resources for meeting these identified needs. Informal measures—such as locally developed surveys and follow-up interviews; group decision seminars with gifted students, parents, and teachers; and expert or panel reviews—are considered content-valid and sensitive to in-house issues.

Needs collected across sources of information, coupled with school system and state directives, help shape the program and steer the subsequent search for resources. Prevention and intervention activities should be conducted on an ongoing basis. Outcomes assessment at the end of the school year should be done to determine overall success of the program and future directions.

Strategies

In keeping with the developmental model of counseling, counselors should take a many-faceted approach to working with highly able children. This involves working with children in a preventive mode through pull-out or small-group work with highly able peers as well as direct intervention. The ultimate purpose of counseling is to listen and hear, see, and respond (Radford 1987). Counselors who wish to help gifted children must make a sincere effort to understand the special characteristics of this population and be willing to try creative strategies in working with these young people.

School counseling curriculum implemented in small-group or pull-out situations can provide a forum for expression of concerns, fears, and frustrations in a supportive environment. This kind of outlet gives children the freedom and relief that comes from knowing they are not alone, that others share their concerns and care deeply. Classroom units such as *Innerchange* and *Magic Circle* (Ball 1974), which encourage introspection and focus on feelings, attitudes, and value-related issues, are particularly significant.

These children are avid readers, so bibliotherapy can be a useful strategy in helping gifted children solve problems through guided reading (Thompson and Rudolph 1988). If properly applied, bibliotherapy offers many possibilities but should not be used in isolation.

As a vehicle for open expression of feelings, attitudes, and values, creative writing can stimulate new ideas or new ways of looking at the familiar. The same freedom of cognitive and affective movement, leading to catharsis, can be found in journaling techniques.

Other strategies should be designed to help gifted children cope with feelings of alienation and to develop questioning, introspective attitudes with regard to who they are, where they are going educationally and professionally, and how they plan to get there. Other areas of emphasis include coping with peer pressure not to succeed, as well as excessive pressure to succeed, valuing all people, and sharing ideas, values, attitudes, and feelings regarding themselves.

Radford (1987) delineated some general strategies for working with gifted children. These include never telling children that they will grow out of it, as this tends to denigrate their feelings. The turmoil and confusion they are feeling are very real and deserve attention. The counselor should assure them that they are capable of finding a solution and give them the tools necessary to understand the conflict as a healthy, though perhaps painful, developmental process. At every step during intervention, the child should be reminded that someone cares and will support his or her effort to work through the problem.

In a comprehensive approach to working with gifted children, parents are a key resource. Their cooperation and active constructive involvement can be essential to the success of any interventive effort. Therefore, any approach to counseling highly able children and adolescents should involve working with parents or guardians to help them deal with the child's psychological and educational growth. This may be a challenge, since parents of gifted children often display the same independence of action evident in their children.

Specific parent effectiveness strategies include self-help through reading, and support groups to promote understanding and discussion of topical issues. Affiliation with national or state organizations such as the National Association for Gifted Children (NAGC) and The Association for Gifted (TAG), a division of the Council for Exceptional Children, might be considered.

When significant domestic problems surface, parents might be referred for personal or family counseling.

SUMMARY

Exceptional children are those with physical, behavioral, emotional, and mental disabilities, as well as the highly able. Exceptional children, at both ends of the continuum, traditionally have not been served well through school counseling, although their needs are often greater than those evident in the general population.

While generalizing across the diverse group of individuals described as "disabled" is not possible, some generic counseling considerations apply. These children do tend to face more barriers than more typical students, especially nonacceptance, discrimination, and stereotypical thinking. Furthermore, they are apt to experience more frustration in day-to-day living, sometimes resulting in low tolerance for stress. Depression may also be more common, which may lead to feelings of hopelessness. In particular, students with deficiencies in cognitive areas have to deal with constant failure. Some counselors may have inadvertently contributed to the difficulties by avoiding these students. Parents, too, may impede their development by being overprotective and cautious.

A collaborative approach across service providers is best, incorporating specialized expertise when indicated. Intervention should consider the areas of self-esteem, personal/social skills, skills for educational success, lifetime recreational and leisure skills, independent living skills, career development, and reduction of dependency on others. Strengths should be maximized and weaknesses minimized. Specific suggestions include relaxation exercises, stress inoculation, cognitive change, problem-solving techniques, assertiveness training, communication training, modeling, and bibliotherapy.

Gifted and talented children also constitute a unique group, and are not generally recognized as having needs for counseling in personal/social, educational, and career development areas. Three prevalent interpersonal characteristics of the highly able are feelings of disapproval, entitlement, and unmet expectations. Sometimes their precocity is stifled by routine and excessive rules that limit their inquisitiveness and natural curiosity. They commonly become underachievers or nonachievers, sometimes in response to peer pressure to not be "different."

Counselors who work with this population should be willing to meet the special challenges exceptional young clients present and utilize stimulating materials focusing on feelings, values, and acceptance. Bibliotherapy and creative writing are two effective strategies with a proven track record. Involving parents in these efforts is encouraged.

REFERENCES

Ball, G. 1974. *Innerchange: A journey into self-learning through group interaction.* Spring Valley, CA: Palomares & Associates.

Commonwealth of Virginia. 1985. *Counseling with handicapped students.* Richmond: Department of Education.

Gowan, J. C., and C. Bruch. 1971. *The academically talented student and guidance.* Boston: Houghton Mifflin.

Kerr, B. A. 1989. *Counseling gifted students.* Indianapolis: Indiana Department of Education.

Mallis, J., and A. Heinemann. 1979. *Reaching the stars: A minicourse for education of gifted students.* Austin, Texas: Multi Media Arts.

Mishne, J. M. 1986. *Clinical work with adolescents* (pp. 166–172). New York: Free Press.

Price, L. 1988. Effective counseling techniques for LD adolescents and adults in secondary and postsecondary settings. *Journal of Postsecondary Education and Disability* 6(3): 7–15.

Radford, J. 1987. *Gifted/talented education counseling guide.* Indianapolis: Indiana Department of Education.

Roberts, Fitzmahan & Associates. 1989. *Natural helpers.* Seattle: Comprehensive Health Education Foundation.

Thompson, C. L., and L. B. Rudolph. 1988. *Counseling children.* 2d ed. Pacific Grove, CA: Brooks/Cole.

6 Counseling with Young Multicultural Clients

Thomas V. Trotter

School Psychology and
Counselor Education Program
University of Idaho, Moscow

$\mathbf{W}$e are evolving into an increasingly multicultural and pluralistic society. As Sue (1989) noted, it is projected that the United States will constitute a "minority majority" by the year 2010. Counselors now must prepare for working with young people who bring unique cultural, language, and social class characteristics to the helping process.

BACKGROUND

The counseling profession traditionally has been oriented toward white middle-class America. Approaches to counseling tend to reflect values the dominant culture prizes: individuality, independence of action, and personal responsibility. Given the collectivistic or group-oriented contexts from which many of our culturally different clientele come, these orientations may be counterproductive. As Triandis (1988, in Verma and Bagley 1988) noted, in collectivistic cultures most people's social behavior is determined largely by goals, attitudes, and values that are shared with some collectivity (group of persons). Collectively determined and perpetuated standards of behavior are clearly evident in Native American, Asian, and Mexican American cultures.

Since the civil rights movement of the 1950s, subsequent minority demands for greater equality, expanded awareness, and affirmative action programs, appreciation has been growing of the need for intervention that fairly recognizes the environmentally determined and reinforced differences between people, as well as their similarities. As counselors, learning how to work effectively with these differences is our goal for action. In short, counselors must take a multicultural approach to intervention that first recognizes the importance of context in assessment, goal formulation, intervention, and evaluation. The emphasis in helping shifts from a focus exclusively on the individual to the relationship between the individual and our pluralistic society, in which ethnic groups maintain their own cultural identity while sharing common elements with the majority culture.

Often, culturally diverse children who enter the schools experience failure. These difficulties sometimes are traceable to a home lacking the material and financial resources that characterize white middle-class households. In addition, they may speak a different language, not hold educational achievement in high regard, and devalue independence of action. When children do not measure up to prevailing school standards that may be foreign to them, they ultimately are blamed for the failure. As Ivey and Authier (1978) noted, even when children are excused because of "cultural deprivation," they are expected to remedy the situation by learning how to comply with institutional demands that may compromise their more natural values and behavioral expectations. In looking at a multicultural orientation to counseling, the basic issue is awareness of the powerful role that context plays in shaping behaviors that come to the counselor's attention.

ISSUES IN MULTICULTURAL COUNSELING

Any approach to counseling that claims to be multicultural in nature must address the many barriers to counseling effectiveness that the helping professionals face. These include:

1. Being neither skilled nor motivated to serve the interests of culturally different clientele. Many counselors are unable or unwilling to consider their lack of multicultural sensitivity in counseling (D'Andrea 1990) and, further, fail to refer clients elsewhere.
2. Experiencing varying degrees of cognitive dissonance, which comes from the discrepancy between the counselor's personal expectations of how culturally different people ought to think, feel, and react to life events and their own thoughts, feelings and reactions.
3. Failing to recognize the negative perceptions of self and the messages of hopelessness that permeate minority group populations and the grim prospect that success on majority group terms may mean compromising important elements of sociocultural identity.
4. Underemphasizing the importance of client culture, holding that "they are just like us" or, conversely, overemphasizing cultural differences to the extent that culturally diverse individuals are considered deviant or are treated like rare and fragile specimens.

5. Failing to see the two overlapping contexts in which culturally diverse people find themselves—that which is dominated by the culture of origin and that which is dominated by the majority culture.
6. Assuming that people have a common understanding of what constitutes "normal" behavior and that this understanding transcends social, cultural, economic, and political situations.
7. Assuming that counseling should be directed primarily toward development of individuals and, in so doing, failing to take advantage of the potential effectiveness of natural support systems—the family, peer group, or community.
8. Defining issues of a multicultural nature from a framework constricted by boundaries drawn by academic disciplines and not exchanging questions and insights with other professionals.
9. Holding to the notion that independence solely on the self is valuable and dependence on others is undesirable.
10. Trying to change individuals to fit the system rather than constructively intervening to influence the system so it becomes more responsive to individuals.
11. Focusing on immediate events as more salient than personal history and denying the role of historical events as antecedents in determining ongoing behavior.
12. Emphasizing individual-centered forms of counseling and competition for status, recognition, and achievement (Pederson 1987, in Sue and Sue 1990).
13. Stressing the importance of verbal expression of emotion and self-disclosure as essential goals in counseling through "talking therapy."
14. Assuming that obtaining insight or understanding into a person's deep, underlying dynamics is mentally beneficial (Sue and Sue 1990).
15. Conducting counseling as an ambiguous and unstructured activity.

These barriers could adversely affect counselors' ability to intervene successfully and are not generalizable to working with all children and adolescents. Counselor orientations, however, may impede the potential to reach the young culturally diverse population, and counselors would do well to correct any counterproductive intervention approaches.

HELPING STRATEGIES

Helping professionals who work with culturally diverse children and youth should take an action-oriented developmental approach to counseling. Two definitions of "developmental" apply to implementation. First, a developmental approach to *intervention* calls for a well-planned and stepwise process through which each stage in counseling builds on the outcomes of the preceding one. Many culturally diverse clients respond to intervention that is structured, direct, and practical in orientation (Sue and Sue 1990). *Prevention* programs also are developmental in that they typically are presented early in the person's life for the purposes of promoting awareness of certain concepts and fostering mastery of selected skills.

Basic conditions must be met before proceeding to subsequent stages in the helping process. After taking these entry-level steps, the counselor concentrates on establishing a working relationship with the young client and the significant others who populate his or her world—in effect, the extended clientele. These people are potential resources. The next stage involves conceptualizing presenting problems within a contextual framework, knowing that intervention means working with a cultural context of origin embedded within or overlapping a majority dominated culture. Problems then must be clearly defined and prioritized, goals for action formulated, and helping strategies appropriate to client lifestyle implemented. Strategies are implemented collaboratively, and evaluated for effectiveness in meeting the formulated goals for action.

Preconditions for Helping

In preparing to work with young multicultural students, counselors should:

1. Have faith in the child's ability to grow and to fully realize his or her potential, given responsive, supportive, and developmental intervention across both cultural contexts in which the child is immersed. Native American children, for example, might benefit from an approach to intervention that incorporates legends and cultural traditions.
2. Examine their personal attitudes and personality style and how these characteristics influence how they behave with culturally diverse clients (Peterson and Nisenholz 1991). Culturally skilled counselors should appreciate their own cultural heritage, values, and biases, and be comfortable with any differences between

them and their clientele (Sue 1981, in Peterson and Nisenholz 1991). They should recognize their limits and be sensitive to conditions warranting referral of minority clients (Sue 1981, in Peterson and Nisenholz 1991).

3. Understand that sociopolitical forces external to the person influence how culturally diverse persons behave. Be prepared to exercise institutional intervention on behalf of multicultural clients when warranted (Sue et al. 1982, in Peterson and Nisenholz 1991). Maes and Rinaldi (in Henderson 1979) suggested that counselors open up more options in the life of the Hispanic child, which usually requires impacting the people and institutions surrounding the child.

4. Become familiar with the differences in world views that characterize minority clients and the implications for counseling. Differences in world views are particularly noteworthy in Native American children, who tend to value cooperation and harmony, generosity, and sharing, living in the present rather than planning for the future, and respect for older people.

5. Have a clear working knowledge of generic approaches to counseling and be able to use the techniques that best accommodate cultural differences and will not aggravate presenting problems in the process.

Establishing an Effective Helping Relationship

Regardless of individual differences, the therapeutic relationship is vital to the total helping process. Without a good relationship, change in the client or prevailing circumstances is less likely to occur. Cormier and Cormier (1985) identified six characteristics of effective helpers that can be applied to working with culturally diverse children and youth:

1. Be competent with regard to cultural diversity and curious enough to know what is happening in the day-to-day life of the young client. Higgins and Warner (in Henderson 1979) indicated that what separates effective and ineffective counselors is more a function of understanding culture and language than the cultural match between client and counselor. Poyatos (1988) supported this perspective in stating that difference is not what makes for divisiveness; rather, lack of appreciation for diversity is what interferes with successful crosscultural communication.

2. Be well-grounded in motivational theory and be able to inspire hope and confidence in clients to apply themselves in counsel-

ing and follow-through. Understand that meaningful reinforcement may be context-specific.

3. Be flexible and know how to adapt techniques to clients rather than force-fitting the client to any one favored approach.

4. Work to reduce anxiety, and promote the emotional security and assurance the client needs to take risks.

5. Be aware of any personal attitudes, thoughts, and feelings that might influence the way in which the counseling relationship develops.

6. Have good will, work on behalf of clients, and resist becoming dependent on the counseling relationship as a source of personal gratification and professional advancement. Always behave ethically and responsibly.

The Cormiers also highlighted the pivotal issue of values. Our values permeate every interaction with clients and are transmitted overtly or covertly. Stereotypical values can interfere when counseling people of different cultures. For example, Smith (in Cormier and Cormier 1985) noted that many of the proverbial conclusions about counseling African American clients (e.g., they characteristically have poor self-concepts, have a nonverbal communication style, and profit only from counseling that is highly structured and action-oriented, may be more myth than reality and tend to reflect majority culture interpretation and values. This same kind of thinking operates in how minority groups are viewed in general and may lead to erroneous diagnostic conclusions and inappropriate prescriptions for intervention.

The fundamental helping skills of empathy, respect, and genuineness are important in our work with young clients.

Empathy

Defined as the ability to understand people from their perspectives, empathy is conveyed primarily by verbal and nonverbal messages (Cormier and Cormier 1985). Traditional methods through which we convey empathy verbally include:

1. Try to make sense of the client's world by clarifying and questioning him or her about relevant experiences, thoughts, and feelings. Some groups are not comfortable disclosing personal information and find the rapid-fire questioning techniques of many North Americans offensive (Ivey 1988). Probing may backfire. Hispanics tend to self-disclose slowly and may need encouragement through storytelling, anecdotes, humor, and prov-

erbs (Thompson and Rudolph 1988). Because of their reliance on the family to resolve problems, Asian American children may be reluctant to disclose in response to probing.

2. By your questions and statements, show that you are aware of what is most important to the client. This necessitates in-depth understanding of the client's world view.

3. Verbally respond in ways that accurately reflect clients' thoughts and feelings and convey understanding of what they imply.

Nonverbal behaviors include making eye contact, assuming a forward-learning body position, and facing the client with an open posture. Nonverbal behaviors are interpreted differently across cultures. Culturally diverse clients also may be more adept at reading nonverbal behavior than their white counterparts are. Counselors who send conflicting verbal and nonverbal messages may be dismissed as untrustworthy. This dimension of the counseling relationship has the potential for overcoming any initial problems between a majority group counselor and a minority group client, depending on compatibility of communication style (Higgins and Warner, in Henderson 1979).

Respect

By valuing the client as a person with worth and dignity, counselors show respect. They are committed to working with clients and seeking to understand their situations by listening, being attentive, and validating clients' concerns. They suspend judgment and convey warmth. Although warmth is communicated through verbal and nonverbal behaviors that have specific meaning within the majority culture, culturally different clients may perceive these same nonverbal behaviors quite differently. For example, whites value direct eye contact and attribute avoidance of eye contact to negative traits; however, some cultures consider avoidance of eye contact or indirect gazing as respectful nonverbal behavior and, as Ivey (1988) noted, consider direct eye contact rude and intrusive.

Genuineness

Genuineness is best conveyed by being willing to work with the individual client and any extended clientele. It also is evidenced through supporting nonverbal and role behavior, congruence, spontaneity, openness, and self-disclosure. The following considerations are important:

1. Eye contact, facial expressions such as smiling, and forward-leaning posture may have a negative impact on culturally di-

verse people, who may interpret these nonverbal expressions as aggressive and intrusive.

2. Although in contemporary Western cultures, too much emphasis on role and position sometimes creates distance in a helping relationship, professional status may prove to be influential, at least initially, with clients who are not culturally programmed to view all people, regardless of credentials, as their equal.

3. Even though self-disclosure often generates an open and facilitative relationship between a majority counselor and client, culturally different people do not necessarily value sharing intimate details and may feel uncomfortable and embarrassed.

The quality of the client-counselor relationship can be enhanced further through counselor characteristics of expertness, attractiveness, and credibility. *Expertness* usually is manifested in counselor credentials, setting, reputation, and role. Beyond qualifications, counselors must evidence awareness of the sociocultural environment from which the child or adolescent comes. *Attractiveness* is best conveyed by structuring the counseling process and leaving little time for open-ended interaction, particularly at the outset. From a multicultural perspective, *credibility* comes from the counselor's providing accurate and reliable information and reacting nondefensively to client challenges or "tests of trust," which are more likely to surface in working with culturally diverse children and youth. The challenge of conveying to the client (and extended clientele) that one is a credible counselor is likely to be greater when working with minority counselees, especially those who deem the family more important than the individual (Sue and Sue 1990).

Conceptualizing the Presenting Problems

Assessment forms the foundation upon which intervention is built. An important dimension is the counselor's ability to conceptualize the presenting problem or the reason for referral. The cognitive-behavioral approach to counseling provides a comprehensive model of assessment that is responsive to contextual variables that contribute to the issues at hand. Understanding the context is essential to fully understanding what might be identified as problem behavior in culturally different children and adolescents. A behavior that the majority culture may perceive as problematic may be considered acceptable behavior in the minority culture of origin. Youngman and Sadougei (in Henderson 1979) described elementary-aged Native American students taking articles off the teacher's desk because in keeping with tribal cultural perspectives this is viewed as sharing between a person of rank (the teacher) and the student. Clearly, this perspective is at odds with the majority culture view of the same behavior.

Assessment should seek out broad-based, unbiased information and avoid diagnostic systems that measure psychological characteristics not readily generalizable across cultures. The cognitive-behavioral approach to counseling, based on principles of learning, can be applied to bring about constructive change in clients. Critical assumptions that have therapeutic implications in working with culturally different clientele include the following:

1. Most counterproductive behavior is learned and, therefore, can be unlearned or be modified.
2. Presenting problems should be described concretely in terms of what the person actually does in situations.
3. The causes of problems—and, therefore, the nature of intervention—are multidimensional and never should be taken out of context.

Client issues usually can be described concretely and connected to contextual events by applying the ABC model of behavior analysis (Cormier and Cormier 1985). Simply defined, this approach to assessment suggests that the behavior (B) that is the focus of concern (and typically the reason for referral) may be influenced by antecedent (A) events that tell a person how to behave, and by consequent events (C) that follow the behavior and strengthen or weaken it. Minority group standards of conduct may be antecedent conditions in determining how a culturally diverse person is likely to respond to certain situations. Minority group reactions and sanctions also may act as consequent events in encouraging or inhibiting behaviors.

Promising methods of collecting evaluative information include the interview, direct observation of client behavior in context, and client self-monitoring. In keeping with the ARC model of problem conceptualization, all three approaches should be structured to clearly describe the behavior in question, identify antecedent events or conditions that cue or trigger behavior, and reinforcing or punishing consequences that follow behavior and in some way influence it. To accurately assess psychological strengths and limitations of minority clients, D'Andrea (1990) recommends determining the internal and external dimensions to the behavior in question and any influential antecedents and consequences. Internal elements that have diagnostic and prescriptive value include thoughts, emotions, and imagery. External considerations include actions taken, contextual events, and relational aspects or connections between the behavior in question and the presence or absence of others.

The first point of contact with the client usually is the initial interview. Interviews with the child and any extended clientele should be conducted in a culturally sensitive manner (D'Andrea 1990). Sue and Sue (1990) offered the following suggestions for conducting an intake session with Mexican American clients, which may be applied as well to other culturally diverse clients.

1. Engage in a respectful and warm conversation with the client. Be sure to pronounce the client's name correctly. It is difficult to establish rapport when the client winces every time you say his or her name.
2. Provide a brief description of what counseling is and the role of each participant. Explain confidentiality.
3. Have the client state in his or her own words the problem or problems as he or she sees it.
4. Paraphrase or summarize the problem as you understand it, and make sure the client knows you understand it.
5. Ask the client to prioritize his or her problems.
6. With the client's help, determine his or her expectations, and develop appropriate goals. Discuss possible outcomes of achieving the goals.
7. Discuss the possible participation of family members, and consider family therapy.
8. Evaluate the role of environmental factors in prompting or maintaining the problem.
9. Explain the treatment to be used, why it was selected, and how it will help achieve the goals.
10. With the client's input, determine a mutually agreeable duration of treatment.

Information sought through interviews may include issues on which the client chooses to focus, a description of presenting problems in terms of observable behaviors and internal events (e.g., thoughts and feelings), identification of influential antecedents and consequences (also in terms of observable/internal events), isolation of any "secondary gains" or payoffs that might sustain behavior, and any previous attempts to resolve the problem. Starr and Raykovitz (1982) designed a multimodel format through which comprehensive assessment interviews can be conducted with children and youth, leading to the formulation of goals for counseling and implementation of intervention strategies. This format is useful in working with culturally diverse clientele.

Interviews with important others may help not only in building a working relationship with prospective collaborators in treatment but also in shedding light on antecedents and consequents of cultural significance. Among the several observational systems that exist, the ABC model calling for direct observations of client behavior in the client's environment is recommended to structure input. Further, individual strengths and limitations can be detected by connecting them to behavioral, antecedent, and consequent events.

Whatever form the assessment-conceptualization process takes, the evaluator should ensure that culturally different clients do not perceive these efforts as evidence of their failure. The more unobtrusive the measures are, the less likely miscommunication will be.

Client participation in the assessment process, or awareness of its outcomes, can be enlightening and even cause the client to make adjustments in behavior that remove the need for additional intervention. Self-monitoring approaches, such as behavioral logs, on which the client records things such as date of occurrence, time, place, description of event, other people present, and personal thoughts and feelings about the event, can be informative and productive.

Information collected across all facets of assessment should lead to identification of priority issues that can be converted to goals for action. These goals enhance counselor credibility as an action-oriented helper, which can motivate clients to follow through. Goals enable focus on areas in need of attention and help counselors determine whether they have the skills necessary to address them. Furthermore, goals structure counseling to meet the client's needs, help identify material and human resources (including extended clientele), and establish an end point toward which progress in counseling is measured. Like the effect assessment sometimes has on clients, collaboratively formulated goals can inspire clients to change. This may be especially inspirational if extended clientele are involved in developing and endorsing goals for action.

Together with the client (both primary and extended), goals for action should be developed to reflect realistic changes in child behavior, to screen for positive and negative consequences of goal accomplishment, and to ensure that the child can manage and is invested in following through. Personal strengths and limitations identified through the assessment process should be incorporated into the goals. The contextual conditions under which these overt and covert behaviors will be applied (location and people usually present) should be specified. Finally, the degree of change expected should be described. An implementation plan, developed with the client, outlines steps to be taken enroute to goal accomplishment through selected helping strategies.

Selecting and Implementing Intervention Strategies

Intervention strategies are plans of action designed to accomplish goals formulated earlier in the counseling process These strategies should be tailored to fit the child (and extended clientele) and not represent a generic, all-purpose approach to counseling especially with culturally diverse clients. Their readiness for transition to actual implementation of strategies depends on a number of considerations: quality of the counselor/client relationship, accuracy of the assessment on which goals for action are based, how realistic and desirable the counseling goals are, client and extended clientele commitment to follow-through, and sufficient baseline data with which to measure progress in counseling intervention.

As with formulating goals, selecting intervention strategies is a shared responsibility, and contingent on the following variables:

- counselor skills and comfort level ("The best helper is the one who has the widest repertory of helping skills and who can readily call upon these skills to meet different needs of any client"—Egan 1990)
- alignment of strategies with counselor values
- degree of fit with the nature of the presenting problem
- the client's response capability

These considerations are especially important in working with multicultural clients.

Contextual factors, particularly the availability and likelihood of reinforcement within both the majority and the minority environments in which the client operates may affect the usefulness of the strategies chosen. As a child advocate, the counselor may have to intervene on the child's behalf to assure accessibility of the needed resources and rewards. Regardless of the intervention strategy, culturally diverse clients must receive strong messages from all elements within their environments, institutional and natural (Shade 1990) that reinforce appropriate behaviors. Perhaps behaviors that are acceptable within the context of origin should be differentiated from those that are appropriate in majority-group situations.

Selected strategies should take into account the client's learning style and preferred response systems. Shade (1990) advocates multisensory presentations that involve all processing channels, as well as supportive material that accesses prior knowledge. The counselor also might consider establishing a contract consisting of a basic description of the selected strategies, goal statements, confirmation of intention ("I agree to ..."), duration of counseling, and statement of informed consent ("I understand what's in this contract ...").

Whatever the course of action, the counselor should provide a rationale for a given approach and an overview of specific steps suggested to implement the strategy. Implementation of any strategy that involves developing appropriate skills should include modeling of goal behavior, opportunities for rehearsal and feedback in counseling, and homework assignments through which the child applies what he or she has learned to life in the real world.

Modeling

When skill deficits (e.g., assertiveness, social skills) are evident, modeling has considerable potential. Modeling is the process of observational learning in which the behavior of an individual or a group, the model, acts as a stimulus for the thoughts, attitudes, or behaviors on the part of another individual who observes the model's performance'' (Perry and Furukawa 1980). Through the modeling approach, children and adolescents can acquire new behaviors, further develop already learned behaviors, or extinguish fears associated with a lack of skills in certain situations. Symbolic, media, and live models should be culturally compatible with the child. In working with culturally diverse children and youth, the counselor can choose from three modeling procedures:

1. *Symbolic modeling.* The model demonstrates target or corrective behavior through written material, audio or videotape recordings, film or slide productions. The characteristics of the model should be similar to those of the client. Practice is important. The client should be allowed to choose the form of media through which modeling is presented.
2. *Self-as-a-model.* The client is filmed or recorded performing the target behavior and later exposed to counselor-edited versions of this same production showing the client demonstrating only successfully mastered skills.
3. *Participant modeling.* A live model is recruited and trained to perform the target behavior for the client, who later performs the same behavior independently after observation and some guided

practice. The live model could be a motivated and respected peer, preferably a person of the same cultural group.

All modeling procedures involve presenting a rationale or reason why the suggested approach is appropriate, a description of how modeling works, identification and subsequent demonstration of target behaviors, guided practice or rehearsal through which the client has an opportunity to try out corrective behavior, and application of learned skills in the real world. Skills learned through modeling should not conflict with behavioral expectations promulgated in the minority context. If they do, situations under which target behaviors are appropriate should be differentiated.

Cognitive Restructuring/Reframing

If a client's thinking about a given situation is clearly counterproductive and causes or aggravates behavior problems, cognitive restructuring and reframing have potential. The assumption behind both strategies is that behavior (how individuals respond to situations) is influenced by antecedent and consequent beliefs, attitudes, and perceptions (or cognitions). Through cognitive change procedures, clients come to understand the relationship between thoughts and resulting behaviors and learn to replace faulty cognitions with more constructive, self-enhancing perceptions.

Irrational beliefs and negative self-statements or thoughts are identified and altered. The implementation sequence to this approach has six steps:

1. Providing a rationale.
2. Identifying counterproductive thoughts in problem situations.
3. Formulating more constructive coping thoughts.
4. Putting these thoughts into practice.
5. Learning to shift from counterproductive to more constructive facilitative thinking.
6. Following up in the real world by gradually trying out replacement thinking or self-statements in challenging situations.

Through cognitive reframing, a client is encouraged to see an issue or a problematic situation from a different perspective. Steps associated with this procedure are:

1. Providing a rationale for taking this approach.
2. Confirming client perceptions (and other responses) in problem situations.
3. Identifying alternative, more plausible explanations.

4. Covert reenactment of the problem situation with revised/replacement perceptions in place.
5. Application of these revised perceptions in the real world through homework or follow-up assignments.

Although it does not fit cleanly into the cognitive change category, Ford (in Thompson and Rudolph 1988) recommended reality therapy, in addition to behavior counseling and systematic counseling, as one of three approaches that should work well with minority group adolescents. Reality therapy was recommended specifically because this approach offers the counselor a method for helping minority clients accept the reality of living in a majority-dominated world.

Problem-Solving

Problem-solving has particular value when the client seems to make habitual inappropriate decisions or readily succumbs to peer pressure. In taking a problem-solving approach to intervention, the critical assumption is that ineffectiveness in resolving problems often leads to behavior and emotional problems. Designed to help individuals identify the most promising alternatives, problem-solving work consists of seven steps:

1. Presenting a rationale as to why and how it works.
2. Working up a concrete definition of the problem.
3. Brainstorming alternative solution strategies with the client.
4. Predicting the likely consequences of each strategy (for the client and significant others).
5. Selecting the "best" strategy.
6. Generating tactics through which the chosen strategy could be implemented.
7. Encouraging follow-through by action planning and securing client commitment to taking action.

Managing Resistance to Intervention

Counselors who work with multicultural clients are more likely to encounter resistance than are their counterparts who are involved with majority-culture populations. Resistance is simply defined as client, counselor, or environmental variables that adversely impact the likelihood of success in counseling.

If the client's resistance stems from a lack of skills or knowledge, the counselor should provide the needed training or more detailed instructions. When the client has minimal or negative expectations, the counselor should acknowledge these thoughts and feelings and, if related to the minority/majority nature of the counseling relationship, validate these concerns and refer to another professional, if warranted. If the resisting client is apprehensive about following through, the counselor should explore these thoughts and feelings, break down the problem into more "bite-sized" tasks, give more support for risk-taking, consider a change of pace or of environment, augment this approach with relaxation exercises or more emphasis on the cognitive dimension, or try bibliotherapy, with sensitivity to cultural compatibility. If resistance is traceable to counselor variables, the counselor should not personalize the resistance but, rather, encourage more client participation in the counseling process, take smaller steps, avoid leaping prematurely to solution strategies, ensure that activities are in keeping with minority group values, attitudes, and beliefs, and be more direct and immediate through confrontation, interpretation, or referrals.

Outcome Evaluation

Evaluative information should be collected throughout the helping relationship. Outcome evaluation specifically refers to process and product operations. Process evaluation designates ongoing measures to determine if the client is making progress. Information gained through process evaluation is useful in pinpointing flaws in the approach and allows counselors to make mid-course corrections in how counseling should proceed. Product evaluation typically is done at the point of termination with the client. It measures the extent to which established goals were attained and determines the overall worth and merit of the approach taken in counseling.

Methods through which outcomes in counseling can be measured include: (1) noting client responses in counseling, (2) observing client behaviors in natural settings, (3) looking for evidence of skills mastery, (4) client self-monitoring of behavior in challenging situations, (5) evaluating performance during role-play or rehearsal activities, and (6) applying valid, culture-free psychological measures conducted as post-tests.

PREVENTION, THE FINAL FRONTIER

School-based counselors are taking a closer, more serious look at developmental school counseling as the program of choice in determining how they carry out their professional responsibilities. Through this approach, counselors are challenged to conduct (together with teachers) classroom activities designed to address needs-driven student competencies. Increased awareness of culturally diverse populations is certainly a student competency deserving of concerted attention in the schools. Other strategies the American School Counselor Association (1988) advocates are:

1. Involve culturally diverse parents on curriculum development planning boards, committees, and other school projects.
2. Develop workshops for culturally diverse parents to orient them to the school system's philosophy of education.
3. Provide awareness workshops for faculty and staff on the dynamics of cultural diversity.
4. Incorporate culturally diverse human and material resources into the educational process.
5. Promote schoolwide activities focusing on differences and contributions of culturally different people.
6. Provide liaison services to facilitate communication among diverse populations in the school and community.
7. Use materials that are free of culturally biased information and urge classroom teachers to do the same.

SUMMARY

As the United States is rapidly evolving into a multicultural and pluralistic society, counselors must be prepared to work with cultural, language, and social class traits that may differ from theirs. This requires understanding the diverse behaviors, values, and lifestyles of the nondominant culture. It means shifting from a focus on the individual to attention to the two different cultures within which the student operates (family and school). These students should not be expected to merely accede to the institutional expectations of the dominant culture.

In working with culturally diverse clients, counselors must be flexible and able to adapt techniques to clients. Understanding nonverbal communication is central to success in counseling, as are empathy, respect, and genuineness.

The most effective approaches with multicultural children and youths entail a structured form of intervention in combination with curricular and other participative approaches to prevention. With regard to intervention, a developmental, action-oriented form of counseling is advocated. It is suggested that cognitive-behavior strategies have a great deal of potential in working with minority group clients. Complementary preventive activities include regular classroom-mediated lessons on awareness of diversity and other approaches to enlist the support of extended clientele.

REFERENCES

American School Counselor Association. 1988. Position statement on cross/multicultural counseling (adopted 1988). Alexandria, VA: ASCA.

Cormier, W., and S. L. Cormier. 1985. *Interviewing strategies for helpers*. 2nd ed. Pacific Grove, CA: Brooks/Cole.

D'Andrea, M. 1990. Training counselors for a pluralistic society. Article submitted to *Counselor Education and Supervision*.

Egan, G. 1990. *The skilled helper: A systematic approach to effective helping*. Pacific Grove, CA: Brooks/Cole.

Henderson, G., ed. 1979. *Understanding and counseling ethnic minorities*. Springfield, IL: Charles C. Thomas.

Ivey, A. 1988. *Intentional interviewing and counseling*. Pacific Grove, CA: Brooks/Cole.

Ivey, A., and J. Authier. 1978. *Microcounseling*. 2d ed. Springfield, IL: Charles C. Thomas.

Perry, M. A., and J. J. Furukawa. 1980. Modeling methods. In F. H. Kanfer and A. D. Goldstein, eds., *Helping people change*, 131–171. New York: Pergamon.

Peterson, J. V., and B. Nisenholz. 1991. *Orientation to counseling*. 2d ed. Boston: Allyn and Bacon.

Poyatos, F. 1988. *Cross-cultural perspectives in nonverbal communication*. Lewiston, NY: C. J. Hogrefe.

Shade, B. 1990. *Cultural ways of knowing, an afrocentric perspective*. Position paper presented at Summer Institute on Restructuring Learning, Council of Chief State School Officers.

Starr, J., and J. Raykovitz. 1982. A multimodel approach to interviewing children. *Elementary School Guidance and Counseling* 16: 267–274.

Sue, D. 1989. *Guidepost*. American Counseling Association 10.

Sue, D. W., and D. Sue. 1990. *Counseling the culturally different. Theory and practice*. 2d ed. New York: John Wiley and Sons.

Thompson, C., and L. Rudolph. 1988. *Counseling children*. 2d ed. Pacific Grove, CA: Brooks/Cole.

Verma, G., and C. Bagley, eds. 1988. *Cross-cultural studies of personality, attitudes and cognition*. London: Macmillan.

7 Counseling with At-Risk Students

James V. Wigtil

Counseling Program
The Ohio State University

JoAnne M. Wigtil

Doctoral Candidate
Family Relations and Human Development
The Ohio State University

A lthough children have always had stress in their lives, the number of children with excessive stress and presenting symptoms with seemingly few coping skills seems to be escalating at an alarming rate (Brenner l984). These children and adolescents under stress are what many today refer to as children at risk—at risk for failure in school, at home, and in the community. As a result of the rapid expansion of knowledge and technological change, coupled with change in attitudes and behaviors, today's children have greater pressures.

David Elkind, author of *The Hurried Child*, posits that children today are hurried to grow up too fast too soon. Pressure to achieve early intellectually, socially, and in organized, competitive sports often leaves the child under considerable stress without the coping skills needed to adapt (Elkind 1981, 1987a, 1987b). Children and adolescents tend to be involved in more adult behaviors, such as sex and drugs, at an early age; these are children growing up without a childhood (Winn 1983). With the pressure to grow up faster, children and adolescents are involved in delinquency, teen pregnancy, substance ahuse, and school failure. Hurried children comprise a large portion of troubled or at-risk children whom professionals see today. Many of these at-risk children and youth are destined to drop out of today's educational system with only a limited potential for becoming productive adults (Dryfoos 1990).

WHO ARE THE CHILDREN AND ADOLESCENTS AT RISK?

The meaning of at risk is unclear in the literature (Sapp 1990; Swanson 1991). In any case, there is a connotation that at-risk students are more likely to drop out of high school. Gross and Capuzzi (1989) suggested that "the term 'at risk' is descriptive of a set of causal/behavioral dynamics that place the individual in danger of a negative future event" (p. 5). Associated with the term *at risk* are factors including behavior problems, low socioeconomic status, poor school attendance, low achievement, poor academic grades, and retention in grade level (Gross and Capuzzi 1989; Sapp 1990; Swanson 1991). Many at-risk students come from minority groups with low socioeconomic status and are referred to by some as the underprivileged or culturally deprived. Still other at-risk students come from dysfunctional families having psychological problems, alcohol and drug abuse, or financial problems (Swanson 1991).

SIGNS AND SYMPTOMS

Knowledge of the signs and symptoms of at-risk children and adolescents is important if counselors are to select appropriate developmentally based interventions for at-risk students. Based on the literature, Gross and Capuzzi (1989) summarized fifteen red flags that are characteristic of youth at risk within an eductional setting:

1. Absent from classes.
2. Failure of at least one grade.
3. Late to school or classes.
4. Low scores in math and reading.
5. Lack of motivation.
6. Low grades.
7. Little identification with school.
8. No perceived relationship of education to life.
9. Bored with school.
10. Rebellious attitude toward authority.
11. Deficient in language and verbal skills.
12. Low tolerance for structured experiences.
13. Behind age group by at least two graduation credits.
14. Acting-out behavior.
15. Truancy.

Beyond this strictly educational perspective on signs and symptoms, several underlying factors/critical events (e.g. abuse, poverty) and at-risk behaviors (e.g., aggression and anger, poor school performance) can place a child or adolescent in a situation that, if not dealt with effectively by counselors, can lead to more serious maladaptive behaviors (e.g., eating disorders, chemical dependency). Table 7.1 contains a summary of the major underlying factors/critical events and behaviors of at-risk children and early adolescents. Maladaptive behaviors (listed

Table 7.1
UNDERLYING FACTORS AND BEHAVIORS OF
AT-RISK CHILDREN AND ADOLESCENTS

Underlying Factors or Critical Events	At-Risk Behaviors	Maladaptive Behaviors
• Abuse*	• Depressive feelings*	• Depression*
• Alcoholism in family*	• Negative body image	• Eating disorder
• Stepfamily*	• Early and unprotected sexual experiences*	• Teen pregnancy*
• Loss (death, divorce)*	• Early use and abuse	• AIDS
• Poverty	• Suicidal ideation*	• Chemical dependency
• Lack of parental bonding	• Aggression and anger	• Suicide attempts or completions*
	• Poor school performance	• Violence and delinquency
		• Failure or school dropout

*Discussed in this chapter

in the far right column) can be an outgrowth of the underlying factors/ critical events (left column), and actual at-risk behaviors (middle column).

To clearly separate these at-risk categories is difficult as they obviously overlap with many additional underlying antecedents— demographical factors such as race and gender; personal characteristics such as low self-esteem and peer influence; family characteristics such as poverty, lack of parental bonding, and parental practice of high-risk behaviors; and community variables such as growing up in a poor urban setting (Dryfoos 1990). For convenience, however, the signs and symptoms are presented separately: first, by four of the underlying factors/ critical events (abuse, parental alcoholism, child in stepfamily, and loss); next, by three of the at-risk behaviors (depressive feelings, early and unprotected sexual experience, and suicidal ideation); and lastly, by maladaptive behaviors (depression, teenage pregnancy, and suicide attempts or completion).

Underlying Factors/Critical Events

Abuse

Abuse (physical, sexual, emotional) is a major underlying factor that can place youth at risk. This is a complex issue because, on one hand, at-risk children and adolescents are victims, but, on the other hand, they may be offenders themselves.

The difficulty in determining the real number of abuse cases is that a majority of cases are not reported (Alford, Martin, and Martin 1990). This is true in spite of laws on reporting, and abuse position statements by professional organizations such as the American School Counselor Association (1988). Some reasons for inaccurate figures are: (1) reporting retrospectively (clients' unreported incidents that occurred in the past), (2) reluctance to report (because of severe offender sanctions), (3) denial (adults' ignoring or choosing not to deal with the problem), (4) sexist beliefs (that girls are the only victims, minimizing the victimization of boys), (5) blame (focusing mainly on victim versus perpetrator), (6) doubt (children telling fictitious stories) (Rencken 1989), and (7) child abuse hysteria (caused by allegations in divorce and custody, as well as overreaction by professionals) (Spiegel 1988; Thompson and Rudolph 1992).

The effects of physical and sexual abuse are difficult to quantify. Some effects are:

- loss of security, trust, and childhood
- feelings, conflicts, and ambivalence: love/hate, guilt/rage, stoicism/fear
- defenses: denial, disassociation, obesity, anorexia; weapons (e.g., hand, mouth, belt); use of alcohol and other drugs; depression; withdrawal from society, family, and reality
- death, such as by suicide (Rencken 1989)

Two important dynamics in physical and sexual abuse involve control and power. Why one family evidences physical abuse and another family harbors sexual abuse is not clear, nor are offender, nonoffending spouse, or child profiles clearly distinguishable for either type of abuse (Rencken 1989).

Abusive parents do differ on some dimensions, but they also tend to have characteristics in common, such as:

- denial (not taking responsibility for one's behavior)
- blame (faulting the victim)
- incongruency (saying one thing and doing another)

- domination (need for power over the children)
- distrust (not trusting their children)
- selfishness (overconcerned with own needs and little for children's rights)
- compulsivity (repeating abusive behavior)
  (McEvoy and Erickson 1990)

Sexual Abuse. England and Thompson (1988) identified six sexual abuse myths: (1) incest occurs infrequently, and, when it does, it is typically found in families with little education and low socioeconomic status; (2) child molesters are sexually attracted to their victims; (3) child molesters usually are strangers to the victims; (4) sexual abuse of children is a recent phenomenon resulting from the sexual revolution, (5) child sexual abuse is typically a violent one-time incident; and (6) many times children fabricate stories of sexual experiences with adults.

Most victims of sex abuse are between the ages of eight and twelve (Finkelhor 1984). Men are the primary perpetrators, abusing about 95 percent of female and 80 percent of male victims (Rencken 1989). Approximately 33 percent of female adolescents are subjected to some type of sexual assault (McEvoy and Erickson 1990).

Children may show some of the signs of sexual abuse listed in Table 7.2. These children do not readily trust anyone and may act out or withdraw. They also have been hurt in the deepest sense by someone close to them that they also may love. If sexual abuse is in the form of incest, the child or adolescent may be in a caregiving or pseudo-adult role. Some adolescents who have been abused sexually have a great deal of difficulty with same-sex friendships (e.g., feel inadequate), others place the prime emphasis in their lives on sex (e.g., are sexually abusive to others), and still others withdraw from sexuality by trying to appear unattractive (Merchant 1990). These abused adolescents are sexually beyond their years but seem much younger or more immature than their chronological age in other areas of their lives.

Physical Abuse. Goldstein, Keller, and Erne (1985) indicated that the number of cases per year ranged from 200,000 to 4 million. Children as young as one to three years of age may develop patterns like that of the abusing parent, such as poor empathy, aggressiveness, and isolation or withdrawal (Main and Goldwyn 1984). When children are abused physically, the negative effects can carry into adolescence and adulthood. Physically abused adolescents typically act out and may trigger a fight for seemingly unimportant things. Others, however, withdraw into submissiveness through fear of the abusing person. Younger adoles-

Table 7.2
PHYSICAL AND BEHAVIORAL SIGNS
OF SEXUAL ABUSE

Physical	Behavior
Discharge in vaginal area	Fear of being with someone
Genital discomfort	Disturbances related to sleep (e.g., bedwetting)
Trouble staying seated or moving about	Eating problems
Pregnancy or venereal disease under thirteen years of age	School behavior changes (e.g., drop in attendance)
	Atypical sexual behavior

Source: Based on "Preventive Sexual Abuse Programs: Problems and Possibilities" by C. Tennant, 1988, in *Elementary School Guidance and Counseling* 23(1), pp. 50–51.

cents (twelve to fourteen years) may begin to show anger in a joking manner through hitting and shoving. This can lead to more intense fighting. Also, younger victims of physical abuse may not know how to be appropriately intimate (Merchant 1990).

Children can be affected by physical abuse in the following ways (Rencken 1989):

- behavior problems
- poor social skills
- lower self-esteem
- antisocial behavior
- general anxiety
- acting out
- serious adolescent adjustment problems
- helplessness/dependency
- less ambition
- fewer friendships
- ineffective peer relationships
- low level of empathy
- inadequate social skills
- aggressive tendencies
- delinquency

- attachment disorders
- neurological abnormalities
- sexual abuse

Physical abuse occurs for many reasons. Our society seems to both tolerate and condone hitting or spanking children (Rencken 1989). Many parents spank their children to show "who is boss," and some schools discipline children in the form of "corporal punishment." Many children watch violence on TV in the form of cartoons and movies. Dysfunctional families that have rigid rules and operate as a closed system are at risk for physically abusive behaviors typically directed toward the children and adolescents.

A study of how physically abused (victim) runaways (43 percent) and nonvictim (physical abuse not an important reason for leaving home) runaways (57 percent) perceived their family environment yielded interesting results. In terms of those who were physically abused at home (Janus, McCormack, Burgess, and Hartman 1987):

1. Victim runaways had lower self-esteem.
2. They were generally dissatisfied with life and wished things were different.
3. Only half of those who were abused physically by their families saw their families as being happy for more than three consecutive days.
4. Negative family environment influenced the runaway's feelings of inadequacy in controlling his or her environment.
5. Lack of adequate coping skills and poor self-concept made it difficult for these runaways to make it in unprotected environments, and victim runaways who left a dangerous family environment were quite vulnerable.

Parental Alcoholism

More than 10 percent of the people in the United States are reared in alcoholic homes (Ackerman 1983). An estimated 6.5 million children live with a parent who is alcoholic (Buwick, Martin, and Martin 1988). In a typical classroom, four to six of the twenty-five students are children of alcoholic parents (Morehouse and Scola 1986). Russell (1989) studied 100 runaways from 2,000 court-referred juveniles and found that 26 percent had parents who were severely alcoholic. Children who have one alcoholic parent have a 50 percent chance of becoming an alcoholic, and children with two alcoholic parents have an 80 percent chance (National Council on Alcoholism 1982).

Alcoholism is a family disease in that family members are part of system. Therefore, all are affected by the alcoholic or chemically dependent parent. Children and adolescents in the family become stuck developmentally as a result of living in a dysfunctional family system in which the alcoholic parent's needs have priority, secrets and privacy are confused, parents are emotionally unavailable to the children, the alcoholic parent's routine determines when and if the children get attention, and, under stress, family roles become rigid. Six dysfunctional roles typically evolve in alcoholic or chemically dependent families:

1. *Enabler.* Typically this family member is the spouse of the alcoholic person, although it can be anyone in the family or close to the family. This person's role is to soften the negative effects of alcoholism by covering up the spouse's drinking.

2. *Hero.* This is usually the oldest child in the family. The hero provides hope and pride for the alcoholic family through activities such as excelling in school.

3. *Scapegoat.* The scapegoat tends to get recognition from peers. Acting-out behavior is typical, and these children develop at-risk behaviors such as early use and abuse of alcohol and other drugs and other maladaptive behaviors.

4. *Lost child.* The lost child is often a middle child who makes few demands at home or school. These children often go unnoticed as they quietly withdraw.

5. *Mascot.* Typically the youngest child is overprotected. This child's clowning behavior helps the family relate somewhat honestly through laughter, reducing anxiety and tension (Wegscheider 1981).

6. *Composite.* This family member can be an only child or a family member who may assume or play all the roles at one time or alternately.

These family roles become more rigid as the alcoholic member progressively gets worse, and the children and adults in the family become as addicted to their roles as the alcoholic parent does to alcohol or drugs. Becoming locked into these roles negatively affects a child's or adolescent's development. Even if the alcoholic stops drinking, the effects of parental alcoholism do not disappear (Thompson and Rudolph 1992).

Children in Stepfamilies

Close to half of married couples in the United States get a divorce. As a result, stepfamilies (blended or remarried families) are becoming more common or normative. In the 1990s, it is estimated that by the time they are eighteen years old approximately a third of all children will spend time with a stepparent. The blended family will be the most common family type by the year 2000 (Whiteman 1991).

Blended families often have some of the following distinctive features (Goldenberg and Goldenberg 1990):

- stepparent—difficulty with parental role
- siblings (stepbrothers and stepsisters)—jealousy and rivalry
- boundaries—ambiguity
- ex-spouses—unresolved conflict
- competition—between stepmother and biological mother, stepfather and biological father
- absent parent—idealized
- intimacy—lacking between nonbiological child and stepparent
- loyalty issues—between children and absent parent, children and stepparent
- loyalty issues—between parent and absent children, parent and stepchildren
- surname—may differ between children and a parent
- new baby—effects from birth of child
- economic support—alimony and child support payments
- custody—adolescent conflicts arising from requests to change

Difficulties in remarried or blended families are attributable to several dynamics: children being part of two different households with unique lifestyles and rules, losses of former relationships, family members with different traditions and family histories, and loss of dreams and hopes within the previous family (Visher and Visher 1988).

Just as individuals and families with children move through developmental stages, so do post-divorce families (custodial single parent and noncustodial parent). The latter have to go through one or two additional phases before restabilizing and continuing their development (Goldenberg and Goldenberg 1991). The formation of a remarried or blended family has three steps: (1) moving into the new relationship; (2) planning and conceptualizing a new marriage/family, and (3) remarriage and restructuring of family (Carter and McGoldrick 1988).

School counselors might discuss the following points with parents who are contemplating remarriage, to facilitate the adjustment of the children involved (Whiteman 1991):

1. Children should be introduced to the potential stepparent in a low-key, natural manner.
2. A relationship between one's children and a new stepparent takes several years to develop.
3. Young children adapt more rapidly to a stepparent than older children and adolescents do.
4. Stepparents should observe family traditions, including giving children and adolescents reasonable gifts at special times.
5. Parents should give children a choice on whether to participate in the wedding.
6. New stepparents who are childless should learn about parenting and child and adolescent development.
7. To expect a child to love or respect the stepparent as much as the biological parent is unrealistic.
8. The new family should reach a compromise on what to call the new stepparent (Mom, Dad, nickname).
9. Parents should spend time with and remind each child that they love the child.
10. Children should listen to and respect the new spouse, but the original parent should be the main disciplinarian.
11. The parent should not take sides with children or with the new spouse. Matters should be discussed privately with the spouse before informing the children of decisions.
12. Transitions can take up to five years; anger and resentment, especially typical of teenagers in blended families, should not be taken personally.

Loss

Loss is very common for children and adolescents and includes: (1) loss of peers and significant others (including boyfriends and girlfriends) through moving, rejection, death, and suicide; (2) parents through rejection, abandonment, divorce, and death; and (3) normal life stages, such as loss of childhood or early adolescence through physical or sexual abuse. Denial of an education may be a critical loss for homeless children (Eddowes and Hranitz 1989).

Specific losses can be grouped into three categories (Frears and Schneider 1981):

1. *Apparent loss*, from illness, death, injury, separation.

2. *Normative loss,* from leaving home, changing schools, moving, divorce.
3. *Unnoticed loss,* from growth, success, remarriage.

In the past, children and adolescents received little help in dealing with loss. More recently, helping professionals have recognized the importance of working through the grieving process•with children so they can complete tasks in their developmental life stage. The grief process enables youth to understand and work through the feelings and behaviors related to loss and separation. The six-stage process of grieving and loss involves (Frears and Schneider 1981):

1. Developing initial awareness.
2. Formulating strategies to overcome the loss.
3. Developing awareness of extent of loss.
4. Completion and healing.
5. Self-empowerment.
6. Going beyond the loss.

The developmental stage also has a bearing on the effects of loss. For example, children in early childhood (four to six years old) and middle school age (six to twelve) think death is temporary, and, they do not have the full capacity to work through loss. Adolescents (age twelve to eighteen) do tend to understand that death is irreversible.

While many losses, such as divorce, can be categorized as normal (Frears and Schneider 1981), such a loss may precipitate other losses, such as familiar environment and lifestyle, in addition to the loss of a parent (Thompson and Rudolph 1992). The resulting disappointment and rejection can lead to at-risk behaviors such as early use and abuse of alcohol and other drugs and poor school performance. If these childhood and adolescent at-risk behaviors are not understood and dealt with, more serious maladaptive behaviors such as chemical dependency, school failure, or dropping out of school, may arise.

At-Risk and Maladaptive Behaviors

Depressive Feelings/Depression

Although not as much attention has been given to depression in childhood as in adolescence, depression does affect many children today (Downing 1988; Hart 1991). An estimated 20 percent of school-age children experience depression (Hart 1991; Worchel, Nolan, and Willson 1987). Within child psychiatric settings, the incidence of childhood depression has been found to be as high as 51–59 percent (Hart 1991).

Childhood depression is difficult to clearly define and identify; however, Lasko (1986) stated that "the child seems down, blue, or irritable and no longer takes interest or pleasure in usual activities" (p. 284). Depression often is associated with feelings of sadness, hopelessness, separation anxiety, and feeling overwhelmed by stressful life events such as being abused, living with an alcoholic parent, experiencing parental divorce or death, or feeling increased pressures to achieve (Downing 1988; Elkind 1987a, 1987b; Newman and Newman 1991).

Some signs of depression in childhood and early adolescence are (Hart 1991; McWhirter and Kigin 1988):

- decrease in motivation
- difficulty with peers
- behavior problems, such as acting-out and aggressiveness
- poor school performance
- low self-esteem
- problems in concentration and thinking clearly
- social withdrawal
- changes in sleeping and eating habits
- irritability

Although many children are unhappy occasionally, it is important to assess whether the child is reacting to a stressful life event, such as a parent's divorce, or whether the depression is chronic, more severe, reappears frequently, and resists change (Downing 1988).

The incidence of depression in adolescence also tends to be unclear, but is considered a significant concern, however. In early adolescence, depression often is linked to suicide, substance abuse, and poor school performance (Newman and Newman 1991). Depression in adolescence also may be heightened by the impact of hormonal changes.

Adolescents may not always experience depression prior to suicide; however, feeling depressed and feeling suicidal (suicidal ideation) do tend to be associated. Thus, depressive symptoms should not be taken lightly, as depression tends to be the most common precipitating factor for those who both attempt and complete suicide (McWhirter and Kigin 1988).

Early and Unprotected Sexual Activity/Teen Pregnancy

Physical and hormonal changes, along with more complex social relationships, occur in adolescence (Newman and Newman 1991). Teens are likely to become involved in dating relationships, and they often are subjected to pressure to become involved in sexual relationships.

The incidence of teenage pregnancy and out-of-wedlock births to adolescent girls has been skyrocketing. This epidemic has implications for the baby, the teen mother, and society. Teenage pregnancy breeds poverty along with babies; teen mothers are seven times more likely to live below the poverty level (Magid and McKelvey 1987). Of the 10 million women in the United States between ages fifteen and nineteen, more than 1.1 million become pregnant each year (Dryfoos 1990). Approximately 125,000 teenage girls under the age of fifteen become pregnant each year.

Dryfoos (1990) suggested that once teens become involved sexually, they are at risk. Not only are the adolescent females at risk for becoming pregnant, but adolescent males and females alike are at risk for contracting sexually transmittable diseases, including AIDS. Dryfoos (1990) posited that society does not adequately address the issue of how to intervene and prevent the negative consequences of early sexual activity. Among the several societal issues is the conflict over the morality of premarital sexual activity (promoting abstinence or providing interventions that focus on instruction of responsible sexual behavior and contraception). And, if the adolescent becomes pregnant, should she be encouraged to place the child for adoption, keep the baby, or have the choice of abortion? In addition, the focus of adolescent pregnancy has been on girls, with little concern for the father (if he is also an adolescent), such as the impact of the pregnancy and the effects of fatherhood on his later development (Newman and Newman 1991).

While pregnancy is one of the consequences of early sexual activity, many teenagers don't regularly use contraceptives (Dryfoos 1990). Young adolescents who become pregnant most likely have come from a single-headed family, had a teen mother themselves, had poor parental monitoring, and delinquent behavior (Dryfoos 1990). Some of the antecedents or underlying factors in early sexual activity include:

- adolescents coming from low-income and uneducated families
- parents providing little support and not communicating well with their children
- living in a poor, segregated neighborhood
- low expectations for the adolescent's future achievement
- poor school performance
- vulnerability to influence by peers

- absence of involvement in school activities (Dryfoos 1990)
- lack of religious socialization or participation in religious services (Newman and Newman 1991)

Other high-risk behaviors, such as truancy and early substance use,
often precede early sex (Dryfoos 1990).

Suicide Ideation/Suicide Attempts or Completion

At-risk behaviors such as suicidal ideation are differentiated from more
serious child and early adolescent maladaptive behaviors such as suicide
attempts (see Table 7.1). As noted, at-risk behaviors typically precede
the development of maladaptive behaviors.

The adolescent suicide rate may be underestimated in that for every
completed suicide, many more adolescents are preoccupied with suicide
ideation (Dryfoos 1990). Statistically, more than 7,000 children and
adolescents commit suicide in the United States each year, and suicide
is the second largest cause of death for adolescents. Approximately a
fourth of all adolescents have some suicidal thoughts, and the adolescent suicide rate has doubled in the past two decades (McEvoy and
Erickson 1990). Of children younger than age fourteen, almost 200
commit suicide yearly (Herring 1990).

Myths that impede understanding of adolescent suicide include
(Capuzzi and Golden 1988):

1. Those who talk about it are not thinking seriously of committing
   suicide.
2. Once a youth is suicidal, he or she is always suicidal.
3. Suicide comes with no warning.
4. An adolescent who survives a suicide attempt usually does not
   try again.
5. Adolescents who commit suicide usually leave notes.
6. Adolescent suicides usually happen in the late evening.
7. The term "suicide" should not be mentioned around adolescents as it may give them ideas.
8. Adolescents who have strong religious convictions do not attempt suicide.

The causes of suicidal behavior in teens include (Capuzzi and
Gross 1989):

- difficulties in the transition to adolescence
- family dysfunction (poor communication, resistance to the grief
  process, difficulties of single parents, blended family confusion,
  midlife transition stressors, abusive interactions)

● environmental pressures (academic achievement, mobility, completion of high school, drug availability, world community)

In children and early adolescents, hopelessness, low self-concept, depression, guilt, and feelings of worthlessness often coincide with suicidal thoughts and attempts. Behavior can be either withdrawn or highly active (Thompson and Rudolph 1992). Other clues are loss of appetite, withdrawal, sleeplessness, and marked behavioral change.

Peck (1984) categorized youth suicide as: (1) the very young (ages ten to fourteen), (2) loners, (3) the depressed, (4) the crisis suicide, and (5) those who commit suicide to communicate something.

The following warning signs deserve immediate attention (Nelson 1988):

● suicidal threats
● sudden behavior change
● isolation and depression
● giving away most valued treasures
● taking care of unfinished business
● prior suicide attempts
● loss in one's life

AN INTERVENTION MODEL

The effects of at-risk and maladaptive behaviors are not only felt and experienced by the students themselves, but also by their siblings, families, peers, teachers, administrators, church personnel, community agencies, and ultimately by society itself. Hathaway, Sheldon, and McNamara (1989) identified at-risk effects according to three classifications: (1) short-term, (2) intermediate, and (3) long-term. These effects can be placed on a three-stage continuum, illustrated in Table 7.3. To reduce these at-risk effects, interventions must be developed.

Intervention Model

Figure 7.1 illustrates a childhood and adolescence intervention model. It shows effective intervening points for childhood at-risk behaviors and adolescent at-risk and maladaptive behaviors. If the underlying factors (1.0) are not addressed, childhood at-risk behaviors (2.0) are likely to develop. If these at-risk behaviors evident in childhood are not dealt with through interventions (5.0) such as prevention or counseling, maladaptive adolescent behaviors (4.0) may become entrenched and will carry into adulthood if the adolescent does not receive counseling, therapy, or other interventions. School counselors can implement intervention strategies (5.0) to help elementary and middle school children (2.0) and high school students reduce or eliminate their at-risk (3.0) and maladaptive (4.0) behaviors. Then, positive/adaptive adolescent behaviors (6.0) can result.

Intervention strategies (5.0) in the form of prevention may be implemented prior to identifying the factors underlying at-risk behaviors (1.0). In fact, Dryfoos (1990) suggested that interventions should take place before the antecedents, focusing on the individual, family, school, and community. Eliminating or reducing these underlying factors can minimize at-risk and maladaptive behaviors of children and early adolescents.

Crisis Response Teams

Child and adolescent at-risk and maladaptive behaviors can precipitate situations or crises that have to be dealt with in the schools. Many schools are developing formal crisis response teams, comprised of counselors and other educators, as well as procedures to address situations that affect students and to deal with their reactions to crises. The crisis teams, consisting of seven or eight trained members, decrease

Table 7.3
CONTINUUM OF AT-RISK EFFECTS

Short-Term	Intermediate	Long-Term
• Low or unrealistically high goals and aspirations	• School failure	• Economic dependence on family or welfare
• Poor self-esteem	• Disempowerment and hopelessness	• Crippling physical, emotional, and mental health problems
• Lack of future orientation	• Alienation	• Criminal involvement
• Poor study habits and learning capabilities	• Disengagement	
• Deteriorated motivation	• Pushout/dropout	

Source: Based on "The Solution Lies in Programs That Work" by W. Hathaway, C. Sheldon, and P. McNamara, in *Youth At Risk: A Resource for Counselors, Teachers and Parents*, edited by D. Capuzzi and D. R. Gross (Alexandria, VA: ACA, 1989), pp. 370–371.

crisis response time, provide opportunities for students to learn coping skills, and conduct debriefing sessions after interventions (Steele 1992). Teams can be formed within one school or on a systemwide basis, and the counselor or counseling department provides the backbone of the crisis plan (Petersen and Straub 1992). Ethical and legal considerations such as student privacy rights and school counselor-client confidentiality have to be taken into account in establishing crisis intervention procedures (Huey 1991). The discussion here ties the intervention to the four underlying factors/critical events and three at-risk maladaptive behaviors described earlier.

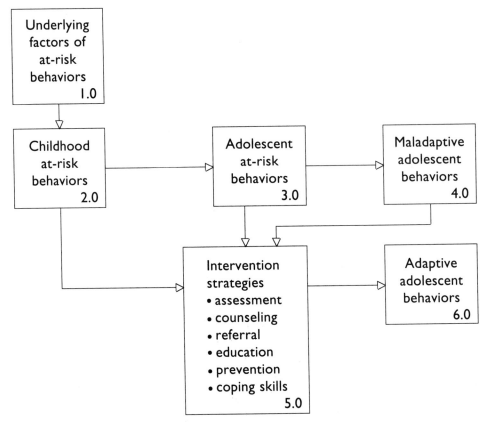

Figure 7.1
INTERVENTION MODEL FOR AT-RISK CHILDREN AND ADOLESCENTS

Underlying Factors/Critical Events
Abuse

Sally was sexually abused by an uncle from age five to fourteen. As a child she had depressive feelings, which are at-risk behaviors. In early adolescence these untreated depressive feelings developed into severe depression, a maladaptive behavior. As a young adult, through intensive counseling and therapy, Sally finally was able to talk about the sexual abuse she endured as a child. One wonders if her school counselors and teachers were aware of her trauma and plight.

School counselors who wish to learn more about child abuse should read the special issue of *Elementary School Guidance and Counseling* edited by Crabbs and Crabbs (1988), on child abuse issues and interventions. In this issue, Vernon and Hay (1988) advocated a preventive approach to elementary-age sexual abuse, incorporating six program areas: accepting yourself, addressing feelings, touch and body parts, making decisions, saying no, and identifying helpers. Activities for each topic can be tailored to various grade levels.

Thompson and Rudolph (1992) offered specific suggestions for counseling abused children:

1. Counselors may have to invest themselves with the abused child and provide frequent evidence that they care.
2. Counselors can use techniques such as visual imagery to address low self-worth and guilt feelings and increase self-esteem.
3. Counselors should not influence the child's verbalizations by asking closed or leading questions but rather seek clarification of nonverbal behavior or words that are not understood.
4. Counselors should determine the child's maturity level before utilizing approaches such as group counseling, role-playing, play therapy, and bibliotherapy.
5. Counselors should provide information on inappropriate/appropriate contact and touching and assure children that selected parts of their bodies should be private.
6. Counselors might provide assertiveness training on how to say no or how to handle potential abuse experiences.
7. Counselors should encourage children to tell someone immediately of an abusive experience.
8. Counselors should deal with issues of trust such as deciding whom to trust and in what situations to be cautious.

One of the school counselor's intervention responsibilities is to report suspected physical or sexual abuse to the proper authorities. This reporting is a legal requirement, and Wilder (1991) suggests the use of a child abuse and neglect form.

Intervention strategies for physical and sexual abuse victims are either immediate or delayed (a year or more after the most recent abusive contact) (Rencken 1989). Intensive individual counseling, small-group work, and family counseling are the major interventions available to school counselors for this at-risk population. Counselors have to practice within the scope of their education and training. If they do not have enough time or the necessary skills, they should make a referral. Helping to make connections for the first visit with a different professional helper and follow-up with these students is important.

Bibliotherapy can be helpful with physically and sexually abused children and adolescents. In the traditional form of bibliotherapy, librarians or counselors develop lists of books and give these to students for therapeutic benefit. A newer form, interactive bibliotherapy, involves facilitated discussions about the readings (Gladding and Gladding 1991). These authors suggest many ways in which school counselors can use interactive bibliotherapy. Krickeberg (1991) also identifies bibliography ideas to use with today's troubled youth.

Children of Alcoholics

Parent training can be an effective intervention for school counselors in working with children of alcoholics (substance abusers) as well as in helping parents and families address the consumption of alcohol and other drugs (U.S. Office of Substance Abuse Prevention 1991). Parents can be introduced to at least five general and interrelated parenting functions: breadwinning, home care, protection, guidance, and advocacy (Alvy 1991). Parents also can be educated in prevention roles (U.S. Office for Substance Abuse Prevention 1991) as:

- role models
- educators or information resources
- family policy-makers and rule-setters
- stimulators of and participants in enjoyable family activities
- monitors
- collaborators
- identifiers and confronters
- interveners
- managers of their own feelings

Roadblocks or barriers to successful parent involvement in parent training include: cost, transportation, care of children, lack of time, lack of interest, lack of ownership of the program, and cultural differences between parents and providers (Kumpfer 1991). School counselors should review, and, if necessary, work to change parenting programs in their school systems to deal with these roadblocks.

"The sooner the better" applies to interventions involving alcoholism and chemical dependency. Programs should be directed to those using and abusing alcohol and other drugs as well as the entire family, including children and adolescents of alcoholic parents, who are at risk. Helping family members understand the disease concept, learn each member's role (enabler, hero, scapegoat, lost child, mascot, composite) in the family disease, and understand formal intervention roles requires a minimum of one or two days and up to six to eight weeks (typically four to six weeks) (Wegscheider 1981). These formal interventions should be facilitated by a trained professional such as the school counselor.

School counselors also can intervene in the lives of substance abusing children of alcoholics through structured student assistance programs focusing on early identification. These programs require trained faculty, assessment, least restrictive interventions, referral to sources outside the school, and follow-up (Palmer and Paisley 1991).

Group (educational, support, life skills, counseling) experiences are among the interventions of choice for children and adolescents of substance-abusing parents. School counselors can offer developmental support groups for children of alcoholics (O'Rourke 1990; Wilson and Blocher 1990). Major techniques should include bibliotherapy, role-playing, rational emotive therapy, gestalt, and awareness activities, assertiveness and relaxation techniques (Wilson and Blocher 1990). The emphasis should be on the children's need for information on alcoholism, exploring feelings, building self-esteem, developing coping skills, managing stress, rehearsing decision-making, and encouraging primary relationships (O'Rourke 1990). Each support group should meet for forty-five minutes to an hour, preferably include five to seven children with a maximum of twelve, and have a two- to three-year maximum age range.

Some families and children protect themselves from alcoholism through defensive distancing (Berlin and Davis 1989). This is characterized by denial of stress, withdrawal, impulsivity, and delinquency, and the adolescents' most frequent contacts outside the family are with substance-abusing groups (O'Sullivan 1992). An alternative is adaptive distancing, in which resilient adolescents and families create a buffer for the adolescent to develop positive self-esteem and goals through some corrective work and awareness of the effects of family alcoholism on themselves. Counselors can teach adaptive distancing through individual counseling as well as psychoeducational and counseling group interventions.

Children in Stepfamilies

School counselors should determine their own attitudes toward the various family configurations, including blended or stepfamilies. Workshops and further course work can help counselors examine their attitudes and values and also improve their skills in intervening with the children and with couples and families.

Because children and families need others' support, counselors should develop skills in training peer facilitators. In addition, counselors should help school faculty improve communication with families, understand family configurations, increase their sensitivity toward noncustodial parents and stepparents in school activities, and understand the extent of family stress (Manning and Wooten 1987).

Depending on their developmental level, children and adolescents can learn from each other through group counseling as well as peer listening and facilitation. Hazouri and Smith (1991) developed a peer listener workbook school counselors can use to train middle school students through a nine-week elective course. Clearly peer-helper interventions can provide support for children and young teens.

When working with youths in blended families, counselors should assess the child or adolescent as well as the family. A combination of individual and family counseling, supportive groups, education, and bibliotherapy may be effective with these students and their families. The primary treatment modality is family counseling, with two exceptions: (1) when the child or adolescent poses a danger to self (in which case hospitalization may be the treatment of choice), and (2) when the family's level of dysfunction is so high that family counseling becomes extremely difficult (Palmo and Palmo 1989).

Couples counseling in concert with family counseling can positively impact dysfunctional family functioning, dynamics, and structure. These counseling sessions should emphasize parenting approaches and relationships. Once parents can learn to refocus and redirect their energy, youths make positive changes (Palmo and Palmo 1989).

Loss

Each child and adolescent has a unique reaction to loss. In working with children on these issues, counselors should ask open-ended questions and communicate interest by listening, understanding, and caring; model accepting behavior by giving support; help the child continue a normal routine to maintain security and structure, yet help the child deal with change and to work through emotions (Bertoia and Alan 1988).

School counselors might help children and adolescents deal with the concept of death through curriculum-based intervention. An example is Moore's (1989) four-week Teen Living Course for ninth-grade students. The content and activities are organized around eight themes (death as a part of living, media influences on beliefs about death, risk-taking behavior, reactions to loss, community support services, coping and helping others cope with loss, preparing for death, and depression and suicide). Some assumptions of this unit are that children and early adolescents are not immune from death, that protecting a child from death does not shield him or her from the stress involved, and that many do not receive education about death from church or home.

Some counseling strategies to use with children who have lost someone through death are (Thompson and Rudolph 1992):

1. Listen to their thoughts and feelings and respond at their developmental level.
2. Encourage them to talk about their grief and pose questions.
3. Help them understand concepts that are difficult to understand (eternity, heaven) if they are developmentally ready. The family's religious leader could also be contacted to provide assistance.
4. Help the child and the parents decide whether the child should attend a funeral of someone known to them.

Group counseling can be an effective intervention concerning death and loss. Landy (1990) suggested the following objectives: provide facts, explain the life cycle, including death, ask and answer questions, and accept and clarify one's feelings. By age group:

Children ages six to eight:	four to eight children per group; six 30-minute sessions. Topics: I feel...today. When my pet died.... When someone I love died.... When I came close to death, I.... When I see a friend of mine upset, I.... Things that concern me about dying are....
Children ages nine to twelve:	four to eight children per group; seven 45-minute sessions. Topics: Things that scared me about death. When my _____ died, I felt.... I have the most

difficult time expressing.... When I'm upset, the expression of kindness I most like is.... If I would know exactly when I am going to die, I would.... What have I learned about death? Death is....

Morganette (1990) described a remedial group that school counselors can lead on the topic of coping with grief and loss. This group for young adolescents is for students currently dealing with an anticipated or a specific loss. The recommended topics for this eight-session group are: getting started, how death happens and what it is, feelings that accompany loss, significance of the funeral, personal memorials, understanding suicide, and how to heal ourselves.

Morganette (1990) also proposed several group sessions to help adolescents work through a divorce in the family. Topics include: getting started, what to call one's new family, living in a new place, thoughts about divorce, expressing your feelings, everybody has problems, and feeling good about yourself.

At Risk/Maladaptive Behaviors
Depressive Feelings/Depression

Feelings of depression stem from many underlying factors, such as the loss of a parent through death or divorce, and stressful life events, such as abuse and parental alcoholism. Depression can be short-lived or persistent. It can range from feelings of loneliness or sadness to suicidal ideation or suicide (Myrick and Folk 1991). Depressed children do not tend to communicate depressive feelings verbally ("I feel sad"). They are more likely to express these feelings behaviorally, through declining grades, anxiety, boredom, and poor social functioning (Hart 1991). Therefore, counselors need to recognize and assess the severity of depression and provide the proper intervention.

Childhood depression often is difficult to assess because of the developmental issues of behaviors and abilities unique to a given age. Children at the concrete operational stage may be unable to recognize the feeling of depression and may think in more abstract or formal operational ways to find solutions to their problems. Young children respond to a question such as, "Amy, has something happened that is making you feel sad?" more readily than "Amy, are you feeling depressed?" (Hart 1991). Depression in middle childhood often takes the form of sadness associated with feeling frustrated, deprived, or rejected. Depression in later childhood often is linked with low self-esteem.

Adolescent depression more often is associated with suicidal ideation (Hart 1991; Newman and Newman 1991).

Identifying the symptoms of depression and assessing it are crucial to treatment and to many school and classroom interventions (Hart 1991). Knowledge of the *Diagnostic and Statistical Manual of Mental Disorders* (DSM III-R) American Psychiatric Association 1987) can be helpful. Self-report instruments, such as the *Children's Depression Inventory* developed by Kovacs (1985), also can be useful to school counselors in assessing depression in children and adolescents ages eight to seventeen. This twenty-seven-item instrument, based on the *Beck Depression Inventory*, also can be used with younger children if the items are read aloud to them (Ollendick and Greene 1990). Referral to agencies outside the school, such as community mental health centers, may be needed, depending upon the severity.

Hart (1991) provided some practical suggestions for school counselors in working with depressed children:

1. Give praise and encouragement to facilitate school performance and peer relationships. When the child's behavior improves, offer a pleasurable classroom event as positive reinforcement for the child.
2. Anticipate possible depression in children who have gone through critical life events, such as abuse, and provide an opportunity for them to express their feelings orally, in writing, or through art.
3. Take a multifaceted approach to helping the child by working with the parents, teachers, and, if a referral is necessary, serve as a liaison with social service agencies.
4. If the child faces repeated failure in the classroom, reduce the schoolwork to help the child achieve mastery and success.
5. Role-play activities and positive self-talk to help the child correct negative thoughts ("I'm bad").
6. Utilize interventions such as enhancement of coping skills, social skills, or even biofeedback or guided imagery.
7. Introduce cognitive restructuring activities within the classroom to role-play difficult situations related to depression (e.g., peer rejection, failure). By involving the entire classs, the role-plays and discussions can be a preventive measure for the entire group, and the depressed child is not singled out.

Adolescence is a time of emotional ups and downs. Breaking up with a boyfriend or girlfriend may trigger feelings of loss that may seem insurmountable, leading to depression (Myrick and Folk 1991; Newman and Newman 1991). Depression in early adolescence is of particular concern; although it is not always an antecedent to suicide, the variables of suicide, substance abuse, and poor school performance are somewhat associated (Newman and Newman 1991: McWhirter and McWhirter 1989).

Myrick and Folk (1991) suggest *peervention*, a prevention program based on what peers can do to help a depressed classmate. In working with depressed young adolescents:

1. Be nonjudgmental.
2. Do not take the adolescent's problems lightly.
3. Ask the appropriate questions.
4. Be supportive.
5. Provide possible options to decrease depression, such as an invitation to lunch.
6. Be aware of and use appropriate referral sources.

Stress management workshops for young adolescents, addressing the issues of stress, depression, and suicide, often are helpful in prevention programs. Myrick and Folk (1991) developed activities, such as "The Stress Box" and the "Gloomy, Doomy Mural," to help adolescents deal with stress (pp. 135–136).

Early and Unprotected Sexual Activity/Teen Pregnancy

Social and peer pressure to engage in sexual activity presents a dilemma for adolescents. The risks of early sexual activity, however, may be considerable: an unplanned pregnancy, sexually transmitted diseases, and AIDS. Discussions on preventing adolescent pregnancy should be based on the adolescent's behavior and sexual experience (Thompson and Sherwood 1989). For example, adolescents who are not sexually involved may be encouraged to continue abstinence until they are mature enough to be responsible for their own sexual behavior.

Abstinence approaches vary from talking with adolescents about the health risks of adolescent sexuality to supporting comprehensive sexuality education programs. Peterson (1990) has offered six topics that school counselors can use in discussing abstinence:

1. *Health concerns*—presenting the dangers of contracting AIDS and other sexually transmittable diseases, future infertility problems, and possible lifelong economic and emotional consequences of adolescent sexual activity.

2. *Values education*—supporting respect for self and others, honesty in relationships, helping adolescents feel good about their independence and decisions about what is right or wrong for their own value system.
3. *Decision-making*—promoting open discussion on the pros and cons of early sexual activity and implications for the adolescent's future family, career, and life plans.
4. *Refusal skills*—presenting activities that help adolescents resist pressure to engage in sexual activity.
5. *Helping parents*—involving parents in seminars and parent-child sexuality classes, which provides an opportunity for parents to share their values with their child.
6. *Comprehensive sexuality education*—Involving coordination of the community, school, home, and church to help young people make good decisions about their life and provide sexuality education programs before they are sexually active.

Howard (1988) developed a peer influence model, Postponing Sexual Involvement Educational Program, in which older adolescents (eleventh- and twelfth-grade students) talk to younger adolescents (under age sixteen) about postponing sexual activity. The older adolescents help the younger ones identify and deal with issues such as social and peer pressures to become sexually active and ways to act responsibly. These educational programs are led jointly by a male and a female adolescent leader. Within the school setting, this program calls for five classroom sessions. The older teens, usually recommended by the school counselor, a teacher, or the principal, undergo a twenty-hour training program.

Another peer influence program enlists, as "peer counselors," adolescents of the same approximate age as those at risk (Howard 1988). These students are trained to assist in providing accurate information, as well as to help with problem-solving when difficult issues arise.

If the adolescent is currently sexually active, he or she can be given counseling and contraceptive information. How these issues are dealt with, however, depends on local community values and school board policy. Therefore, school counselors must be knowledgeable of the community values and school policies and handle adolescent concerns accordingly. In addition, adolescents who are pregnant need a comprehensive intervention to deal with the multiple problems involved in teen pregnancy, such as medical care, financial concerns, and child care (Newman and Newman 1991; Thompson and Sherwood 1989).

Keat (1990) suggested multimodal therapy as a comprehensive approach that can be used with children, adolescents, or adults facing multiple problems. The multimodal approach (Corey 1991; Lazarus 1984) is eclectic in that the assessment considers seven modalities related to individual functioning. The BASIC ID incorporates *behavior* (habits and behaviors that can be observed), *affect* (emotions and moods), *sensation* (the five basic senses, such as touch, hearing), *imagery* (memories and how we see ourselves), *cognition* (attitudes, rational and irrational thoughts, beliefs), *interpersonal relationships* (getting along with others), and *drugs/biology* (physiological functioning, health concerns, nutrition). The pregnant adolescent typically has deficits in several of these areas, and the multimodal approach provides the framework for utilizing multiple intervention techniques applicable to multiple problems (Keat 1990; Newman and Newman 1991; Thompson and Sherwood 1989).

Cindy, a fifteen-year-old girl, came into the school counselor's office pregnant, anxious, and scared. She was functioning poorly in all areas of her life—academically, interpersonally, and emotionally. She seemed unable to cope with the many concerns of becoming an adolescent unwed mother.

Cindy was anxious (*affect*) about telling her parents of the pregnancy and talking to her teachers about her decline in academic performance (*behavior*). The counseling sessions included rehearsing how to communicate with her parents and her teachers about the situation and helping Cindy with her anxiety by using imagery and deep breathing exercises and accepting her nonjudgmentally as a person. The area of *sensation* involved attending to her physical concerns about her health and the health of the baby. She also became involved in childbirth/parenting classes. In the *imagery* intervention, positive imagery helped Cindy visualize herself as capable and as possessing a good self-image. *Cognitive* interventions provided information about nutritional needs through bibliotherapy, educational and career counseling, and information about programs and funding available for pregnant adolescent health care. To help Cindy with her academic problems, study skills were highlighted. Interventions in *interpersonal relationships* included helping her rehearse and role-play communicating with her parents and her boyfriend, gaining conflict resolution skills, improving social skills with peers, and assertiveness training. In the *drug/biology* modality, Cindy received information about dietary needs for herself and the unborn baby. (Adapted from Thompson and Sherwood 1989)

Group counseling is another effective option in the area of adolescent pregnancy. Thompson and Sherwood (1989) suggested that the multimodal approach to group counseling can be aimed at helping pregnant adolescents deal with excesses and deficits in each of the seven modalities. They proposed developing "modality profiles" for each of the group members to assess individual problems and generate possible interventions. One important goal of group counseling is to help members identify coping skills to use in handling specific problems, such as improving interpersonal relationships or completing school. Thompson and Sherwood also advocated teen parent support groups for pregnant adolescents. These support groups are designed to help adolescent parents develop the skills to become self-sufficient.

Additional considerations that school counselors should keep in mind in helping adolescents deal with sexuality and pregnancy are to (Lamb and Elster 1985, Newman and Newman 1991):

1. Further their own knowledge about sexuality, prevention programs, and teen pregnancy programs.
2. Involve the family, schools, and community agencies in adolescent pregnancy issues such as prevention and parenting (Newman and Newman 1991).
3. Help adolescents improve their self-esteem, interpersonal relationships, and problem-solving skills.
4. Include adolescent fathers in adolescent pregnancy programs and counseling to help them deal with their feelings about the pregnancy and the child (Lamb and Elster 1985; Newman and Newman 1991).
5. Introduce school-based intervention programs that incorporate the issue of sexuality as part of life-skills development (Dryfoos 1990).
6. Address the need for family planning, parent education, and educational/employment counseling for adolescent mothers and fathers (Newman and Newman 1991).

Suicidal Ideation/Suicide Attempts and Completions

Some of the interventions school counselors may use to prevent youth suicide are (Thompson and Rudolph 1992):

1. Encourage parents to consult a doctor or psychiatrist if you think the child is having serious suicidal ideations.
2. Work with parents so they are aware of the child's thoughts and feelings, know how to listen and converse with the child, and have a plan to recognize and handle potential future crises.
3. Consult with or refer children who are suicidal to specialists in suicide prevention (e.g., a suicide center).
4. Apply strategies to raise the self-concept of children with suicidal ideations.
5. Use behavior modification techniques with children who have tendencies toward self-destruction or self-mutilation.
6. Follow up on cues or threats (e.g., "you'll miss me") right away with active listening to determine what triggered the self-destructive thoughts and feelings.
7. Talk to a child if you sense that he or she has suicidal ideations, as this may create the opportunity to talk, which the child needs.
8. Give suicidal children your name (or other's), phone number, and encouragement to call in times of stress or crisis.
9. Talk with and listen to children who have suicidal ideations about what recently happened in their lives (situations involving loss, shame, trauma) and let them express themselves without being judged or denied the right to their feelings.
10. If a child has suicidal ideations, ask about his or her plan (one danger signal is a well-developed plan).
11. Ask children about their fantasies and dreams or to draw or write about their feelings and thoughts.
12. Watch for a "sudden recovery" after a severe depression; it could be a warning sign that the child has decided to end his or her life.
13. Give depressed or disturbed children special attention for months after a suicide attempt.

Jason, a thirteen-year-old middle school student, was the second suicide in the county within a short time. The counselor met with the school faculty to attain consistency in working with the 150 students who had been in contact with Jason daily. Class-sized groups helped students say good-bye (let go) and explored coping methods. An empty seat (Jason's) was placed in each of the classes. Based on their comfort level, students were invited to speak to the empty seat, say good-bye or imagine saying good-bye, or telling him what they would have wanted him to know.

Several students took the opportunity for further individual, dyadic (pairs), or small-group counseling. One group (an initial group) met for one session, in which the students were asked to think about Jason and his death, to express their feelings on paper with colors, and then to process the experience. A subsequent group (long-term) then met weekly for three months. This group was composed of six girls (three from the initial group). These intense sessions resulted in four members sharing that they had attempted suicide and two members indicating that they had considered it (Alexander and Harman 1988).

School counselors also can use puppets or stories to intervene with depressed and suicidal children. Mutual storytelling is one intervention that can be used with children as young as five years old and preferably with children ages nine to fourteen (Stiles and Kottman 1990). This intervention has two parts: First the child tells a "made up" story about anything, and the counselor listens, noting the child's metaphors and possible psychological meanings. Second, the counselor tells a story using the same characters to solve the issues and conflicts more effectively.

School counselors should become skilled in evaluating suicidal potential. Davis and Sandoval (1991) have offered several models for school-based intervention and prevention, including a no-suicide contract. Developmentally, young children do not know that death is not reversible. Adolescents should be helped to develop a short-term commitment that is both realistic and clear (Bradley and Rotheram-Borus 1989).

Finally, Siehl (1990) has presented a convincing case for suicide postvention in the schools. The school counselor can initiate a suicide disaster plan, with ten considerations:

1. Identify and train a team to address the emotional crisis.
2. Develop and hold inservice workshops for staff and for students on causes, signs and symptoms, and referral sources.
3. Develop a strategy to inform and debrief faculty.
4. Establish temporary, accessible, private crisis centers in the schools.
5. Help teachers by making a checklist of activities.
6. Develop a plan to monitor signs and symptoms in other students after a student suicide.

7. Make home visits.
8. Hold an event (e.g., a memorial service for students to deal with the loss and recognize more positive solutions.
9. Identify one school official to deal with media coverage.
10. Carefully monitor high-risk students for at least two months and on a more informal basis for up to two years.

SUMMARY

Children and adolescents today are facing many societal changes that can cause them to become more vulnerable to stress and, therefore, at risk. Associated with the term "at risk" are factors such as behavior problems, poor academic grades, and low socioeconomic status. To understand at-risk youths, counselors must have knowledge of at least three developmental stages (elementary school age, middle school age, adolescence) and the tasks appropriate to each of these stages, as well as knowledge of the signs and symptoms of each at-risk category.

A model of underlying at-risk factors and critical events (abuse, child of alcoholic parent(s), child in stepfamily, loss), at-risk behaviors (depressive feelings, early and unprotected sexual experiences, and suicidal ideation) and maladaptive behaviors (depression, teen pregnancy, suicide attempts or completion) is a helpful conceptualization for school counselors to understand at-risk children and early adolescents. Selected developmentally based intervention strategies can be applied to these underlying factors/critical events and the at-risk and maladaptive behaviors.

REFERENCES

Ackerman, R. J. 1983. *A guidebook for educators, therapists and parents.* Indiana, PA: Learning Publications.

Alexander, J. C., and R. L. Harman. 1988. One counselor's intervention in the aftermath of a middle school student's suicide: A case study. *Journal of Counseling & Development* 66(6): 283–285.

Alford, P., D. Martin, and M. Martin. 1985. A profile of the physical abusers of children. *School Counselor* 33: 143–150.

Alvy, K. T. 1991. Parent training as a prevention strategy. In *Parent training is prevention: Preventing alcohol and other drug problems among youth in the family* (DHHS Publication No. ADM 91-1715, pp. 11–26). Washington, DC: U.S. Government Printing Office.

American Psychiatric Association. 1987. *Diagnostic and statistical manual of mental disorders.* 3d ed., rev. Washington, DC; APA.

American School Counselor Association. 1988. The school counselor and child abuse/neglect prevention. *Elementary School Guidance and Counseling* 22(4): 261–263.

Berlin, R., and R. B. Davis. 1989. Children from alcoholic families: Vulnerability and resilience. In T. J. Dugan and R. Coles, eds., *The child in our times: Studies in the development of resiliency* (pp. 71–82). New York: Brunner/ Mazel.

Bertoia, J., and J. Allan. 1988. School management of a bereaved child. *Elementary School Guidance and Counseling* 23(1): 30–38.

Bradley, J., and Rotheram-Borus, M. 1989. *Evaluating suicial youth in community settings: A training manual.* Tulsa: University of Oklahoma Press.

Brenner, A. 1984. *Helping children cope with stress.* Lexington, MA: Lexington Books.

Buwick, A., D. Martin, and M. Martin. 1988. Helping children deal with alcoholism in their families. *Elementary School Guidance and Counseling* 23(2): 112–117.

Capuzzi, D., and L. Golden. 1988. Adolescent suicide: An introduction to issues and interventions. In D. Capuzzi and L. Golden, eds., *Preventing adolescent suicide.* Muncie, IN: Accelerated Development.

Capuzzi, D., and D. R. Gross. 1989. I don't want to live: Suicidal behavior. In *Youth at risk: A resource for counselors, teachers and parents* (pp. 271–304). Alexandria, VA: American Counseling Association.

Carter, B ., and M. McGoldrick. 1988. Overview: The changing family life cycle: A framework for family therapy. In B. Carter and M. McGoldrick, eds., *The changing family life cycle: A framework for family therapy.* 2d ed. Needham Heights, MA: Allyn and Bacon.

Corey, G. 1991. *Theory and practice of counseling and psychotherapy.* 4th ed. Pacific Grove, CA: Brooks/Cole.

Crabbs, S. K., and M. Crabbs, eds. 1988 Special issue: Child abuse issues and interventions. *Elementary School Guidance and Counseling* 22(4): 259–352.

Davis, J. M., and J. Sandoval. 1991. *Suicidal youth. School-based intervention and prevention.* San Francisco: Jossey-Bass.

Downing, J. 1988. Counseling interventions with depressed children. *Elementary School Guidance and Counseling* 22(3): 231–240.

Dryfoos, J. G. 1990. *Adolescents at risk: Prevalence and prevention.* New York: Oxford University Press.

Eddowes, E., and J. Hranitz. 1989. Educating children of the homeless. *Childhood Education* 65: 197–200.

Elkind, D. 1981. *The hurried child: Growing up too fast too soon.* Reading, MA: Addison-Wesley.

Elkind, D. 1987a. Do we push our kids too hard? *Good Housekeeping,* September, pp. 117–119.

Elkind, D. 1987b. Super kids and super problems. *Psychology Today,* May, pp. 60–61.

England, L. W., and C. L. Thompson. 1988. Counseling child sexual abuse victims: Myths and realities. *Journal of Counseling and Development* 66: 370–373.

Finkelhor, D. 1984. *Child sexual abuse.* New York: Free Press.

Frears, L. H., and J. M. Schneider. 1981. Exploring loss and grief within a holistic framework. *Personnel and Guidance Journal* 22: 341–345.

Gladding S. T., and C. Gladding. 1991. The ABC's of bibliotherapy for school counselors. *School Counselor* 39(1): 7–13.

Goldenberg H., and I. Goldenberg. 1990. *Counseling today's families.* Pacific Grove, CA: Brooks/Cole.

Goldenberg, I., and H. Goldenberg. 1991. *Family therapy: An overview.* 3d ed. Pacific Grove, CA: Brooks/Cole.

Goldstein, A. P., H. Keller, and D. Erne. 1985. *Changing the abusive parent.* Champaign, IL: Research Press.

Gross, D. R., and D. Capuzzi. 1989. Defining youth at risk. In D. Capuzzi and D. R. Gross, eds., *Youth at risk: A resource for counselors, teachers and parents* (pp. 3–18). Alexandria, VA: American Counseling Association.

Hart, S. L. 1991. Childhood depression: Implications and options for school counselors. *Elementary School Guidance and Counseling* 25(4): 277–289.

Hathaway, W., C. Sheldon, and P. McNamara. 1989. The solution lies in programs that work. In D. Capuzzi and D. R. Gross, eds., *Youth at risk: A resource for counselors, teachers and parents* (pp. 367–394). Alexandria, VA: American Counseling Association.

Hazouri, S. P., and M. F. Smith. 1991. *Peer listening in the middle schools: Training activities for students.* Minneapolis: Educational Media Corp.

Herring, R. 1990. Suicide in the middle school: Who said kids will not? *Elementary School Guidance and Counseling* 25(2): 129–137.

Howard, M. 1988. *How to help your teenager postpone sexual involvement.* New York: Continuum.

Huey, W. C. 1991. Crisis intervention procedures and student privacy. *NASSP Bulletin* 75(534): 36–41.

Jagucki, J. E. 1989. Children of alcoholic parents. In J. C. Bleuer and P. A. Schreiber, eds., *Counseling young students at risk* (pp. 69–84) Ann Arbor, MI: ERIC Counseling and Personnel Services Clearinghouse.

Janus, M. D., A. McCormack, A. W. Burgess, and C. Hartman. 1987. *Adolescent runaways: Causes and consequences.* Lexington, MA: Lexington Books.

Keat, D. 1990. Change in child multimodal counseling. *Elementary School Guidance and Counseling* 24(4): 248–262.

Kovacs, M. 1985. Children's depression inventory (CDI). *Psychopharmacology Bulletin* 21: 995–998.

Krickeberg, S. K. 1991. Away from Walton Mountain: Bibliographies for today's troubled youth. *School Counselor* 39(1): 52–56.

Kumpfer, K. L. 1991. How to get hard-to-reach parents involved in parenting programs. In *Parent training is prevention: Preventing alcohol and other drug problems among youth in the family.* (DHHP Publication No. ADM 91-1715, pp. 87–95). Washington, DC: U.S. Government Printing Office.

Lamb, M. E., and A. B. Elster. 1985. Adolescent mother-infant-father relationships. *Developmental Psychology* 21, 768–773.

Landy, L. 1990. *Child support: Through small group counseling.* Mount Dora, FL: Kidsrights.

Lasko, C. A. 1986. Childhood depression; Questions and answers. *Elementary School Guidance and Counseling* 20: 283–289.

Lazarus, A. A. 1984. Multimodal therapy. In R. J. Corsini, ed., *Current psychotherapies* (pp. 491–530). Itasca, IL: Peacock.

Magid, K., and C. A. McKelvey. 1987. *High risk: Children without a conscience.* New York: Bantam Books.

Main, M., and R. Goldwyn. 1984. Predicting rejection of her infant from mother's representation of her own experiences: Implications for the abused-abusing intergenerational cycle. *Child Abuse and Neglect* 8: 203–217.

Manning, D., and M. Wooten. 1987. What stepparents perceive schools should know about blended families. *The Clearing House*, 606: 230–235.

McEvoy, A. W., and E. L. Erickson. 1990. *Youth and exploitation.* Holmes Beach, FL: Learning Publications.

McWhirter, J. J., and T. J. Kigin. 1988. Depression. In D. Capuzzi and L. Golden, eds., *Preventing adolescent suicide* (pp 149–186). Muncie, IN: Accelerated Development.

McWhirter, J. J., and B. T. McWhirter. 1989. When life seems darkest: Adolescent depression. In D. Capuzzi and D. R. Gross, eds., *Youth at risk: A resource for counselors, teachers and parents* (pp. 121–139). Alexandria, VA: American Counseling Association.

Merchant, D. A. 1990. *Treating abused adolescents.* Holmes Beach, FL: Learning Publications.

Morganette, R. S. 1990. *Skills for living: Group counseling activities for young adolescents.* Champaign, IL: Research Press.

Moore, C. M. 1989. Teaching about loss and death to junior high school students. *Family Relations* 38(1): 3–7.

Morehouse, E. R., and C. M. Scola. 1986. *Children of alcoholics: Meeting the needs of the young COA in the school setting.* South Laguna, CA: National Association for Children of Alcoholics.

Myrick, R. D., and B. E. Folk. 1991. *Peervention: Training peer facilitators for prevention education.* Minneapolis: Educational Media Corporation.

National Council on Alcoholism. 1982. *Facts on teenage drinking.* New York: NCA.

Nelson, R. E. 1988. Overview of prevention. In D. Capuzzi and L. Golden, eds., *Preventing adolescent suicide* (pp. 249–268). Muncie, IN: Accelerated Development.

Newman, B. M, and P. R. Newman. 1991. *Development through life: A psychosocial approach.* 5th ed. Pacific Grove, CA: Brooks/Cole.

Ollendick, T. H., and R. Greene. 1990. Behavioral assessment of children. In G. Goldstein and M. Herson, eds., *Handbook of psychological assessment.* 2d ed. (pp. 403–422). New York: Pergamon Press.

O'Rourke, K. 1990. Recapturing hope: Elementary school support groups for children of alcoholics. *Elementary School Guidance and Counseling* 25(2): 107–115.

O'Sullivan, C . M. 1992. Adolescents in alcoholic families. In G. W. Lawson and A. W. Lawson, eds., *Adolescent substance abuse: Etiology, treatment and prevention* (pp. 419–427), Gaithersburg, MD: Aspen.

Palmer, J. H., and P. O. Paisley. 1991. Student assistance programs: A response to substance abuse. *School Counselor* 38(4): 287–293.

Palmo, A. J., and L. A. Palmo. 1989. The harmful effects of dysfunctional family dynamics. In D. Capuzzi and D. R. Gross, eds., *Youth at risk: Resource for counselors, teachers and parents* (pp. 43–69). Alexandria, VA: American Counseling Association.

Peck, M. 1984. Youth suicide. In H. Wass and C. A. Corr, eds., *Childhood and death*. Washington, DC: Hemisphere.

Petersen, S., and R. L. Straub. 1992. *School crisis survival guide.* West Nyack, NY: Center for Applied Research in Education.

Peterson, L. 1990. *Adolescent abstinence: A guide for family planning professionals.* Washington, DC: U.S. Government Printing Office.

Rencken, R. H. 1989. Bodily assault: Physical and sexual abuse. In D. Capuzzi and D. R. Gross, eds., *Youth at risk: A resource for counselors, teachers and parents* (pp. 71–95). Alexandria VA: American Counseling Association.

Russell, C. 1989. Children of divorce. In J. C. Bleuer and P. A. Schreiber, eds., *Counseling young students at risk* (pp. 49–68). (Report No. ISBN 1-56109-009-3). Ann Arbor, MI: ERIC Counseling and Personnel Services Clearinghouse.

Sapp, M. 1990. Psychoeducational correlates of junior high at-risk students. *High School Journal* 73(4): 232–234.

Siehl, P. M. 1990. Suicide postvention; A new disaster plan: What a school should do when faced with a suicide. *School Counselor* 38(1): 52–57.

Spiegel, L. 1988. Child abuse hysteria and the elementary school counselor. *Elementary School Guidance and Counseling* 22(4): 275–283.

Stiles, K., and T. Kottrnan. 1990. Mutual storytelling: An intervention for depressed and suicidal children. *School Counselor* 37(5): 337–342.

Steele, W. 1992. *Preventing self destruction: A manual for school crisis response teams.* Holmes Beach, FL: Learning Publications.

Swanson, M. S. 1991. *At risk students in elementary education: Effective schools for disadvantaged learners.* Springfield, IL: Charles C. Thomas.

Tennant, C. 1988. Preventive sexual abuse programs: Problems and possibilities. *Elementary School Guidance and Counseling* 23(1): 48–53.

Thompson, C. L., and L. B. Rudolph. 1992. *Counseling children.* 3d ed. Pacific Grove, CA: Brooks/Cole.

Thompson, R., and A. Sherwood. 1989. Female, single, and pregnant adolescent unwed mothers. In D. Capuzzi and D. R. Gross, eds., *Youth at risk: A resource for counselors, teachers and parents* (pp. 195–230). Alexandria, VA: American Counseling Association.

U.S. Office for Substance Abuse Prevention. 1991. *Parent training is prevention: Preventing alcohol and other drug problems among youth in the family* (DHHS Publication NO. ADM 91-1715). Washington, DC: U.S. Government Printing Office.

Vernon, A., and J. Hay. 1988. A preventative approach to child sexual abuse. *Elementary School Guidance and Counseling* 22(4): 306–312.

Visher, E. B., and J. S. Visher. 1988. *Old loyalties, new ties: Therapeutic strategies with stepfamilies.* New York: Brunner/Mazel.

Wegscheider, S. 1981. *Another chance: Hope and health for the alcoholic family.* Palo Alto, CA: Science and Behavior Books.

Whiteman, T. 1991. *Innocent victims: Helping children through the trauma of divorce.* Wayne, PA: Fresh Start.

Wilder, P. 1991. A counselor's contribution to the child abuse referral network. *School Counselor* 38(3): 203–214.

Wilson, J., and L. Blocher. 1990 The counselor's role in assisting children of alcoholics. *Elementary School Guidance and Counseling* 25(2): 98–106.

Winn, M. 1983. *Children without childhood.* New York: Penguin Books.

Worchel, F., B. Nolan, and V. Willson. 1987. New perspectives on child and adolescent depression. *Journal of School Psychology* 25: 411–414.

Applications to Groups, Classrooms, Families, and School Personnel

Part *II*

8 Small-Group Counseling

James J. Bergin

Department of Student Development Programs
Georgia Southern University, Statesboro

S mall-group counseling with children and adolescents is becoming more popular in the school setting. Group and individual counseling both provide a facilitative environment characterized by trust, caring, acceptance, understanding, and support. Group counseling, however, uniquely allows children and adolescents to be understood and supported by peers as well as the counselor. This is especially valuable to students whose primary concerns are in the areas of social interaction and self-expression. Moreover, the group provides an excellent opportunity for them to observe and learn from each other. Behavior modeling not only teaches new behaviors, but it also can be a powerful force in motivating group members to try out alternative behaviors and practice specific skills such as stress reduction, study skills, and social skills (Ehly and Dustin 1989).

The group itself can become a primary source of support for the individual because it creates an atmosphere in which potentials and skills can be discovered, explored, developed and tested. Through group participation, members maximize the opportunity to help themselves and others (Grayson 1989). As Gladding (1991) pointed out, "It is often through helping others that an individual's own self-esteem and self-confidence are increased" (p. 286).

This chapter covers the definition of group counseling, goals of group counseling with children and adolescents, stages of the group process, counselor role, and ethical considerations in group work with minors. Practical procedures such as selecting participants, determining the size of the group, planning the number of sessions, establishing group rules, and planning for evaluation are discussed. Three types of counseling groups are described, with outlines of procedures for each, and suggested resources for designing group activities.

DEFINITION OF GROUP COUNSELING

One of the most useful definitions of group counseling is that offered by Gazda, Duncan, and Meadows (1967).

> Group counseling is a dynamic, interpersonal process focusing on conscious thought and behavior involving the therapy functions of permissiveness, orientation to reality, catharsis, and mutual trust, caring, understanding, acceptance, and support. The therapy functions are created and nurtured in a small group through the sharing of personal concerns with one's peers and the counselor. The group counselees are basically normal individuals with various concerns which are not debilitating to the extent of requiring extensive personality change. The group counselees may utilize the group interaction to increase understanding and acceptance of values and goals and to learn or unlearn certain attitudes and behaviors. (p. 306)

This definition underscores the concept that involvement in counseling creates a dynamic interactive process among peers and, as such, it can exert strong influences on the individual members in a number of ways.

1. The group's offer of caring, acceptance, and support for each member encourages mutual trust and sharing of individual concerns.
2. The group's orientation to reality and emphasis on conscious thought leads individuals to examine their current thoughts, feelings, and actions and to express them in a genuine manner.
3. The group's overt attempt to convey understanding to each member encourages tolerance and an accepting attitude toward individual differences in personal values and goals.
4. The group's focus on personal concerns and behavior encourages the individual to consider alternative ways of behaving and to practice them within the context of a supportive environment.

This definition also points out that members of counseling groups are normal individuals who have the ability to deal with their own concerns and do not have extensive personality problems. Instead, individuals make educated choices about their personal behaviors. They can help not only themselves but also, with the counselor, participate in the development of all group members.

GOALS OF GROUP COUNSELING WITH CHILDREN AND ADOLESCENTS

The major goal of group counseling is to create the opportunity for individuals to gain knowledge and skill that will assist them in making and carrying out their own choices. The intent is to promote personal growth and resolve problems or conflicts. To this end, the group process engages individuals in activities that explore personal thoughts, feelings, attitudes, values, and interests, and the way these factors influence personal choices. It also examines the individual's skills in communication, cooperation, and decision-making, particularly as they pertain to interpersonal interaction and problem-solving.

Group counseling seems ideally suited to the needs of elementary, middle, and secondary school students. Developmentally, children and adolescents alike lack knowledge and skill to deal with the challenges of growing up. Much of the curriculum that covers these areas of knowledge and skill is addressed appropriately through large-group guidance activities. For students who require additional assistance, more personalized information, or emotional support, however, group counseling provides an atmosphere that is highly conducive to remedial training, self-exploration, and peer support.

Group counseling is also a valuable supplement to individual counseling. Students who are being counseled individually may present problems and concerns that can be addressed best in a group context. For example, a student who has difficulty making decisions and committing to a course of action may benefit a great deal from a group experience focused on the tasks of communication and cooperative decision-making. Similarly, a young child who has difficulty articulating thoughts and feelings, perhaps because of delayed language development, can enhance vocabulary and expressive skills by participating in a "feelings" group. In addition, group counseling can be an effective supplement to individual counseling for students with behavior problems at home and at school (Vander Kolk 1985).

Group counseling with children differs from group work with older students in some respects. Although the basic principles of group counseling apply to all ages, the group must be adapted to the social, emotional, and intellectual development of young children, as well as their verbal communication skills (George and Dustin 1988). Young children tend to feel most natural in play and activity groups, as they are accustomed to acting out their needs as a way of expressing themselves (Lifton 1972). Play media with small groups (two to four members) often are recommended for preschoolers and primary grade level youngsters. In his book *Group Counseling: A Developmental Approach*, Gazda (1989) set out a thorough description of these kinds of groups and the application of play therapy techniques in a school setting.

During the elementary and middle school years children rapidly gain verbal ability, which enables them to participate readily in the verbal exchange that typifies most counseling groups. Hence, most groups in this age range focus on activities similar to those for adolescents. Even though these students may be quite articulate and expressive, many require some training in social interaction, especially in functioning as a member of a group. Therefore, counselors in elementary and middle schools incorporate into group procedures the opportunity for participants to learn group roles and practice active listening skills that will facilitate the group process. Some practitioners have developed specialized group activities targeting the acquisition of these skills for group participants (Bergin 1991; Myrick 1987).

Group counseling may be the preferred intervention for adolescents (Corey 1990). They strongly desire peer acceptance and affiliation, and the group context affords them easy access to peer feedback and support. Moreover, the struggle for independence from authority and the preoccupation with self that characterizes this developmental stage can make adolescents reluctant to seek individual counseling with an adult. Unlike younger children, who more readily trust counselors, adolescents tend to feel threatened by any suggestion that they seek counseling. The invitation to join a group and to work with peers is more appealing, as it reduces the chances of being put on the "hot seat"; at the same time, it increases the opportunity to relate with peers and gain their approval. Other than the additional emphasis on trust and peer acceptance, group counseling procedures with adolescents are generally the same as with adult groups.

STAGES IN THE GROUP PROCESS

Groups typically proceed through four stages: initial, transition, working, and termination. In the *initial stage*, activities are geared to bring about cohesion among group members. Icebreaker activities frequently are employed to introduce members to each other and help them feel comfortable interacting with other participants. This stage also provides for discussion of the group's purpose and objectives, as well as members' commitment to work with and help each other. The group agrees upon and establishes the rules. Each rule is clarified for the group to ensure understanding, especially concerning confidentiality. Once these issues have been clarified, the group sets about building rapport with each other by demonstrating caring, attention, and a desire to know and understand each other. The trust that develops in the group allows group members to self-disclose and address their personal concerns through problem-solving techniques (the focus of the working stage).

The group's movement to the working stage is seldom smooth and uniform. Some individuals are ready to self-disclose before others, and many are reluctant to give up the warm feelings experienced in the trusting atmosphere of the group. Hence, most groups go through a *transition stage*, during which members confront reluctance to proceed, reiterate the group's purposes, and recommit themselves to supporting each other to accomplish the group's objectives. The behavior most commonly associated with this stage is resistance. Resistance may be in the form of avoidance behaviors such as coming late to sessions, failing to listen attentively to each other, engaging in chitchat, or withholding ideas and opinions from the group. It also may take the form of challenges to the counselor. Participants may question the "real" purposes of the group, why the members were chosen for the group, and how confidentiality can be guaranteed. The key ingredient in group success is trust. As individual members confront their concerns in a caring and accepting manner, they reinforce other members' trust and commitment to the group's progress.

The *working stage* is reached when the group addresses its primary purpose of helping individual members deal with their present concerns. These concerns may revolve around a developmental need, situation, or experience common to many or all group members, or it may be an issue of immediate concern to an individual. In any case, the manner in which the issue or concern manifests itself in the life of the individual is unique. The group process assists individual members in clarifying their concerns and exploring alternative ways of achieving their personal goals. Activities such as role-playing and modeling afford members the opportunity to express themselves, receive feedback from others, and observe, practice, and learn new ways of behaving, which they can choose to transfer to their environments outside the counseling group.

The major function of the final stage, *termination*, is to help members evaluate their progress toward personal goals during involvement in the group process. Members engage in self-evaluation, provide feedback to each other, and are reinforced for their participation in the group process. They formulate and discuss plans for implementing what each member has learned. Follow-up and evaluation arrangements also are made at this time.

THE COUNSELOR'S ROLE

The counselor is the primary facilitator of the group process. Initially he or she assesses student needs, defines the group purposes and objectives, identifies and selects prospective group members, arranges permission for members to join, organizes the schedule of sessions, plans the group activities, and arranges space for the group to meet. While carrying out these responsibilities, the counselor enlists the support of parents, school administrators, teachers, and other faculty members.

During the group process, the counselor concentrates on promoting the development of group interaction, establishing rapport among group members, leading the group progressively through all four stages, and encouraging individual members' self-exploration and personal decision-making. The counselor guides the group as it discusses individual and joint concerns, models appropriate attending and responding behaviors, and reinforces members for supporting each other during their individual self-exploration. In addition, the counselor confronts resistance sensitively, redirects negative behavior, and encourages the group's efforts to become self-regulatory. The counselor safeguards the group's integrity by enforcing the rules the group establishes for itself.

After completion of the group process, the counselor evaluates the group as a whole and helps the group conduct an evaluation of the group process. After the final session, in which members assess their personal progress and contributions to the group, the counselor conducts a follow-up evaluation with the members to gain their opinions of the group's effectiveness. The counselor also contacts the teachers and parents of the members to get their impressions of the group's impact regarding members' functioning in settings outside of the group. *Group Counseling Techniques* (Corey, Corey, Callanan, and Russell 1988) and *Group Counseling: Strategies and Skills* (Jacobs, Harvill, and Masson 1988) give comprehensive explanations of the stages and group leadership techniques.

ETHICAL CONSIDERATIONS IN GROUP WORK WITH MINORS

When engaging children and adolescents in the group counseling process, one of the most important issues a counselor must consider is each client's welfare. Adult clients presumably have the ability to care for themselves and make wise choices regarding their present and future behavior. Minors, however, are dependent upon their parents or guardians to assist them in these matters. Therefore, the counselor has to accept ethical responsibility for advising children and adolescents of their rights to choose how they participate in the group process and deal with their personal feelings, beliefs, values, and behaviors. Likewise, because parents and guardians normally have a deep interest in the welfare of their children, as well as being legally responsible for them, the counselor should collaborate with parents and keep them apprised of their children's progress and needs as revealed through the counseling group process. Other adults, such as teachers and school administrators, who actively participate in the child's growth and development also have ethical and legal rights to be informed of the counselor's work with group members, especially if the parents grant these other adults these privileges.

The counselor should prepare an information sheet describing the group process, purpose, activities, rules, and number of sessions to present to parents along with a request for their written consent allowing the child to participate in the counseling group. The counselor must clarify and emphasize the group rule regarding confidentiality. The group counseling context offers less assurance of maintaining confidentiality than does individual counseling, so the counselor cannot guarantee to the group anyone's confidentiality other than the counselor's. Even if the counselor adheres to the rule of confidentiality, some group members may question it when the counselor is known to be consulting with the member's parents, teachers, and other adults. Therefore, during pregroup interviews and again in the first session, the counselor must explain the importance of maintaining confidentiality, inform members of the potential consequences of intentionally breaching it, and clarify the specific conditions under which the counselor will reveal information about a member to parents, guardians, teachers, or others.

Corey and Corey (1992) have presented a number of guidelines concerning the issue of confidentiality when working with minors. They recommend that the counselor ask participants to sign a contract agreeing not to discuss what happens in the group, to obtain written parental consent even when not required by state law, and to scrupulously abide by school policies regarding confidentiality. Counselors must practice within the boundaries of local and state laws, especially laws regarding child neglect and abuse, molestation, and incest (pp. 58–61). Group leaders who videotape or audio-record sessions should inform members of the ways the recordings will be used and the manner in which their security will be maintained. Whether they are being used for supervision of counseling interns or as a part of a research project, the counselor should obtain written release of information signed by the parents (Vander Kolk 1985). Huey and Remley (1988) discuss these issues, as they pertain to counseling with groups of public school students in their book *Ethical and Legal Issues in School Counseling*.

LOGISTICS OF GROUP FORMATION

Selecting Participants for the Group

Perhaps the most significant factor in the ultimate success of the group is the membership of the group itself. Group cohesion and productivity are most likely when members share a common goal and have the desire and ability to work cooperatively with each other. The counselor has to identify the common needs of prospective members and conduct interviews with potential group members to determine their interest in and suitability for group membership.

Assessment of student needs forms the basis for establishment of goals for the group and for those of its individual members (Vander Kolk 1985). The counselor observes students directly, interprets data from educational achievement tests and career development inventories, analyzes students' self-reports, and accepts referrals from parents, teachers, and other professionals. Some authorities recommend conducting a systematic needs assessment of the entire school to identify the needs of a broad spectrum of students (Ohlsen, Horne, and Lawe 1988; Worzbyt and O'Rourke 1989). The results can be used to target the needs of prospective members for group counseling as well as to highlight the prevalence of issues and problems impacting specific groups within the student population. In addition, the counselor might give students self-referral forms to describe their interests in joining a group and the topics they would like to discuss. The counselor can use the self-referral information to construct special groups addressing the current concerns of these students while they are highly motivated toward self-improvement.

In determining students' needs, the counselor is advised to consult with parents and teachers and seek their collaboration throughout the group's existence. Observations of teachers and parents, and the data they supply by completing needs assessment surveys, can help the counselor pinpoint students' concerns and identify the abilities of prospective group members. Further, consultation with parents and teachers can help the counselor deal with any concerns these people may have about the group counseling process. Conducting orientation sessions for parents and teachers encourages understanding of and support for the group counseling process (Duncan and Gumaer 1980). At a minimum, the counselor should contact parents and teachers to arrange scheduling for the group sessions and to secure permission for students to be released from class to attend the group sessions. Prior to being enrolled in the group, each prospective group member should be interviewed.

The interview is intended to ascertain the student's willingness to work on self-improvement, desire to assist others in their efforts toward growth, commitment to the group's progress toward its goals, and the student's compatibility with other group members. The counselor explains the purpose and goals of the group to the individual, clarifying the reasons the individual was selected, describing the procedures, activities, and materials to be used in the group process. The counselor defines the meaning of "confidentiality" (and the conditions under which it is broken), and specifies the time and space arrangements for the meetings, duration of the group, group rules, and requirements for membership. The counselor listens carefully to the student's questions, responds to each, and makes sure the questions are answered to the prospective member's satisfaction. The emphasis on clarifying these issues assures that the students (and their parents) can give informed consent to group membership.

These issues should be discussed again with all the group members during the first session and reiterated throughout the group process as necessary, especially when group members are young children. From a legal standpoint, the counselor, when asking parents for written permission for their child's participation in the group, should provide this information in writing. This information also can be used to create a "contract" that students sign to indicate they understand the group's purposes and are committed to becoming part of it.

The interview also allows the counselor to assess whether the individual is compatible with other group members and whether the group goals and setting are appropriate for the individual. According to Carroll and Wiggins (1990), the ingredients for good group composition include members' acceptance of each other, willingness to self-disclose, voluntary participation, and a balance of personal characteristics among group members. Individuals who are initiators, cognitive, expressive, other-oriented, and willing to risk self-disclosure should be included in the group to balance those who are primarily followers, reflective, quiet, self-oriented, and low risk-takers.

Creating a heterogeneous mix of minority and majority viewpoints, males and females, and various cultural backgrounds adds to the interchange of ideas. Including individuals who are better adjusted and more experienced concerning the group's major issues helps build cohesion in the group, and these members can be models for other members. Carroll and Wiggins (1990) also urge counselors to be intuitive regarding a prospective member's effect upon the potential interaction of all the members and to avoid poor risk combinations such as individuals who are withdrawn, paranoid, psychopathic, or are unable to conceptualize or verbalize at the average level of functioning within the group.

Level of functioning is especially important when working with groups of children. Differences in physical maturation and verbal ability may preclude their participation with peers or older children in group activities that demand strength, coordination, or verbal fluency. To avoid differences of this nature and to take advantage of students' natural preference for same-age companions, elementary school students tend to be grouped by grade level for counseling. This also makes scheduling easier and allows group members to transfer what they learn in the group to their interactions within the school setting. During the middle school years, students sometimes express a strong preference for same-sex peers, so some counselors conduct separate counseling groups for boys and girls. Generally, however, heterogeneous grouping is acceptable for any age group and is recommended for adolescent groups in particular, to promote better communication between the sexes.

Counselors should avoid including "best friends" or "worst enemies" in the same group, as these relationships can interfere with the group's efforts to be cohesive and maintain its focus. Similarly, students with severe disciplinary problems bring their own agenda to the group and can be highly disruptive. These individuals, as well as those who show a lack of concern for others, should be considered for individual counseling or some other strategy that emphasizes the consequences of antisocial behavior (Vander Kolk 1985). In addition, suicidal or severely depressed students who may need immediate help might be better served by individual counseling and monitoring (Lifton 1972).

Size of the Group

In determining the number of members to include in the group, the primary consideration is the leader's ability to manage the group's interactions. With primary-grade youngsters engaged in play therapy, group size should be limited to three or four members. Groups for older children and adolescents usually have six to eight members but can range from five to ten, depending on the group's focus and the skills of the members and their counselor. A group with fewer than five members runs the risk of limiting the opportunities for individuals to interact with a variety of peers and benefit from a broader range of suggestions and support.

The counselor also must take into account student absenteeism. Young students are prone to childhood diseases, and absentee rates of at-risk students are often higher than those of their peers. Transience in the student population also portends dropouts. At the other extreme, expanding the group membership beyond ten strains the counselor's ability to attend and respond to all the interactions in the group.

Larger groups can be managed by the counselor working with a co-leader, and some experts highly recommend co-leaders for smaller groups as well. By collaborating in planning and managing the group process, a co-leader helps the counselor broaden his or her skills as a leader. A thorough discussion of co-leadership is provided in Corey and Corey's (1992) work, *Groups: Process and Practice* (4th ed.).

Length and Number of Group Meetings

Groups need time to warm up, build cohesion, address their problem focus, and come to closure. To maintain continuity and momentum, groups should meet weekly for 90 to 120 minutes. Counselors in public schools, however, often are restricted in the amount of time they can arrange for group counseling. Convincing teachers and parents to release students from class for an extended time weekly is difficult, especially when state officials and the public pressure the schools to assume greater accountability for student achievement. Once-a-week sessions are often disrupted by school special events and holidays. Therefore, many school counselors arrange for their groups to meet for a normal class hour once or twice a week over eight to twelve weeks. Groups for younger students usually meet for two thirty-minute sessions each week, as this time frame more closely fits their regular instructional class periods and their average attention spans.

Counselors have different preferences in scheduling. Some find that group continuity and momentum are enhanced by meeting more frequently over a shorter time. This may be especially advantageous for topic-specific groups on coping with suicide, dealing with a death or natural disaster, or other crisis. Some counselors schedule developmental groups for elementary school students to meet daily for a two-week period. Holding the sessions during a different class session each day minimizes the time students miss a given instructional period (Myrick 1987).

Group Rules

Early on, the group should establish a set of clearly defined rules governing members' behavior. Members typically commit to:

- joining the group voluntarily
- attending and coming on time to all group sessions

- working on self-improvement
- helping others improve themselves
- maintaining confidentiality concerning what others say and do in the group
- obeying the rules the group adopts

The group may set additional rules initially or as the need arises during the group process. Examples of group-specific rules include:

- only one person speaking at a time
- speaking directly to individuals
- listening and attending to the speaker
- participating in the group discussions
- dealing with the here and now
- no fighting or shoving
- no put-downs or verbal assaults

The number of rules is left to the discretion of the counselor and the members themselves. The guiding principles are that each member must assume responsibility for choosing what he or she does and says in the group and that each is committed to taking an active role in growth and maintenance of the group (Anderson 1984). The counselor and the members are bound by the rules the group sets for itself, and they share responsibility for maintaining them. Only the counselor, however, has the right to remove someone from the group.

EVALUATION

In planning the evaluation for the group process, the counselor should allow members to receive feedback from the group and should arrange for data gathering to assess the group's perceived effectiveness. Feedback can be offered to members if the counselor devotes the last sessions (the termination stage) to self-reflection and summarization of members' observed behaviors during the group process. Group members should be given time to assess how far they have progressed, summarize their observations of other members' behaviors, and make recommendations for their personal growth and that of other members. The counselor should instruct members to evaluate their growth in terms of the group's stated purposes, and encourage them to make positive comments and suggestions in their feedback to each other. Based upon this reflection and feedback, students can devise a personal plan of action that they can follow after the group terminates. Whenever possible, the counselor should arrange for the group to hold a follow-up meeting after a few months to allow members to discuss their progress in the personal plans they designed for themselves. If this meeting is not possible, the counselor should arrange to meet with members individually.

The effectiveness of the group process itself usually is determined by analyzing information obtained from the members, their parents, and teachers. In the follow-up session with students, data are gathered regarding members' opinions of the group's effectiveness in meeting its goals. The counselor can create a brief questionnaire or rating sheet for students to fill out. Change in student attitude can be ascertained by having members complete an attitude scale or survey prior to beginning the group process and again following termination. Examples of inventories that can be used in both pre- and post-group assessment are included in Morganett's (1990) book, *Skills for Living: Group Counseling Activities for Young Adolescents.* Similar procedures can be employed with parents and teachers to obtain their perceptions of students' new knowledge and skills targeted in the group. The counselor may wish to interview these adults to discuss their observations of any changes in students' behaviors or attitudes following the group experience. Additional counseling needs or other follow-up interventions also may be discussed during this consultation session.

TYPES OF COUNSELING GROUPS

Counseling groups can be divided into three types: developmental, problem-centered, and topic-specific. Certain basic elements are common to all three types.

First, all groups must have a definite purpose, which the counselor clearly defines and states. As Gladding (1991) pointed out, "If leaders are not sure of the types of experiences they wish to set up and for whom, the group will most likely fail'' (p. 131). Group purposes are defined and delineated in the stated goals and objectives the counselor prepares for the group process prior to selecting members. The goals may target the needs of an identified group of students who, for example, may be deficient in certain academic, vocational, or interpersonal skills, or the goals may focus on the expressed needs and interests of individual students. In either case, the goals direct the group process from its inception through post-group evaluation. The objectives clarify the goals by stating expected outcomes for members to derive from the group experience. The objectives also guide the counselor in selecting activities and discussion procedures for conducting the group sessions.

They are the basis for evaluating how well the group attains its purposes.

Second, all three types of groups must have requirements for member participation and impose rules for membership. Group members, screened from a pool, are expected to commit to rules of conduct the group establishes and to be accountable to the group itself. Because the group process takes place within an educational institution and the group members are minors, the group must operate within certain legal restrictions, organizational policies, and the expectations of parents, teachers, and school administrators.

Third, all three types of groups must include structured procedures. Each type of group proceeds through the same four stages of group development previously identified. Each limits the time for length of sessions and for duration of the meetings by establishing a beginning and an end. Although the roles of the counselor and the members vary depending on the purpose of the group, the age and characteristics of the students, and the counselor's theoretical orientation, the counselor and the group collaborate to bring about cohesion among the members and sustain an atmosphere of mutual trust, caring, understanding, acceptance, and support. This dynamic interaction is what provides the core structure for all of the group's activities.

Finally, it sould be noted that incorporating structured activities in the group process is intended to serve as a stimulus for group interaction and self-reflection. The activities should not be used to limit the thoughts and expressions of group members or to substitute for lack of communication among group members. The counselor's focus should be on helping members identify their unique personal reactions (thoughts, feelings, opinions, and values) as they emerge in the context of the group process in response to the stimulus each activity provides.

DEVELOPMENTAL GROUPS

Developmental groups help students meet the challenges of everyday, normal activity in the process of growing up. Like large-group guidance activities, they address the individual's need to gain knowledge and acquire skills in the areas of personal identity, interpersonal interaction, academic achievement, and career planning. They are oriented to growth and prevention rather than remediation and are directed toward development of specific behaviors and skills that will enhance the individual's ability to function independently and responsibly.

Group membership is open to all students but usually is targeted to children and adolescents who seem to be delayed in comparison to peers of the same ability levels and social and academic backgrounds. Prospective group members often are identified by parents and teachers during consultation with the counselor as students who are experiencing problems in the areas of underachievement, absenteeism, tardiness, low self-esteem, or lack of social involvement with peers. Other students volunteer for groups to enhance their skills or knowledge.

The groups usually have a central theme related to the student's level of understanding, personal interests, and perceived needs. For example, a group dealing with interpersonal communication skills might be called "The Friendship Group" for younger students, or "Dating Conversation Made Easy" for adolescents. Other group titles might be "How to Study Better and Get Better Grades," "My Special Talents," and "How to Create a Personal Career Plan." Some groups teach specific skills such as assertiveness training, steps in problem-solving, stress management; or they may present models to help students understand their communication styles, as in transactional analysis (Thompson and Rudolph 1988). Developmental groups frequently incorporate media such as videos, films, and books. Games, worksheets, simulations, and role-plays also can encourage discussion.

Descriptions of developmental groups and small-group activities are available in the literature. Group themes for elementary school students include:

- listening skills (Merritt and Walley 1977)
- dealing with feelings (Morrison and Thompson 1985; Omizo, Hershberger, and Omizo 1988; Papagno 1983; Vernon, 1989a)
- social skills and friendship (Brown and Brown 1882; Keat, Metzgar, Raykovitz, and McDonald 1985; Rose 1987; Vernon 1989a)
- academic achievement (Gerler, Kinney, and Anderson 1985)
- self-concept (Omizo and Omizo 1987a)
- career awareness (Rogala, Lambert, and Verhage 1991)
- problem-solving/decision making (Bergin 1991; Vernon 1989a)

Themes and descriptions of groups for secondary students include:

- social skills and making friends (Morganett 1990; Vernon, 1989b)
- communication and assertiveness training (Huey 1983; Morganett 1990; Myrick 1987)
- personal identity and self-esteem (Lee 1987; Morganett 1990; Tessier, 1982; Vernon 1989b)

- dealing with feelings and managing stress (Leaman 1983; Morganett 1990; Vernon 1989b)
- achievement motivation and school success (Campbell and Myrick 1990; Morganett 1990)
- problem-solving/decision-making (Vernon 1989b)
- career exploration and planning (Rogala, Lambert, and Verhage 1991)

A developmental group for adolescents is described on the following pages.

Developmental Group: Polishing My Self-Image

Group Goals:
- To build group cohesion, cooperation, and communication
- To develop an understanding of self-concept formation
- To identify the effect of positive and negative reinforcement on self-esteem
- To identify personal strengths and weaknesses
- To develop a plan for enhancing personal self-image

Session 1:

Objectives:
- To demonstrate cooperative behaviors
- To make positive, reinforcing statements and suggestions to each other
- To establish rules for the group

Procedure: The counselor leads the group in a discussion of the group's purpose and goals and facilitates the establishment of group rules. Members sign the individual contracts negotiated in the initial counselor/student interviews. The contracts confirm the individual member's commitment to the group. Members then are paired and invited to participate in a "Who are you?" icebreaker activity: One member spends two minutes asking his or her partner, "Who are you?" and the partner answers. (Example: "Who are you?" *An eighth grader.* "Who are you?" *Someone who likes rock and roll music.*) After two minutes, the partners reverse roles. At the end of the time, each member of a pair introduces the other member to the entire group and tells at least two things about the person that he or she discovered during the

"Who are you?" activity. Following the icebreaker activity, the counselor asks questions such as:

- Did you learn anything about yourself by participating in this activity?
- Did you learn anything about others?
- What are you looking forward to in the next group session?

Session 2:

Objectives:
- To describe strengths and weaknesses
- To realize that all individuals have both strengths and weaknesses

Procedure: The counselor provides a journal for each group member and explains that members are to record their personal reactions to all of the group's activities and discussions. Members then complete a "Personal Coat of Arms" activity (Canfield 1976), which requires them to think of symbols representing the following: a personal achievement, something they've recently learned to do, something they'd like to do better, a special talent, a weakness, and a bright idea they have had. They draw their symbols on a paper shield the counselor provides. The counselor asks members to display the shields and encourages each to explain the symbols on his or her shield. The counselor can facilitate discussion by asking questions such as:

- Which symbol was the most difficult to think of?
- How did you feel when you shared your symbols?
- How did it feel to talk about your strengths?
- Is it bragging or just telling it like it is?
- What was it like to share a weakness? Does having weaknesses mean you are not a good person? (The counselor should stress that everyone has strengths and weaknesses but that this doesn't affect a person's overall worth.)
- What did you learn about yourself in this activity?

Session 3:

Objectives:
- To describe personal characteristics using metaphors
- To explain how these metaphors describe their perceptions of themselves
- To state and describe their perceptions of each other using metaphors

Procedure: The counselor explains and gives examples of metaphors. Members complete the metaphorical statements, "If I were a(n) _____ I would be a(n) _____ " using items of their choice from the following categories: *animal, building, home appliance, movie, car, book*. The counselor invites members to share their responses and offer additional positive metaphors to each other. The counselor asks each person who offers an alternative metaphor to explain his or her response.

The counselor leads the group in discussing the following questions:

- Was it difficult to think of metaphors?
- What did you learn about yourself by identifying metaphors?
- What metaphors would you use to describe your best qualities as a friend? as a student? as a member of the group? as a worker?

Session 4:

Objectives:
- To identify how self-concept develops
- To identify ways in which self-worth is affected by positive and negative feelings

Procedure: The group views the videocassette, *I Like Being Me: Self-Esteem* (Sunburst Communications 1990). This program describes the origins of self-worth, the ways feelings and beliefs about self-worth can be changed, and the ways positive and negative feelings affect self-worth. After reviewing the major points of the program, the counselor leads the group in a discussion of self-worth:

- Describe a time when you felt good about yourself.
- Describe what it means to *value* yourself.

● What can you do to change your feelings about yourself?

Session 5:

Objectives: ● To identify the negative effects of "put-down" statements on self-esteem
● To identify self put-downs

Procedures: The counselor directs the group in a "put-downs" activity (Vernon 1989b) in which volunteers read aloud negative statements such as, "stupid idiot," "dumb jerk," "fat, ugly creep," and "lazy good-for-nothing." The statements are read as though the reader is making them about himself or herself. The counselor then leads a group discussion about the effects of negative self-talk on a person's self-esteem. To stimulate discussion, the counselor asks questions such as:

● What do you accomplish by putting yourself down?
● What positive statements can you use to stop yourself from making personal put-downs?

Session 6:

Objective: ● To describe positive statements and actions that can be used to stop negative self-talk

Procedure: The counselor facilitates a group discussion of situations in which group members find themselves engaging in negative self-talk. The group identifies the put-down statements and then brainstorms positive, alternative statements and behaviors to reinforce feelings of self-worth and esteem. The counselor helps the group select some scenarios to role-play. First the members role-play the negative statements, then the situations using the positive statements they have proposed. To emphasize the concepts, the counselor can ask questions such as:

● How did it feel when you made the positive statement instead of the put-down?
● What positive statements can you use to keep from making personal put-downs?

Session 7:

Objectives: ● To identify personal goals for improving self-concept
● To describe ways to achieve these goals

Procedure: The counselor leads the group in a discussion of goal-setting. Members are encouraged to develop a personal plan for self-improvement. The counselor instructs group members to write their plans in their personal journals. To help members develop goals and strategies, the counselor makes statements and asks questions, such as the following, to stimulate ideas:

● What goals do you want to set for yourself?
● How do you need to change your behavior to meet these goals?
● How can you encourage yourself when others put you down? when you make mistakes? when you don't seem to be making progress toward your goals?

Session 8:

Objectives: ● To share what was learned during the group sessions
● To give positive suggestions for accomplishing personal goals

Procedure: The counselor encourages members to share what they have learned with the group by reviewing and summarizing their journal entries. Members are invited to share plans for self-enhancement with the group. The counselor makes statements and asks questions that facilitate the group's sharing of suggestions to improve self-concept. The counselor and the group plan a follow-up session. To facilitate this activity, the counselor asks questions such as:

● Which suggestions from the group can you use to help you reach your goals?
● How much progress do you think you can make toward meeting these goals before the group's follow-up session?
● How has this group been helpful to you?

Problem-Centered Groups

The problem-centered group is open-ended, and topics are determined by whatever is of concern to participants at the time of the meeting. According to Thompson and Rudolph (1988), these case-centered groups are comprised of children "...working on different problems. Each child has the opportunity to receive the group's full attention to his/her problem" (p. 260). Members' commitment to the group entails helping others with their concerns and fostering problem-solving processes. The emphasis is on here-and-now experiences of individual group members. They are encouraged to explore their problems, examine the alternatives open to them, consider the probable consequences of each alternative, and decide upon a course of personal action. The counselor and other group members attempt to empower the individuals to take action on their decisions by providing support, feedback, and the opportunity to practice new behaviors within the group. In addition, the counselor encourages members to try out new behaviors as homework between scheduled group meetings.

While membership in problem-centered groups is open to all students, members preferably should have skills in articulating personal concerns, attending and responding to others, and some knowledge of their personal needs and aspirations. Intermediate, junior, and senior high school students, because of their level of maturation and social experience, are more likely to have these skills than are primary grade youngsters. Therefore, counselors may wish to establish problem-centered groups exclusively with this population. For younger children, play therapy techniques can be effective in promoting problem-solving skills. To facilitate communication in problem-centered groups, counselors might first involve students in developmental groups specifically designed to teach listening skills and cooperative behaviors that will enhance appropriate interaction in group counseling activities.

The issues and concerns targeted for group sessions are unique to the individuals who comprise the group. Each member is responsible for explaining to the group his or her specific problem and, with the group's assistance, for developing and implementing strategies to resolve the problem. Group members are selected not only because they are committed to self-improvement but also because they have the desire and ability to help their peers. Thus, each individual's problem becomes an issue for the group. The counselor and other group members attempt to provide feedback to the individual in a manner that he or she can understand and act upon. As Ehly and Dustin (1989) pointed out:

> When members help the individual identify a specific area of behavior that causes problems for the individual and for the other students, the problem seems real. What may have been seen as only something bothering a teacher now becomes the student's problem as group members indicate how much they also dislike the behavior. (p. 94)

Members of problem-centered groups are selected for a variety of reasons. Frequently they are referred by teachers and parents who are concerned about the students' behaviors at home or at school. For example, these adults may hear the student complaining that "no one likes me" or notice that the student doesn't interact much with peers. Many students volunteer to join groups to focus on issues of particular concern to them, such as resolving conflicts with parents or peers. Counselors invite some members to join a group as a follow-up to individual counseling, especially if the individual's problems are interpersonal in nature. Counselors also may select some members specifically because they can articulate ideas and feelings, are effective problem-solvers, and so can serve as good role models.

Because group members usually are close in age and share the same school environment, their concerns tend to be similar, and common topics often emerge in problem-centered groups. Some of the topics common to elementary school students are: attitudes toward family members, conflicts with parental and school authority figures, relationships with friends, cliques within the peer group, and making the transition to middle/junior high school. Adolescents often are concerned with issues such as relationships with friends, dating and attitudes toward sex, dealing with teachers, homework, and school, working in addition to going to school, preparing for the future in terms of career, marriage, and post-secondary education, and relationships with parents (Ehly and Dustin 1989).

A sample outline for a problem-centered group follows. Additional examples and a comprehensive examination of strategies for conducting this type of group are found in *Elements of Group Counseling* by Carroll and Wiggins (1990); *Counseling and Therapy for Children* by Gumaer (1984); and *Working with Children and Adolescents in Groups* by Rose and Edelson (1987).

Problem-Centered Group

Group Goals: • To build group cohesion, communication and cooperation
• To define and analyze personal concerns

● To generate solutions to personal concerns through problem-solving
● To establish personal plans of action to resolve problems
● To accept responsibility for transferring what is learned in the group process to solving problems in one's personal life

Session 1:

Objectives: ● To demonstrate cooperative behaviors
● To establish group rules and develop group cohesion
● To self-disclose concerns the individual wishes to address in the group

Procedure: The counselor leads the group in discussing the group's purpose and goals and in establishing rules for the group. (Rules should be written on posterboard and displayed during each session.) Members sign the contracts they negotiated in the individual counselor/member interviews, which represent commitment to the group process. Individuals introduce themselves by sharing one thing that others can't tell by looking at them.

The counselor then employs an inclusion activity, "Group Logo" (Bergin 1989), to begin to build group identity and promote cohesion. In this activity the members cooperate in drawing overlapping shapes on a large piece of posterboard. Together they agree upon a picture they see emerging from the lines they have drawn, and then outline, color, and title the picture. The title and picture become the group's logo, which can be displayed throughout subsequent group sessions.

Following the group-building activity, the counselor invites students to identify personal concerns they want to bring up in subsequent sessions. The counselor can facilitate the group's discussion by asking questions such as:

● Why do you think joining this group can be helpful to you?
● How do you feel about the group logo?
● How can you feel more comfortable in the group? What are you looking forward to?

Sessions 2–8:

Objectives:
- To identify individual problems
- To brainstorm ways to solve these problems
- To encourage self-disclosure of feelings, concerns, and opinions
- To try out new behaviors and responses to problem situations through role-playing
- To establish plans for resolving personal problems

Procedures:
Individual members present their personal concerns and describe thoughts, behaviors, and feelings about those problems. The group focuses on the here and now. Members respond to each other to clarify feelings, perceptions, and concerns, and suggest alternative ways of dealing with the issues. To stimulate dialogue, the counselor might briefly review and summarize the previous session, then ask group members to share how their problem-solving "plans" worked or how the problem has evolved since the last session. During the sessions, the counselor prompts members to speak directly to one another and links members by pointing out similarities in the problems, feelings, or experiences they describe.

The group must adhere to the rules it has established. The counselor must insist that members wait their turn and allow everyone to have the opportunity to speak. The counselor must allow reticent members to proceed slowly until they are comfortable with self-disclosure. The counselor can encourage the group by making statements such as:

- I'd like to hear each of you give your opinion about what Jill has told us.
- When Trent is ready, he will tell us more about his feelings.
- Kara, you seem to understand how Andy and Chago are feeling. Can you tell us how your feelings are similar?

The counselor leads the group in brainstorming problem-solving behaviors. The members suggest alternative courses of action and identify and evaluate probable consequences of these proposed solutions. Role-playing is one means of trying out alternative behaviors. The counselor suggests homework assignments to help members try out new behavior and encourages members to report the results during subsequent sessions. For closure, the counselor can initiate a round robin sharing of an "I learned" or an "I feel" or an "I will" statement relative to the issues discussed.

Sessions 9–10:

Objectives:
- To share what was learned during group sessions
- To share personal goals and strategies for resolving the problems shared with the group

Procedure: The counselor begins a discussion to allow group members to share what they have learned during the group process in regard to themselves and their personal problems. Each member defines a plan for applying problem-solving skills in his or her environment. Members make positive statements, reinforcing each other for their communication and cooperation while in the group. The counselor and members plan a follow-up session. To facilitate the discussion, the counselor might ask questions such as:

- How do you feel about your problems right now?
- What progress do you think you've made toward resolving the problems?
- What must you continue to do to resolve the problems?
- What's the next step you need to take?
- What things have you learned in this group that will help you reach your goals?

Topic-Specific Groups

Topic-specific groups are designed to meet the needs of students who are having difficulty with situational circumstances that create negative feelings and stress that interferes with normal functioning. These groups are similar to developmental groups in that new knowledge and skills are taught to the members, but the theme is helping these students learn to handle more serious concerns rather than to resolve typical developmental problems. In topic-specific groups, members all share similar concerns about a given situation or condition. Because of the commonality of problems, topic-specific groups are also much like problem-centered groups, which center on open discussion about a current issue.

The group setting allows the opportunity for members to understand the issue in more depth, to explore and express feelings, and to identify coping strategies. Students learn that their feelings are normal, that their peers often feel the same way, and that they have options to help them deal more effectively with the problems and thus reestablish personal autonomy and happiness. Students also receive feedback and support from others who understand what they are experiencing because they have similar problems.

Although they are not primarily crisis intervention groups by design, topic-specific groups often arise out of crisis events such as a classmate's accidental death or suicide. In instances such as these, the immediate purpose of the group is to provide support to group members who are dealing with the crisis situation. Later, a follow-up group can be organized to help them explore the incident more fully, along with any other concerns related to the larger issue (Myrick 1987).

The themes targeted in topic-specific groups range from dealing with physical or sexual abuse and coping with death and loss to adjustment situations such as moving away and parental divorce and remarriage. Like developmental groups, topic-specific groups frequently use media and structured activities to stimulate discussion of the topic and present relevant information to members. They may make extensive use of role-play and homework exercises to promote specific coping skills.

References to topic-specific groups for elementary school students are:

- obesity (Lokken 1981)
- physical abuse (Baker 1990)
- grief and loss (Peterson and Straub 1992)
- sexual abuse (Powell and Faherty 1990)
- aggressive behavior (Amerikaner and Summerlin 1982)
- divorce and separation (Bradford 1982; Burke and Van de Streek 1989; Cantrell 1986; Gwynn and Brantley 1987; Hammond 1981; Kalter 1988; Omizo and Omizo 1987b; Snyder 1985; Tedder, Scherman, and Wantz 1987; Yauman (1991)

Topic-specific issues for adolescent groups include:

- children of alcoholics (Emshoff 1989)
- separation and divorce (Camiletti and Quant 1983; Morganett 1990; Omizo and Omizo 1988)

- suicide (Morganett 1990; Peterson and Straub 1992; Florida 1990)
- death of family member (Furman and Pratt l985)
- avoiding drug abuse (LeCoq and Capuzzi 1984)
- teen parenting (Huey 1987)
- teen pregnancy (Blythe, Gilchrist, and Schinke 1981)

Group membership usually is targeted to students who are currently having difficulty with a specific issue or are considered to be at-risk. Some members, however, may be chosen because of their past experience with the issue and success in coping with it. These students can help stabilize the group atmosphere and build a sense of hope and confidence that the group process will lead to similar successes for all group members. They also serve as role models, especially in behavior modification groups, who exemplify the coping skills group members desire. Further, counselors can provide powerful reinforcement by linking the models with targeted group members. A sample of a topic-specific group for elementary school students who have trouble adjusting to divorce follows.

Topic-Specific Group: Support Group for Children of Divorce

Group Goals:
- To build group cohesion, cooperation and communication
- To develop mutual support
- To correct misinformation about the causes of divorce
- To identify and express feelings about divorce
- To plan strategies for coping with divorce

Session 1:

Objectives:
- To establish rules for the group
- To demonstrate cooperative behaviors
- To develop group cohesion an commitment
- To state what members hope to achieve while in the group

Procedure: The counselor leads group members in a discussion of the purpose and goals of the group. Members are then asked to establish group rules and sign individual contracts, negotiated during counselor/client interviews, symbolizing the individual's commitment to the group. The counselor or a volunteer writes the group rules on a large piece of posterboard for display throughout each session.

The counselor then asks each member to introduce himself or herself to the group and initiates an icebreaker activity as follows: The counselor distributes magazines and a nine-inch square of tagboard to each student. They cut out pictures describing themselves and paste them on the tagboard. Then they cut their picture into four to six pieces and put them in an envelope. Students exchange envelopes, put the puzzles together, and share what they learned about each other from the "people puzzle."

Following this activity, the counselor describes the goals of the group and invites members to say what they would like to learn. Questions such as the following may stimulate this sharing:

- What do you want to learn while you are in this group?
- Now that you have heard everyone tell what they want to learn, what do you have in common?
- How did you feel about describing your goals to the group?

Session 2:

Objectives:
- To describe the changes divorce has made on the family
- To identify similarities and differences in experiences with divorce

Procedure:
The counselor distributes paper and colored markers to group members and invites them to draw pictures of their families and their homes. The counselor instructs the members to divide the paper into six spaces and draw pictures to represent:

- your family
- a good time you've had with your family
- how your family has changed recently
- what you miss about the way your family used to be
- a good thing about the way your family is now
- how you feel about the way things are now

The counselor then asks each member to display his or her picture and tell the group about it. Other members listen and then share their own experiences, which may be similar or dissimilar. The following questions can stimulate discussion:

● How did it feel to describe your family picture?
● What changes has divorce made in your family life?
● After hearing others in the group describe the changes in their lives, what changes do you think are similar for everyone?

Session 3:

Objectives:
● To encourage expression of feelings
● To learn to express feelings through pantomime
● To identify feelings common to all group members
● To identify ways to cope with negative feelings

Procedure:
The counselor leads members in an activity in which they identify their feelings by responding in pantomime. The counselor has participants draw a feeling word out of a sack and asks them to show how they look or act when they are bored, angry, happy, sad, confused, worried, frustrated. Each group member is able to see the expressions on the other faces and identify with those feelings.

Following the pantomime, participants are invited to draw situations, such as the following, out of the bag and identify how they feel.

● Mom is angry with Dad or Dad is angry with Mom.
● You are home alone.
● You don't get to see Mom or Dad very often.
● You think you're the cause of your parents' divorce.
● Your parents don't have as much time to spend with you.
● Your friend makes fun of your family.

Individual members are encouraged to verbalize these feelings. The counselor helps the group think of ways to cope with the feelings. Members describe what they do to relieve sad, angry, or lonely feelings. Members are encouraged to brainstorm ways of coping by doing positive things. The counselor records all the positive suggestions on a large piece of posterboard to use in later sessions. The counselor debriefs the activity by asking students:

- Was it hard to identify feelings?
- Did others share similar feelings?
- What did you learn about ways to deal with negative feelings?

Session 4:

Objectives:
- To learn that they are not the cause of divorce
- To identify reasons some parents divorce
- To suggest ways to cope with negative feelings caused by the changes divorce brings

Procedure: Members view the videocassette *When Your Mom and Dad Get Divorced* (Sunburst Communications 1991), which reassures youngsters that they are not responsible for divorce. The program describes ways children can help themselves feel better. The counselor facilitates discussion by asking the group to respond to questions such as:

- What are some reasons parents get a divorce?
- Do children cause divorce?
- Can children do anything to prevent divorce?
- What positive things can children do to cope with the changes the divorce causes?

The counselor then displays the posterboard listing the coping behaviors brainstormed by the group in session 3. The counselor asks the group to look at the posterboard and determine which suggestions for coping with sad, lonely, and angry feelings might be used to help deal with feelings caused by divorce.

Session 5:

Objectives:
- To describe the negative situations divorce causes
- To listen and reflect others' feelings

Procedure: The counselor asks each group member to describe the divorce-related events that "bother me the most." The counselor helps the group set up a role-playing activity in which to act out some of these events. A volunteer acts out problem events for group members, who then attempt to help the individual clarify the reasons the events bother him or her the most. The counselor and the other group members express their appreciation for the individual's willingness to share his or her experiences and feelings with the group. The counselor then asks questions such as:

- Are your situations similar or dissimilar to those of others?
- How do you feel about discussing things that bother you?
- Is it helpful to have others listen and understand?

Session 6:

Objectives:
- To express concerns about divorce to a divorced adult
- To simulate parent/child discussions about divorce
- To identify strategies to cope with the changes precipitated by divorce

Procedure:
The counselor invites a divorced parent to attend the group session and respond to members' questions about divorce. The counselor emphasizes the importance of parent/child dialogue to help children and parents adjust to the changes in their lives resulting from the divorce.

Volunteers are asked to use adult and child puppets in demonstrating situations that can be stressful for children. These situations could include:

- talking with the custodial and the noncustodial parent about the divorce
- meeting new adults in their parents' lives
- adjusting to changes in the home environment
- taking on new responsibilities that parents may place on the child

The counselor leads the group and guest in a discussion of the puppet simulations and may wish to ask questions such as:

- What is the child feeling in this situation?
- How does the parent feel?

- How does the other adult feel?
- What are the puppets saying and doing that make the parent and/or child feel bad?
- How can they make each other feel better?
- How can they make themselves feel better?

Session 7:

Objectives:
- To state personal goals for coping with divorce
- To identify strategies to help reach the goals
- To identify people who can offer support after the group ends

Procedure:
Based upon work done in previous sessions, the counselor encourages and helps each individual make a plan for coping with his or her own problems relating to the divorce. The counselor leads the group in brainstorming a list of people such as peers, family members, clergy, and significant others who can provide support to group members. The counselor can facilitate the activities by asking the following kinds of questions:

- What things continue to upset you the most about divorce?
- When do you feel most upset?
- What can you do to feel better?
- What can other people do to help you?

Session 8:

Objectives:
- To express current feelings about the divorce
- To state what members have learned during the group sessions
- To offer support and encouragement to each other

Procedure:
The counselor distributes index cards and invites participants to write the following:

- one thing you learned by being in the group
- something you can do about your negative feelings
- someone who can help you if you need help
- one way you've changed because of the group.

Members are further encouraged to offer each other feedback and positive suggestions for coping and to share the statements they wrote on their cards. The group and the counselor plan a follow-up session in which the counselor brings closure to the group by asking questions such as:

- How do you feel now compared to how you felt when you first became a member of the group?
- How have the other group members been helpful to you?
- What do you plan to do to help yourself between now and the group follow-up session?

SUMMARY

Group counseling can be a valuable intervention in school settings. Given the normal developmental concerns of students in general, and the more serious problems of many young people, school counselors see group counseling as an efficient, effective, and viable approach to helping children and adolescents both remedially and preventively.

Group counseling can reach a larger number of students than individual counseling and it provides the added dimension of immediate feedback and support from peers. The major goal of group counseling is to offer the chance for each member to gain knowledge and skills for decision-making and problem-solving. The main difference between group counseling at the elementary level and at higher levels is in the students' verbal capacities. Play media is therefore often used in the lower grades.

Stages in the group process are: initial, transition, working, and termination. The group proceeds from building rapport and trust, which allows for helpful interchange and the dynamic of developmental growth, to personal problem-solving, and evaluation of progress.

The counselor, the primary group facilitator, organizes the group in terms of its times and setting, purposes and objectives, assessment of needs, group activities, as well as group size and composition. In counseling with minors, ethics and confidentiality are important issues, and these limitations must be understood by the counselor, the group members, and the parents/guardians. Parental cooperation throughout the group experience is desired, as they can be a contributing resource to the group's success.

Three types of counseling groups are developmental, problem-centered, and topic-specific. Developmental groups are directed at helping students meet the challenges of everyday, normal life; they are oriented to growth and prevention. Problem-centered groups center on issues of concern to group members at the time of the meeting, and problem-solving techniques are emphasized. Topic-specific groups focus on critical issues and circumstances that interfere with normal functioning. Common themes at the elementary level are divorce aftermath, obesity, abuse, grief and loss. For adolescents, themes typically are organized around alcoholism in the family, separation and divorce, suicide, death of a family member, avoiding drug abuse, teen pregnancy, and teen parenting.

REFERENCES

Anderson, J. 1984. *Counseling through group process.* New York: Springer.

Amerikaner, M., and M. Summerlin. 1982. Group counseling with learning disabled children: Effects of social skills and relaxation training on self-concept and classroom behavior. *Journal of Learning Disabilities* 15(6): 340–343.

Baker, C. 1990. *Development of an outreach group for children ages five through thirteen who have witnessed domestic violence* (Report No. CG 022 667). Nova University. Fort Lauderdale, FL. (ERIC Document Reproduction Service No. ED 325 737)

Bergin, J. 1989. Building group cohesiveness through cooperation activities. *Elementary School Guidance and Counseling* 24(2): 90–95.

Bergin, J. 1991. *Escape from pirate island* [Game]. Doyleston, PA: Mar*Co Products.

Blythe, B., L. Gilchrist, and S. Schinke. 1981. Pregnancy prevention groups for adolescents. *Social Work* 26(6): 503–504.

Bradford, A. 1982. *Parting: A counselor's guide for children of separated parents* (Report No. CG 016 519). Columbia: South Carolina State Department of Education. (ERIC Document Reproduction Service No. ED 227 391)

Brown, C., and J. Brown. 1982. *Counseling children for social competence: A manual for teachers and counselors.* Springfield, IL: Charles C Thomas, Publisher.

Burke, D. and L. Van de Streek. 1989. Children of divorce: An application of Hammond's group counseling for children. *Elementary School Guidance and Counseling* 24(2): 112–118.

Camiletti, Y., and V. Quant. 1983. Anticipatory counseling for adolescents of divorced parents. *School Guidance Worker* 39(1): 20–23.

Campbell, C., and R. Myrick. 1990. Motivational group counseling for low-performing students. *Journal for Specialists in Group Work* 15(10): 43–50.

Canfield, J. 1976. *100 ways to enhance self-concept in the classroom.* Englewood Cliffs, NJ: Prentice Hall.

Cantrell, R. 1986. Adjustment to divorce. *Elementary School Guidance and Counseling* 20(3): 163–173.

Carroll, M., and J. Wiggins. 1990. *Elements of group counseling: Back to the basics.* Denver: Love Publishing.

Corey, G. 1990. *Theory and practice of group counseling.* 3d ed. Pacific Grove, CA: Brooks/Cole.

Corey, G., M. Corey, P. Callanan, and J. Russell. 1988. *Group techniques.* rev. ed. Pacific Grove, CA: Brooks/Cole .

Corey, M., and G. Corey. 1992. *Groups: Process and practice.* 4th ed. Pacific Grove, CA: Brooks/Cole.

Duncan, J., and J. Gumaer. 1980. *Developmental groups for children.* Springfield, IL: Charles C Thomas.

Ehly, S., and R. Dustin. 1989. *Individual and group counseling in schools.* New York: Guilford Press.

Emshoff, J. 1989. Preventive intervention with children of alcoholics. *Prevention in Human Services* 7(1): 225–253.

Florida, State of. 1990. *Youth suicide prevention.* Ann Arbor, MI: Author.

Furman, J., and J. Pratt. 1985. *Coping with the ultimate change, death of a family member: A support group for bereaved adolescents* (Report No. CG 018 340). National Association of Social Workers meeting, New Orleans. (ERIC Document Reproduction Service No. ED 259 239)

Gazda, G. 1989. *Group counseling: A developmental approach.* 4th ed. Boston: Allyn and Bacon.

Gazda, G., J. Duncan, and M. Meadows. 1967. Group counseling and group procedures—Report of a survey. *Counselor Education and Supervision* 9: 305–310.

George, R., and D. Dustin. 1988. *Group counseling: Theory and practice.* Englewood Cliffs, NJ: Prentice Hall.

Gerler, E., J. Kinney, and R. Anderson. 1985. The effects of counseling on classroom performance. *Journal of Humanistic Education and Development* 23(4): 155–165.

Gladding, S. 1991. *Group work: A counseling speciality.* New York: Macmillan.

Grayson, E. 1989. *The elements of short-term group counseling.* Washington, DC: St. Mary's Press.

Gumaer, J. 1984. *Counseling and therapy for children.* New York: Free Press.

Gwynn, C. and H. Brantley. 1987. Effects of a divorce group intervention for elementary school children. *Psychology in the Schools* 24: 161–164.

Hammond, J. 1981. *Group counseling for children of divorce: A guide for the elementary school.* Flint, MI: Cranbrook Publishing Co.

Huey, W. 1983. Reducing adolescent aggression through group assertive training. *School Counselor* 30(3): 193–203.

Huey, W. 1987. Counseling teenage fathers: The "maximizing a life experience" (MALE) group. *School Counselor* 35(1): 40–47.

Huey, W., and T. Remley. 1988. *Ethical and legal issues in school counseling.* Alexandria, VA: American Counseling Association.

Jacobs, F., R. Harvill, and R. Masson. 1988. *Group counseling: Strategies and skills.* Pacific Grove, CA: Brooks/Cole.

Kalter, N. 1988. *Children of divorce: Facilitation of development through school-based groups; Grades 4 and 5. A replication manual* (Report No. CG 022

143). Lansing: Michigan State Dept. of Mental Health. (ERIC Document Reproduction Service No. ED 313 620)

Keat, D., K. Metzgar, D. Raykovitz, and J. McDonald. 1985. Multimodal counseling: Motivating children to attend school through friendship groups. *Journal of Humanistic Education and Development* 23(4): 166–175.

Leaman, D. 1983. Group counseling to improve communication skills of adolescents. *Journal for Specialists in Group Work* 8(3): 144–150.

LeCoq, L., and D. Capuzzi. 1984. Preventing adolescent drug abuse. *Journal of Humanistic Education and Development* 22(4): 155–169.

Lee, C. 1987. Black manhood training. *Journal of Specialists in Group Work* 12(1): 18–25.

Lifton, W. 1972. *Groups: Facilitating individual growth and societal change.* New York: John Wiley & Sons.

Lokken, M. 1981. *Weight: Helping kids keep it off!* (Report No CG 016 388). (ERIC Document Reproduction Service No. ED 225 040) Educational Resources Information Center, National Institute of Education, U. S. Dept. of Education, Washington, DC.

Merritt, R., and D. Walley. 1977. *The group leader's handbook: Resources, techniques, and survival skills.* Champaign, IL: Research Press.

Morganett, R. 1990. *Skills for living: Group counseling activities for young adolescents.* Champaign, IL: Research Press.

Morrison, K. and M. Thompson. 1985. *Feeling good about me.* Minneapolis: Educational Media Corp.

Myrick, R. 1987. *Developmental guidance and counseling: A practical approach.* Minneapolis: Educational Media Corp.

Ohlsen, M., A. Horne, and C. Lawe. 1988. *Group counseling.* 3d ed. New York: Holt, Rinehart & Winston.

Omizo, M., J. Hershberger, and S. Omizo. 1988. Teaching children to cope with anger. *Elementary School Guidance and Counseling* 22(3): 241–245.

Omizo, M., and S. Omizo. 1987a. The effects of group counseling on classroom behavior and self-concept among elementary school learning disabled children. *Exceptional Child* 34(1): 57–64.

Omizo, M. and S. Omizo. 1987b. Group counseling with children of divorce: New findings. *Elementary School Guidance and Counseling* 22(1): 46–52.

Omizo, M., and S. Omizo. 1988. The effects of participation in group counseling sessions on self-esteem and locus of control among adolescents from divorced families. *School Counselor* 36(1): 54–60.

Papagno, N. 1983. *A single model counseling group across all special needs children* (Report No. CG 400 198). American Psychological Association meeting, Anaheim, CA. (ERIC Document Reproduction Service No. ED 237 923)

Peterson, S., and R. Straub. 1992. *School crisis survival guide.* West Nyack, NY: Center for Applied Research in Education.

Powell, L., and S. Faherty. 1990. Treating sexually abused latency age girls. *The Arts in Psychotherapy* 17: 35–47.

Rogala, J., R. Lambert, and K. Verhage. 1991. *Developmental guidance classroom activities for use with the national career development guidelines*. Madison: Vocational Studies Center, University of Wisconsin.

Rose, S., and J. Edelson. 1987. *Working with children and adolescents in groups*. San Francisco: Jossey-Bass.

Rose, S. 1987. Social skills training in middle childhood. *Journal for Specialists in Group Work* 12(4): 144–149.

Snyder, K. 1985. An intervention program for children of separated or divorced parents. *Techniques: A Journal for Remedial Education and Counseling* 1(4): 286–296.

Sunburst Communications. 1990. *I like being me: Self-esteem*. [Filmstrip]. Pleasantville, NY: Author.

Sunburst Communications. 1991. *When your mom and dad get divorced*. [Filmstrip]. Pleasantville, NY: Author.

Tedder, S., A. Scherman, and R. Wantz. 1987. Effectiveness of a support group for children of divorce. *Elementary School Guidance and Counseling* 22(2): 102–109.

Tessier, D. 1982. A group counseling program for gifted and talented students. *The Pointer* 26(3): 43–46.

Thompson, C., and L. Rudolph. 1988. Counseling children. 2d ed. Pacific Grove, CA: Brooks/Cole.

Vander Kolk, C. 1985. *Introduction to group counseling and psychotherapy*. Columbus, OH: Charles E. Merrill.

Vernon, A. 1989a. *Thinking, feeling, behaving: An emotional educational curriculum for children*. Champaign, IL: Research Press.

Vernon, A. 1989b. *Thinking, feeling, behaving: An emotional education curriculum for adolescents*. Champaign, IL: Research Press.

Worzbyt, J., and K. O'Rourke. 1989. *Elementary school counseling: A blueprint for today and tomorrow*. Muncie, IN: Accelerated Development.

Yauman, B. 1991. School-based group counseling for children of divorce: A review of the literature. *Elementary School Guidance and Counseling* 26(2): 130–138.

Designing a
Developmental
9 Counseling Curriculum

Toni R. Tollerud

*Department of Educational Psychology,
Counseling, and Special Education
Northern Illinois University, DeKalb*

Robert J. Nejedlo

*Department of Educational Psychology,
Counseling, and Special Education
Northern Illinois University, DeKalb*

Think back to your school days and recall your school counselor. Did you know the counselor's name? Under what conditions did you talk to the counselor? Do you remember a counselor during all grades or just in high school?

Chances are that your initial thoughts about the school counselor were vague or minimal. Often, students used to see the counselor to help set their schedule, look at college information, or if they got into trouble. Most recollections are negative or minimal, at best. Even more rare is the recollection that the school counselor came to the students' classroom and did any kind of teaching to address students' developmental needs. Historically, counselors have followed a traditional format of counseling that has been more reactive, remedial, and crisis-oriented. Counselors in middle and high school settings have had to take on, in addition, the cumbersome administrative role of scheduler, which can consume much time and energy.

The days of the school counselor solely as disciplinarian, scheduler, and crisis counselor are numbered. The role of school counselor in the school setting is in transition. Ellis (1991) said:

> A new school of thought is emerging among educators and counselors. Unlike the reform movement of the past decade, this new movement takes full account of students' personal needs in formulating educational goals. Proponents of this school of thought recognize the close relationship between students' academic development and their personal growth; accordingly, they are seeking to place guidance at the heart of the educational process. (p. 70)

To meet this challenge, today's counselors need to broaden their roles to include teaching as part of the counseling process within the school setting. Dealing with crises and doing remedial work will continue to be important. In addition, however, they must move into an arena that includes the developmental/preventive component. In this approach, the counselor acts in a proactive, goal-oriented way that is comprehensive and integrated into the school's total educational process. This comprehensive approach is called developmental guidance and counseling.

DEVELOPMENTAL/PREVENTIVE MODELS

Several models advocate a strong developmental/preventive focus. Developmental guidance and counseling models (Gysbers and Henderson 1988; Myrick 1987; Vernon and Strub 1990–91) came on the scene in the early 1970s. In 1979, the American School Counselor Association adopted this approach and issued the following definition of developmental guidance:

> Developmental guidance is that component of all guidance efforts which fosters planned interventions within educational and other human services programs at all points in the human life cycle to vigorously stimulate and actively facilitate the total development of individuals in all areas: i.e., personal, social, career, emotional, moral-ethical, cognitive, and aesthetic; and to promote the integration of the several components into an individual's life style. (ASCA Revised, 1984)

The developmental guidance and counseling program is a comprehensive approach that integrates a curriculum of counseling into the total educational process for all students in the school, rather than seeing it as peripheral or tangential.

Incorporated into the developmental guidance and counseling model are seven principles identified by Myrick (1987):

1. Developmental guidance is for all students.
2. Developmental guidance has an organized and planned curriculum.
3. Developmental guidance is sequential and flexible.
4. Developmental guidance is an integrated part of the total educational process.
5. Developmental guidance involves all school personnel.
6. Developmental guidance helps students learn more effectively and efficiently.
7. Developmental guidance includes counselors who provide specialized counseling services and interventions.

In addition, we believe the following principles are applicable in developmental models:

1. Developmental guidance and counseling helps students cope

with issues and problems that are normal to growing up and becoming adults.
2. Developmental guidance and counseling considers the nature of human development, including the general stages and tasks of normal maturation.
3. Developmental guidance and counseling encompasses three approaches: remedial, crisis, and preventive.

COUNSELING ALL STUDENTS IN THE CLASSROOM

The core component of a developmental guidance and counseling program is the preventive aspect. Certainly prevention can be integrated into individual and small-group counseling, but its primary infusion comes through the counseling and guidance curriculum offered in the classroom. This counseling program is available to *all* students in the school, not just those few who can be aided through individual counseling. Through the classroom curriculum, students at every grade level, throughout the entire academic year, are offered programming that attends to students' developmental level and personal needs.

The developmental guidance and counseling model spans the K–12 years. It is based on the concept that children pass through various developmental stages as they grow and mature. For children to develop in a healthy manner, they must successfully progress through certain kinds of learning and development. Therefore, within the model, student competencies, based on developmental learning theory, are identified for each grade level. These student competencies become the objectives from which the school counselor begins to develop a counseling curriculum.

Student competencies differ among school districts and states. The American School Counselor Association (1990) published a guide for school counselors that suggests student competencies for each grade level. States and school districts use these to write their own list of competencies applicable to their situations and settings. Student competencies typically are organized around three domains of development: personal/social, career/vocational, and academic/learning (discussed later in the chapter).[1]

Since Gysbers's seminal work in the 1970s, developmental models have been adopted throughout the country by state departments of

---

[1]For further information on student competencies, write ASCA, 5999 Stevenson Avenue, Alexandria, VA 22304.

education (e.g., Wisconsin, Oklahoma, Louisiana, Iowa), and by school districts (i.e., San Antonio, Texas, and Lincoln, Nebraska). Presentations and workshops are offered on how to design and implement this programming in school settings, and counselor education training programs have begun to teach this model to school counselors in training.

Some reasons for this national trend are:

1. Today's youth are trying to grow up in a complicated and fast-changing society. Their complex needs of personal and social adjustment, academic proficiency, and career and vocational awareness can be met best through a comprehensive, integrative program.
2. Counselors in the schools cannot effectively use a one-to-one counseling approach alone, as it provides services to only a few students. Developmental programming in the classroom enables counselors, teachers, and people in the community to impact all students in their personal, academic, and career development.
3. As the developmental approach is implemented, it becomes cost-effective by providing services to all students in an accountable manner.

THE COUNSELOR'S NEW ROLE AS EDUCATOR

In the past some teachers went into the field of counseling to escape the classroom. Today's developmental counselors must see the classroom as the "front line" of their work. In returning to the mainstream of education, counselors must have the professional skills needed to fulfill all the roles they will be called upon to perform: teacher, therapist, group facilitator, career specialist, crisis manager, consultant, administrator, researcher, college specialist, test interpreter. When administrators hear an explanation of the curriculum of counseling, they generally are highly supportive and willing to help make it possible.

A fully developed counseling curriculum requires approximately 20–25 percent of the counselor's time. Many counselors wonder how they will have the time to implement a counseling curriculum. It is a matter of administrative support and program management. The following time utilization plan has proved workable at the high school level:

individual and group counseling ...25–30%
developmental programming 20–25%
placement (internal and external)........18%
administrative coordination.................15%
information-giving 10%

testing 5%

evaluation/follow-up 2%

Even though large-group counseling is vital to the developmental/ preventive focus, counselor time still must be allocated to small-group counseling and individual counseling, as suggested above.

As with any comprehensive program, developmental programming must incorporate a team approach if it is to effectively meet the needs of all students. This means that teachers must be active participants. Counselors who are trained and prepared in the developmental model take the lead in establishing the curriculum, but they do so in collaboration with teachers, drawing upon their expertise. Counselors can train teachers in the types of lessons and the process desired for a curriculum of counseling. As counselors meet with the large groups, they can model the teaching of personal/social, academic, and career lessons that enhance and promote academic growth. Team teaching is encouraged. Ideally, classroom teachers assume some of the responsibility for teaching the lessons and meeting the objectives identified in the counseling curriculum. For example, students might be given an assignment to write an essay on a career option.

Because time during the school day is at a premium, creative planning is necessary to implement developmental programming. This may be easier at the grade school level because the suggested thirty minutes a week for counselors to come into the classroom is easier to fit into the teacher's schedule. In the upper grades, where students are attending classes in periods, the counselor may have to negotiate alternatives for leading classroom programs. In some schools, teachers of English, science, social studies, physical education, or other classes allow the counselor to deliver the curriculum in the classroom within agreed-upon timeframes. In other schools a guidance and counseling period has been established around homerooms or split lunch periods. Myrick (1987) suggested implementing a program in which teachers, serving as student advisors become involved in developmental guidance and counseling during homeroom or other designated periods.

Cooperation is a key to planning and delivering an effective developmental program. The counselor is under heavy scrutiny to use classroom time effectively and efficiently. Students, faculty, and administrators are critics of how the program is evolving. An evaluation procedure is necessary to establish accountability. Developmental counseling programs must have some system in place to measure outcomes of the student competencies and objectives of the established curriculum.

Reporting outcomes to the faculty and administration is a positive step in gaining support. In addition, counselors should install evaluation guidelines to improve effectiveness in future student programming.

Becoming active in reforming school counseling, and changing it from an ancillary role to an integral role in the total educational process, is no easy task. From a developmental perspective, working as an educator in the classroom may require major shifts in the counselor's role and behaviors. Infusing objectives from a curriculum of counseling into other areas of teaching requires creativity by classroom and subject teachers. With careful planning, this change can be highly productive and is well worth the effort. Students will benefit by having access to a curriculum of counseling over their school years that assists in their positive development and refinement of skills for living, through better decision-making, self-awareness, and coping abilities. Schools will benefit from a curriculum that addresses the complex personal developmental needs of its students, in addition to their academic subject matter needs. The curriculum will give students the tools to approach life's challenges, minimizing the number and severity of student difficulties.

For school counselors, this new role means becoming more active and taking an integral role in the total school curriculum. It means moving into the classroom, becoming curriculum specialists, and holding themselves and their programs accountable. The profession can no longer hide behind closed doors or unclear goals. To move into the developmental program is to put one's expertise on display and to be accountable for one's work. It is a worthy challenge.

MAJOR PRINCIPLES IN A CURRICULUM OF COUNSELING

A curriculum of counseling is based on the premise that all students need assistance throughout their school years in accomplishing developmental tasks. Successfully achieving these skills can lead each student to a sense of personal fulfillment and enhance the quality of life as a productive person in society.

A curriculum of counseling provides a systematic approach for exposing students to lessons appropriate to their developmental level. The lessons are presented so that students are able to learn, understand, and eventually master aspects of personal-social development, vocational/career development, and academic/educational development. The primary goal is to present learning in these areas so students can develop healthy ways to cope and deal with situations that arise during their life's journey. Students can work through developmental and situational crises if they are able to call upon the skills they learned to confront difficulties when they arise. As an example, students might role-play appropriate ways of handling their feelings when they are angry at school. Having the students explore alternative ways of reacting and consider the consequences of their behaviors in situations that are not emotionally charged gives students a better understanding without the emotional component. When the students are faced with a real situation in their personal lives, they will be able to make more appropriate, positive decisions.

Like any other curriculum in the educational schema, a curriculum of counseling must be comprehensive and ongoing, sensitive to the student's readiness to learn in the areas of personal-social, vocational, and academic development. Lessons emphasizing prevention should begin at the elementary level and progress to more difficult or abstract levels as the student's cognitive and emotional development allows. All students can benefit from lessons that promote positive self-esteem, for example, but the way the counselor approaches this will be quite different, depending upon the grade level. Adults and preschoolers can benefit from lessons on this topic as well. Main ideas and themes must be repeated each year in ways that enhance the student's learning and relate to age-level experiences. One way this can be done is to establish monthly themes for each grade level each year. Units taught during that month reflect the theme in a developmentally appropriate lesson. One school district that has adopted this approach has established the following themes (Winneconne Developmental Guidance Program 1990, 6):

August	• Getting Acquainted/Orientation/Transition
September	• Academic Fitness/Self-Evaluation/Goal-Setting
October	• Choices and Consequences/Decision-Making
November	• Liking Me/Self-Esteem
December	• Family
January	• Wellness/Lifestyles/Stress Management
February	• Friendship/Interpersonal Relationship Skills
March	• Citizenship/Civic and Social Responsibility
April	• Feelings/Communication/Coping
May	• Careers/Exploration/Planning

The curriculum must have organization and format. Activities should be sequential and follow a simple and consistent format. Goals related to student competencies should be set for each grade level and outcomes observed. When students understand the meaning behind their educational programming and know what to expect, they will benefit and will likely become the program's most avid supporters. Students, along with other faculty, staff, and parents, need to see the counseling curriculum as an integral component within the total instructional program.

Within the organizational structure of the curriculum of counseling, units and lesson plans must be designed for each grade level. Developing the curriculum to fit the needs of a school system is a major task. Counselors must be willing to delve into the plethora of materials available from publishers and glean from them what they believe will be the most appropriate. Curriculum resources can be organized into three-ring binders so they can be shared with other counselors in the school district or neighboring districts. Some of the materials can be used in classroom guidance and counseling programming. These materials should be reviewed and customized according to the unique characteristics of the setting. (Designing a lesson plan for a developmental program and teaching the lesson in the classroom are discussed in detail later in this chapter.)

A curriculum in counseling must be flexible. As new areas of need arise in a program, the curriculum should be amenable to revision and embellishment without beginning again. The toughest time will be at the start-up, when guidance and counseling units have to be created. After a unit has been taught, additional units can be added, and changes made. When appropriate, outside experts can serve as resources within the curriculum. For example, local police officers might come into the classroom to teach a unit on drug awareness. Some school districts hire local professional substance abuse centers to teach a prevention program to their students at all grade levels. Flexibility enables the counseling curriculum to fit the ever-changing needs and circumstances of the setting and the students.

Finally, a curriculum in counseling must be accountable, which requires good planning from the start of a program. Goals and objectives for the curriculum should be written in behavioral and measurable terms. An evaluation should be done at the end of the units to determine if the students understood and grasped the topic or issue presented. To accomplish this, students might respond to a game or informal test that would not be used for grading. Classroom teachers could respond to any new behaviors they observe in the students. Year-end evaluations should be done to reflect the work and curriculum put forth by the counseling program. By planning ahead and developing evaluative materials from the beginning, the counseling curriculum has a much better chance to be successful and find favor with parents, faculty, and administrators.

All the components in a curriculum of counseling must work

together in a holistic and meaningful way. This comprehensive approach helps the counselors involved in the curriculum to see how their work contributes to students' healthy development. The developmental approach centers on the development and attainment of student competencies in three areas of living: personal/social, career/vocational, and academic/learning. To do a thorough job, planners involved in the developmental model need to carefully consider three components for each area: life themes, life transitions, and life skills that affect human beings as they grow and develop. We have adopted the concept of life themes, life transitions, and life skills from Drum and Knott (1977) in designing student development programs for high schools and university counseling and development centers.

THE STUDENT DEVELOPMENT PROGRAM MODEL

Developmental counseling programming is a structured, sequenced, large-group activity, directed to the needs and interests of all students in the school, and sensitive to the developmental competencies and interests of students at different grade levels. It is a helping process in which the counselor and teacher present a series of lessons representing a curriculum of counseling. Figure 9.1 depicts the student development program model and the interrelatedness of each aspect with the three areas of development discussed. The developmental approach targets the accomplishment of student competencies in three areas of living: personal/social, career/vocational, and academic/learning development.

1. *Personal/social*: Identifies competencies that will assist students in understanding and expressing self, as well as looking at how they relate to others as individuals and in groups; helps students see how their thinking, feelings, and behaviors shape their personality, their being, and their interpersonal relationships.
2. *Career/vocational*: Targets competencies that will assist students in exploring career possibilities and opportunities; helps students with career decision-making and enables them to make a successful transition from school to the world of work.
3. *Academic/learning*: Provides activities and experiences that develop competencies leading to a student's educational success; promotes optimum development of each student's learning potential.

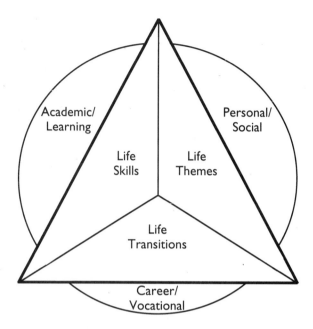

Figure 9.1
STUDENT DEVELOPMENT PROGRAM MODEL

When students are taught a curriculum emphasizing these three areas at every grade level, the preventive aspect is clear. The goal is to teach the students how to deal with normal developmental issues that will lead to self-awareness, increased self-esteem, positive relationships with others, goal-setting, decision-making, career exploration, and study skills. Knowledge of these concepts then can be translated into skills or tools that will lead to healthy choices and responses when students face difficulties or decisions.

Planners of the student development program model also identify specific goals, issues, and situations, addressed in the classroom experience, in the areas of:

1. *Life themes*: major recurring situations and issues throughout the lifespan that can be addressed developmentally so people can adequately respond to and deal with them. Certain situations occur again and again throughout life. Each time they appear, they may have to be addressed differently, perhaps at a more intensive level, requiring modifications or different skills. Life themes are best approached by teaching life skills that relate to

specific recurring situations. As people grow and mature, the best method to handle or cope with these situations may change. Examples of life themes are friendship and love, stress, personal safety, and responsibility.

2. *Life transitions*: major changes and passages throughout the lifespan that impact on a person and necessitate adapting and restructuring current behaviors and realities. Life transitions are specific to points in a person's life at which significant changes occur. Some of these are common to most people, such as starting school and obtaining a driver's license, moving, and the like. Other transitions occur at varying times, such as first job, first love, or death of a significant grandparent or parent. Some students go through painful life transitions before most people do, such as serious illness, divorce of parents, and serious injury. Including life transitions in the curriculum is critical so students can begin to prepare for anxious times and crises by identifying life skills that may help them cope effectively when the situation does present itself.

3. *Life skills*: learned behaviors that enable a person to perform the essential tasks of normal developmental growth throughout the lifespan. These are taught in the counseling curriculum continually. Most relate heavily to the personal/social area and include self-acceptance, listening, communication, problem-solving, values clarification, and the like.

Life themes and life transitions necessitate learning life skills to be able to handle recurring situations, issues, changes, and life passages. As we identify the themes and transitions in the lives of students preschool–12, we should design and implement programs that will:

- create an awareness of the dynamics involved in each life theme and transition
- help individuals understand how the themes and transitions affect them
- teach them how to change or modify their behaviors to adjust to or resolve specific life themes or transitions

For example, in teaching about stress, we explain that sometimes unpleasant circumstances result in an upset stomach or other physical manifestation. When students can discuss how they feel about unpleasant situations and the effects of these situations, we can teach them how to develop coping skills to deal with the unpleasant situations.

Working Within the Structural Framework

As a curriculum of counseling is developed, certain essential topics have to be included at every grade level throughout the curriculum. Counselors are encouraged to prioritize the essential topics and develop units and lessons one topic at a time across the K–12 curriculum. Some planners set up their curriculum to focus on decision-making in fifth grade and careers in sixth, for example. Haphazard or unsequential planning should be avoided. In the most effective programs, essential topics appear throughout the K–12 curriculum; these topics are presented each year so they can be sequential and build upon each other. Suggested essential topics are listed in Table 9.1.

Another set of topics can be termed "special needs." Special needs topics may be instituted in a school or community because of the unique needs or characteristics of the local community. As examples, units on death or loss may be needed if a school has had a series of suicides or catastrophic deaths of some of its students; units on gangs may be needed in some schools.

Figure 9.2 contains a structural framework form that can assist counselors in designing classroom guidance and counseling programs. Often the hardest step in a developmental guidance and counseling program is getting started. This format can be used to begin a new program or to reassess an ongoing program. In using the form:

1. Select a grade level.
2. Read and review the ASCA student competencies or a source that addresses student needs based on their developmental level.
3. Consider other pertinent information gathered from needs assessments of students, teachers, parents, and administrators.
4. In the appropriate column, list important life themes, life transitions, and life skills you think should be accomplished at that grade level.

The suggested essential K–12 topics for a student development curriculum of counseling (as listed in Table 9.1) cover the personal/ social, career/vocational, and academic/learning areas. Within each area, the three components of life skills, life themes, and life transitions add meaningful organization to the specific units for each of the developmental areas. This structural framework enables counselors to identify the core areas of the counseling curriculum, topics essential in all programs and topics unique to the individual school setting.

Identifying topics is only the first step, however. Objectives should be developed for each topic from kindergarten through the senior year in

Table 9.1

K–12 TOPICS IN THE ESSENTIAL AREAS

Personal/Social Area

Life Themes	Life Transitions	Life Skills
Self-Concept Development	Family Changes (new siblings, death, divorce)	Self-Awareness
Friendship and Love	New School Orientation	Self-Acceptance
Change	Significant Life Events (puberty, driver's license, first job)	Listening Skills
Conflicts		Communication Skills
Stress		Values Clarification
Values		Problem-Solving
Personal Safety		Relationships Skills
Responsibility	Loss of Friends and Loved Ones	Coping Skills
Grief and Loss		Behavior Management

Career/Vocational Area

Career Exploration	Career Fantasy to Career Exploration	Planning
Use of Leisure Time	Exploration to Tentative Career Choice	Goal-Setting
Attitude Toward Work		Career Decision-Making
Dual-Career Couples	Career Decisions	Employment-Seeking Skills

Academic/Learning Area

Motivations	Preschool to Elementary	Study Skills
Learning Styles	Elementary to Middle School	Time Management
Learning Deficiencies	Middle School to High School	Speech and Test Anxiety Reduction
Discipline vs. Procrastination	High School to College	Critical Thinking
Lifelong Learning	High School to Work	Analysis and Synthesis

high school. These objectives will serve as the basis for creating units and lessons on each of these topics into a sequential, grade-level curriculum. Vernon and Strub (1990–91) identified objectives for the self-concept topic as follows:

Steps:
1. Identify school level (i.e., elementary, middle, or high school).
2. Identify developmental tasks and needed competencies.
3. Utilize professional assessment and/or needs assessment.
4. Identify developmental program based on the model.

Definitions:

Life Themes: Major recurring situations and issues throughout the lifespan which need to be addressed developmentally so that people can adequately respond to these situations and cope with these issues.

Life Transitions: Major changes and/or passages throughout the lifespan that impact on a person in such a way as to necessitate adaption and restructuring of current behaviors and realities.

Life Skills: Learned behaviors which enable a person to perform the essential tasks of normal developmental growth throughout the lifespan (e.g., problem-solving).

	LIFE THEMES	LIFE TRANSITIONS	LIFE SKILLS
Academic			
Personal/ Social			
Career			

Figure 9.2
STRUCTURAL FRAMEWORK FORM FOR A DEVELOPMENTAL COUNSELING PROGRAM

Primary

To identify physical characteristics.

To recognize/appreciate physical similarities and differences between people.

To identify ways in which individuals are unique.

To learn that people have many different kinds of qualities and characteristics.

To recognize how people grow and change.

To identify personal strengths.

To learn that everyone makes mistakes.

To identify individual interests.

To learn that people aren't better or worse just because they are different.

To learn that interests and abilities change.

To develop an awareness of behavior in various situations.

To learn to make positive self-statements.

To recognize special personal traits.

To identify how exercise and nutrition affect mental health.

To describe specific ways to care for one's body.

To identify personal abilities.

To describe one's own unique physical characteristics.

To describe one's own unique abilities.

To identify personal limitations.

To recognize that personal strengths and limitations will change.

Intermediate

To learn that making mistakes doesn't make one good or bad.

To identify personal mistakes and what was learned from them.

To develop an awareness of individual responses in different situations.

To recognize that negatively comparing their physical differences, characteristics, or abilities to others is unnecessary.

To learn that "being perfect" isn't possible.

To recognize that certain aspects of one's self can be changed and that certain aspects can't change.

To differentiate between poor performance in one area vs. being a complete failure.

To identify personal abilities/strengths.

To differentiate between positive and negative self-talk (messages).

To learn to use positive self-talk.

To identify positive/negative behaviors.

To identify ways in which one's body is special.

To recognize ways in which they are important to themselves and to others.

To identify personal characteristics valued in self.

To describe ways in which abilities and interests change over time.

To learn that a person is special regardless of how he or she behaves.

To learn that being male and female are equally special.

To identify sexist/nonsexist ways to describe males and females.

To learn to describe individual abilities without stereotyping them as male/female.

Junior High

To identify the physical, intellectual, emotional, social, and spiritual aspects of self.
To recognize degrees of control over personal success and failure.
To learn to accept compliments and criticism.
To identify positive ways to maintain a healthy body, mind, and spirit.
To identify "self put-downs" and learn to apply positive self-talk.
To identify sex-role stereotypes and how this limits both male and females.
To learn the difference between "who one is" and "how one behaves"; poor behavior doesn't imply that the person is no good.
To identify one's positive and negative attitudes and to develop ways to avoid excess negativity.
To learn ways to value self even if others don't treat you as a worthwhile person.
To identify positive ways to behave in a variety of situations.
To differentiate between "bragging" and sharing positive aspects of self.
To identify unique aspects of one's personality.
To learn to compare their abilities to others without self put-down.
To learn the relationship between caring for and valuing self and treating one's body in healthy ways.
To identify positive aspects of being a male or a female.
To identify characteristics they value in themselves.
To recognize positive ways of displaying a sense of humor.
To identify ways to develop a sense of personal power: an "I can" attitude.
To identify ways in which individuals become self-motivated.

High School

To identify personal values.
To identify one's interests and abilities in order to formulate personal goals.
To identify positive ways of "taking care of" oneself.
To differentiate between self-defeating and self-enhancing behaviors and how they relate to one's view of self.
To learn that failure and rejection are not a reflection on one's self-worth.
To learn ways to access personal strengths and positive self-talk in coping with difficult situations.
To differentiate criticism of "who one is" from "what one does."
To identify how one's wants and needs influence future planning.
To develop an understanding of the various roles people play.
To recognize the connection between how one views him/herself and how she/he behaves.
To identify sources of personal strengths/limitations.
To clarify goals and aspirations.

To identify personal skills that contribute to satisfactory physical and mental health.

To describe ways in which sex-stereotyping limits individual options.

To identify risk-taking behaviors.

To describe personal risk-taking behavior and to learn to assess the positive/negative impact of such behavior.

To learn to identify one's responsible and irresponsible behaviors.

To distinguish between self-defeating and self-enhancing behaviors.

To identify areas of personal accomplishment and achievement.

To develop an understanding of how individual contributions impact society. (pp. 26–28)

Once objectives have been established, the counselor is ready to design the appropriate units and lesson plans to meet those objectives.

How To Design A Lesson

School counselors who have been trained in a teacher preparation program have a distinct advantage in developing classroom developmental counseling lessons. Motivation, student behavior and achievement, and discipline are among the key considerations for counselors entering the classroom. Counselors who have never had formal training should at least familiarize themselves with affective instructional programs for the classroom.

A Knowledge Base of Teaching Skills

Good (1979), Hunter (1976), and Stallings (1984) have developed instructional programs that provide classroom teachers a format and process shown to be effective. Other programs also can increase the knowledge and confidence of school counselors who work in the large-group setting, by offering innovative techniques for use in the classroom. One of these approaches is called *cooperative learning* (Johnson and Johnson 1987). According to Jones and Jones (1990) a cooperative learning approach "not only enhances learning and positive attitudes toward both subject matter and school in general, but it also creates positive peer relationships and enhances students self-esteem'' (p. 233). Because self-esteem is always a by-product and sometimes even the prime objective in a classroom guidance unit, methods that enhance its potential are imperative.

Another methodology with a strong impact on what takes place in the classroom has been introduced by Purkey and Schmidt (1990) and Purkey and Novak (1984). Called "invitational learning," this approach attempts to elevate the importance of school and learning in an environment that heavily emphasizes the unique worth, respect, and dignity of each student. It moves beyond the premise that self-esteem is something that should be the theme of an occasional classroom activity and, instead, holds that the entire educational experience should validate individual worth.

Purkey and Schmidt (1990) stressed that school counselors and teachers must act in a way that makes school inviting to children. By modeling and demonstrating concrete humanistic behavior, the counselor and teacher can help the student relate to the environment, become assertive by developing a sense of control within the classroom, be willing to try new things and make mistakes, and be able to cope with the world. Models such as Johnson and Johnson's and Purkey's provide a base of knowledge for the counselor who will be active in the school setting as the large-group leader, enabling what is learned and experienced within the classroom to be generalized into the entire school, the family, and the community.

Given this background on teaching methodology, the counselor needs to undertake the extensive planning and specific preparation described here before implementing developmental counseling programming in the classroom.

Format for Developmental Counseling Units and Lessons

The most common approach for a counseling curriculum is to develop units organized around a theme or central idea. These themes may arise out of the life-themes, life-transitions, or life-skills components discussed earlier. The unit may evolve as the result of a needs assessment or an identified outcome desired from the students, or it may reflect grade level developmental competencies. Myrick (1987) suggested that many units should be done yearly, with appropriate readiness skills for each grade level, and other units may be created in response to specific needs or events. For example, if the school is beginning to see the inklings of gang activity, the counselor may elect to introduce a unit on gang awareness, taking care to provide appropriate sequences in units that match the developmental level.

Units usually have an overall theme and are composed of several lessons or sessions. Although the number of sessions varies with the topic, time allocation, and age level, anywhere from four to ten sessions is appropriate. Each unit also should include general objectives and goals the counselor intends to meet throughout the sessions. A unit format should include the following:

Grade Level
Unit Name or Topic
Appropriate Grade-Level Competencies
Rationale for Unit
Unit Purpose
Unit Objectives
Number of Sessions
Evaluation Criteria and Method

Sometimes a brief rationale, explaining why this unit is important, should be included in the curriculum. This rationale can be presented to the administration, staff, and faculty, synopsizing the "what and why" of the curriculum. This is especially important if the counselor develops units on sensitive issues such as AIDS or death and loss.

The classroom lesson is the heart of the developmental counseling program. Building upon a model developed by Vernon (1989), it is suggested that each lesson should contain the following components:

1. *Purpose and Objectives*
   Begin the lesson with a purpose and an objective that you intend to accomplish in that lesson. Write the objectives in specific terms of a performance/measurable outcome. For example: The student will respond to another by using an "I message" appropriately. Avoid broad objectives like: The student will develop an understanding of better communication skills.

2. *Stimulus Activity*
   Design a well-planned activity that will assist you in fulfilling that objective. This stimulus activity may be a story, film, role-play, speaker, simulation, reading assignment, etc. Be careful not to use all your allotted time in the activity. It is not the most important part of the lesson but should only "set the stage" for what you want to accomplish with the students . Be sure to include a list of materials and/or supplies you will need in this lesson.

3. *Content-Level Discussion*
   Discuss the stimulus activity at a *content* level. For example, ask the students to share in pairs what they thought was going on in the story, or work in small groups and tell what the main problem in the video was. Again, keep this section relatively short and simple. Focus on what students did in the activity and what main concepts were presented.

4. *Personal-Level Discussion*
   Discuss the stimulus activity at a *personal* level. For example, one may ask students to think of when they may have had a similar experience, or if it has happened to them, or how they felt. One may also brainstorm ideas as to what students think should be done, or what they would do to handle the situation. In this component the students apply the main concepts to their

personal situations. Be sure to give this component ample time; *it is the key to the lesson.* In addition, counselors will find that most of the materials applicable to the units will not contain questions that focus on the personal level; thus, the counselor will need to pay special attention to this and spend time developing these questions.

5. *Closure*

Process the session and bring some closure to the group: With this step one can utilize the group process skills in asking the students what they learned in the session. This might include new insights about themselves or about others.

The final step requiring consideration in the developmental counseling unit is evaluation, which must be planned from the start. It becomes essential in reporting the value and benefit outcomes to administrative and school board personnel. It also benefits the classroom teacher and the student by calling attention to the work he or she is doing and the potential impact it is having on students' thinking, feeling, and behavior.

Evaluations can be done at the end of each session or at the end of a unit. The evaluations should be kept simple and appropriate to the grade level, and they can be creative. Art or creative writing projects can be used. The students might form small groups and role-play to the rest of the class what they have learned. Checklists or surveys should pinpoint the objectives identified at the start of the unit. The most important purpose of the evaluations is to gain insight into the effectiveness of the unit so it can be changed when the unit is taught again in the future. In an effective developmental counseling program, evaluation and accountability go hand-in-hand.

Utilizing this lesson plan format shown in Figure 9.3, two examples of lessons are provided, one for the elementary school and one for the secondary school. Both have the theme of problem-solving/ decision-making

Unit development and lesson design are challenging and require creativity. Ideas can be found in affective education materials or borrowed from other counseling programs. When using ready-made curricula, it should be adapted, as necessary, to the unique needs and objectives of your situation. A resource list of suggested affective education materials is found at the end of this chapter.

How to Conduct Classroom Guidance and Counseling Lessons

For counselors, teaching in a classroom is much different from counseling in an office. Counselors with prior teaching experience may find the

Lesson #_____ Topic _____

(1) Lesson Objectives _____

_____

Materials _____

(2) Stimulus Activity _____

(procedure) _____

_____

(3) Content-Level Discussion Questions

    a) _____

    b) _____

    c) _____

(4) Personal-Level Discussion Questions

    a) _____

    b) _____

    c) _____

(5) Closure _____

Evaluation (may be optional)_____

Notes:

Figure 9.3
LESSON PLAN FORMAT

LESSON EXAMPLE ON PROBLEM-SOLVING/ DECISION-MAKING ACTIVITY, GRADES 1–2.

Lesson #3 of 6

Topic: Big and Little Choices

Lesson Objective: To learn to distinguish between major and minor problems and to recognize that these perceptions can change.

Materials: Magazine pictures of people in different situations; a large piece of posterboard per each two students; crayons or markers as needed

Stimulus Activity: Big and Little Choices

Procedure:
1. Display a variety of magazine pictures showing people in each of the following situations: grocery shopping, reading the classified ads, looking at a new house to buy, and trying on some new shoes.
2. Discuss each picture and identify the decisions connected with the pictures: selecting food to eat, a new job, a new house, a new pair of shoes.
3. Categorize each decision as being either major (big) or minor (little), and explain that one determines whether a decision is major or minor by considering the consequences of the decision (what the long-term effects will be, whether the decision will mean big changes in one's life, etc.).
4. Illustrate that, regardless of whether a decision is major or minor, the decision-making process follows the same steps: gathering information, identifying alternatives, and understanding consequences. For example, in deciding what shoes to buy (a minor decision), you first need to know where you can get shoes. Then you need to look at all the sizes, styles, colors, and prices. What happens if you select a black pair instead of brown? Hightops instead of lowcuts? In deciding whether to buy a new house (a major decision), a person needs to know what houses

are available and where, as well as how much they cost and how much money the person can afford to spend. What are the neighborhoods like? How will it affect a family to move? Is moving something the family really wants to do?

5. Have students select a partner and together create a display chart of big and little decisions, using additional magazine pictures.

6. Direct sharing of completed charts.

Content-Level
Discussion Questions:
1. What is the difference between a big (major) decision and a little (minor) one?

2. Can the same decision be a big one for one person and a small one for another person? (An example would be a teenager's choosing a new after-school job and a parent's choosing a new job to help support a family.)

3. What makes a decision major or minor?

Personal-Level
Discussion Questions:
1. Has anyone in your family ever made a major decision? What was it? How did it affect your family?

2. What kinds of decisions do you usually make?

3. Why is making good minor decisions important practice for you?

Closure
(To the Leader):
Children often minimize the importance of their decision-making because they know their decisions are most often minor ones. It is necessary to develop childrens' sense of their own power and pride in making even small decisions. Furthermore, it may be helpful to remind children that effective decision-making skills are learned and, as such, require practice that can be provided by making good minor decisions on a daily basis.

Source: From *Thinking, Feeling, Behaving* by A. Vernon (Champaign, IL: Research Press, 1989), 57–58.

LESSON EXAMPLE ON PROBLEM-SOLVING/ DECISION-MAKING ACTIVITY, GRADE 10

Lesson #2 of 6

Topic: Decision-Making

Lesson Objective: To know that decisions range from minor importance to major importance.

To know that different decisions require different degrees of thought.

Materials: Handout, "Decisions Come in All Colors"

Stimulus Activity: Decisions Come in All Colors

Procedure: 1. Give a brief explanation that we make many decisions each day, some of which are routine and may be important or unimportant, and others that have much more importance and require more attention.
2. Distribute handouts to students and ask them to rate the ten decisions according to the scale.

Content-Level
Discussion Questions: 1. What are the differences between major decisions and minor decisions?
2. As decisions become more important, what thought processes must we go through before taking action on a decision?

Personal-Level
Discussion Questions: 1. Perhaps not everyone will agree on the same degree of importance for each decision. Why?
2. Think of some decisions that you will be making in the next day and year. Choose a minor decision and a major decision and discuss with your partner its degree of importance and how you will go about making that decision.

Closure

(To the Leader): We make many decisions each day, some of which are routine and unimportant, and others that have more importance and require more attention. Still others may be of great importance and likely will require a good deal of time and study before reaching a decision. We must be able to differentiate major and minor decisions in order to know relatively how much time to spend on a given decision.

Decisions Come in All Colors

Let's look at the scale below:

1	2	3	4	5
Not under your control; made primarily by others.	Made almost routinely without thinking about it.	Think about it but do not really study it.	Do some self-study, and/or talk to some others before deciding.	Much time, thought, and investigating before deciding.

Read the ten decisions listed below that you may have to make. Following each statement, record how you would classify its relative importance according to the above scale. If the statement does not apply to you, write in one that does apply.

1. Whether to ride the bus to school. _____
2. Whether to attend math class or skip and talk to a friend. _____
3. What clothes to wear today. _____
4. Whether to get a part-time job. _____
5. Whether to brush my teeth this morning. _____
6. Whether to get a job or go to college. _____
7. What I must do to get an A in English. _____
8. Whether to study at home tonight. _____
9. Whether to break up with my boy/girlfriend. _____
10. Whether to cheat on a test. _____

Is your classification of each of these decisions the same as the other members of the group? Why or why not? _____

This program is concerned primarily with decision-making as it pertains to decisions one could classify in Category 4 or 5 above, especially Category 5.

rewards of classroom teaching to be an enjoyable part of their total counseling work. In conducting classroom developmental programming, the counselor and the classroom teacher have to work together. The counselor teaches some lessons. Others are led by classroom teachers or qualified community people in a six-week unit on feelings. For example, the counselor may teach three sessions and the teacher the last three sessions. The school counselor is responsible for implementing the counseling curriculum and for assisting and coordinating teachers who are also involved. This may include in-service training, team teaching, or modeling by the counselor.

Whereas normal classroom teaching centers on subject matter, teaching a counseling curriculum, or developmental programming, centers on content that is much more personalized. The curriculum of counseling (life themes, life transitions, and life skills) necessarily means the counselor or teacher has to personalize the content to each student. Teachers have to differentiate teaching academic content from teaching a curriculum that is more process-focused and phenomenological. Students integrate learning into their own individual, family, and social environments. Thus, the counselor and teacher alike strive to have the students internalize the content as it relates to their academic, and personal/social lives and then make behavioral changes. In this process of personalizing, the counselor has to be facilitating and empowering in the classroom.

A curriculum of counseling also involves teaching aspects that are more factual and objective. A unit on self-awareness, for example, may include information on nutrition, stress reduction, or using positive self-statements. Those objectives can be infused intentionally into the total school curriculum and become part of a health, English, or reading lesson. Career exploration may be incorporated into a social studies class. In these ways, a curriculum of counseling is integrated within the total curriculum, and attempts to meet the needs of the whole student. The key to this approach is for classroom teachers to be consistent in how they address the objectives within the counseling curriculum, to ensure that students are exposed to developmental, sequenced programming. The counselor should administer this curriculum and be responsible for seeing that age-level competencies and objectives are clearly and appropriately met.

Teaching the curriculum of counseling is one of the most effective ways to develop students' potential, as the content is developmental and preventive, and the counselor or teacher is working with fifteen to thirty or more students at the same time. Teaching a developmental counseling curriculum can further the potential of many individuals. To see potential develop can provide a real source of pride and enjoyment in one's work.

Necessary Classroom Skills

Some skills important to successfully teaching the curriculum of counseling include:

- classroom management
- operation of audiovisual equipment
- time management
- delivery of a presenting stimulus or lecturette
- directing structured activities from dyads to total group
- active listening
- open-ended questioning
- facilitating the group process
- nonjudgmental responses
- pacing
- balancing flexibility and staying on task
- involving all students
- noting cues for follow-up work with individual students

In some cases counselors and teachers may have to renew some of these skills. Counselors and teachers often attend professional development workshops or conferences to become updated on the skills and knowledge necessary to develop and implement a counseling curriculum.

Steps in Classroom Lessons

The following steps in conducting classroom lessons may be helpful:

1. Prepare materials and handouts in advance
2. Place all materials in a filing folder that can be pulled later to update and reuse.
3. Arrange ahead of time for any audiovisual equipment, and know how to operate that equipment or have someone operate it.
4. Be generally knowledgeable and familiar with the entire unit and totally familiar with the lesson that is to be taught that day.
5. Arrive early, and start on time.
6. While keeping the classroom atmosphere relaxed, maintain proper decorum using classroom management skills.
7. Follow the structure of the lesson plan to teach the unit using group-process skills.

8. With an eye on time management, strive to personalize the content with a balance of task orientation and flexibility.
9. Utilize various-sized groups (dyads, triads, groups of six, or total group) for maximum effectiveness in given activities.
10. Vary the traditional classroom style to circles or sitting on the floor.
11. As appropriate, make use of student demonstrations, role-plays, homework with nonthreatening assignments,.
12. Conclude by generalizing the content to applicable situations in the students' world.

Leading classroom lessons has some pitfalls that can be avoided just by being aware of what could happen. Detailed storytelling by the facilitator and students should be avoided. If the counselor is overly flexible, students can ramble in their discussions. Some of the content can be sensitive material for students and their families (e.g., sexual responsibility). It might be well to let parents know in advance about such material. Presented to parents tactfully, their reaction might be defused and actually much appreciated.

THE FUTURE OF DEVELOPMENTAL PROGRAMMING

The promises of developmental programming far outweigh the pitfalls. Developmental programming through classroom lessons is done to avert students' problems or "nip them in the bud." Because the content of developmental programming is preventive in nature, students should be enabled to reach their potential sooner than they would without this intervention.

Practical research is needed to determine the extent to which developmental programming is helpful in problem-solving, fosters achievement, reduces dropout rates, alleviates social/emotional problems, promotes readiness for major transitions, and so on. Collaborative research must be done to evaluate its effects. Developmental programming holds much promise in the development of students' potential and their achievement in the learning/academic, career/vocational, and personal/social areas of the guidance and counseling curriculum.

SUMMARY

This chapter has presented a strong rationale for a counseling curriculum that reaches all students and that is delivered by counselors in collaboration with other student services staff, teachers, and community resource persons. Teachers, properly trained, have an integral role in the delivery of this curriculum when the content of their class activities relates directly to the topics in the counseling curriculum. This curriculum is based on an identification of students' developmental needs pre K–12. A model curriculum has three components: (1) academic learning, (2) career/vocational, and (3) personal/social. In each of the components the curriculum addresses life themes, life transitions, and life skills. The chapter includes information on how to design and implement the counseling curriculum, how to conduct classroom lessons, and examples of lessons and resources. The design and implementation of a developmental counseling curriculum is an effective and productive means for students to succeed academically, interpersonally, and vocationally. In addition, counselors are viewed as providing an essential part of the total school curriculum designed to facilitate change and develop the potential of all students.

REFERENCES

American School Counselor Association. 1990. *Counseling paints a bright future: Student competencies and guide for school counselors.* Alexandria, VA: ASCA.

Drum, D. J., and J. E. Knott. 1977. *Structured groups for facilitating development: Acquiring life skills, resolving life themes, and making life transitions.* New York: Human Sciences Press.

Ellis, T. 1991. Guidance—The heart of education: Three exemplary approaches. In G. R. Walz (compiler), *Counselor quest* (p. 70). Ann Arbor: University of Michigan. (ERIC Counseling and Personnel Services Clearinghouse)

Good, T. 1979. Teacher effectiveness in the elementary school. *Journal of Teacher Education* 30: 52–64.

Gysbers, N. C., and P. Henderson. 1988. *Developing and managing your school guidance program.* Alexandria, VA: American Counseling Association.

Hunter, M. 1976. *Improved instruction.* El Segundo, CA: TIP.

Johnson, D., and R. Johnson. 1987. *Learning together and alone: Cooperative, competitive, and individualistic learnings.* 2d ed. Englewood Cliffs, NJ: Prentice Hall.

Jones V. F., and L. S. Jones. 1990. *Comprehensive classroom management: Motivating and managing students.* 3d ed. Boston: Allyn and Bacon.

Myrick, R. D. 1987. *Developmental guidance and counseling: A practical approach.* Minneapolis: Educational Media Corp.

Purkey, W., and J. Novak. 1984. *Inviting school success. A self-concept approach to teaching and learning.* 2d ed. Belmont, CA: Wadsworth.

Purkey, W., and J. J. Schmidt. 1990. *Invitational learning for counseling and development*. Ann Arbor: University of Michigan. (ERIC Counseling and Personnel Services Clearinghouse)

Stallings, J. 1984. *An accountability model for teacher education*. Nashville, TN: George Peabody College for Teachers, Vanderbilt University, Stallings Teaching and Learning Institute.

Vernon, A. 1989. *Thinking, feeling, behaving: An emotional education curriculum for children*. Champaign, IL: Research Press.

Vernon, A., and R. Strub. 1990–91. *Developmental guidance program implementation*. Counseling and Human Development Foundation Grant Project. Department of Educational Administration and Counseling, University of Northern Iowa, Cedar Falls, IA.

Winneconne School Counselors. 1990. *Winneconne developmental guidance model*. rev. ed. Madison, WI: Department of Public Instruction.

SELECTED RESOURCES FOR DEVELOPING A COUNSELING CURRICULUM

Elementary

Anderson, J. 1985. *Thinking, changing, rearranging: Improving self-esteem in young people*. Eugene, OR: Timberline Press.

Lessons and activities covering areas such as self-esteem, where hurt comes from, beliefs that cause problems, changing language, and changing destructive thoughts. Includes teacher's guide with spirit duplicating masters and student paperback book. Ages 10+.

Berne, P., and L. Savary. 1981. *Building self-esteem in children*. New York: Continuum.

Sixty-eight effective, practical techniques to help parents, educators, and other concerned adults develop healthy relationships with children and foster the attitudes and atmosphere in which self-esteem can flourish.

Borba, C., and M. Borba. 1978. *Self-esteem: A classroom affair—101 ways to help children like themselves*. Minneapolis: Winston Press.

More than 100 ways to build self-esteem in children. Activities teach students to communicate better, use their talents, and be responsible. Provides Me dolls, People recipes, Happygrams, A Picture Dictionary of Feelings, awards, puppets, bulletin boards, and more.

Bowman, R. P., and R. D. Myrick. 1991. *Children helping children: Teaching students to become friendly helpers*. Minneapolis: Educational Media Corp.

Written for elementary and middle school counselors, teachers, and principals who want to improve the learning climate in their schools. Designed to help young students take a more active role in the learning and helping process.

Canfield, J., and H. Wells. 1976. *100 ways to enhance self-concept in the classroom.* Englewood Cliffs, NJ: Prentice Hall.

A good source of quotations, cartoons, and activities that can be used in developing self-awareness and enhancing positive self-concepts. K–12.

Castell, J. D. 1978. *Learning to think and choose: Decision-making episodes for the middle grades.* Santa Monica, CA: Goodyear Publishing.

Provides thirty ready-to-use classroom exercises based on five different ways to reach decisions. Worksheets for individual and group decision-making activities are included.

Cihak, M., and B. Heron. 1980. *Games children should play: Sequential lessons for teaching communication skills in grades K–6.* Glenview, IL: Scott Foresman.

Games that teach children essential communication skills: how to state feelings, needs, and wishes clearly; how to listen to others; how to go through a problem-solving process, assert rights, and discover feelings.

Commissiong, W. 1991. *The best face of all.* Chicago: African-American Images.

The author takes young readers through a litany of facial features and choices asking each time "Which eyes are best?" or "Which are the best noses?" The answers are sometimes practical, sometimes heartwarming, and always insightful.

DUSO Kits (1, II)—Developing understanding of self and others. Circle Pines, MN: American Guidance Service.

Affective education programs for primary students. Puppets, tapes, manual, stories.

El-Shamy, S. 1979. *28 ways to vent anger.* Bloomington, IN: Crescent Publishers.

Applicable for all ages, especially elementary. Safe ways to vent anger and reduce stress.

Feshbach, N., and S. Feshbach. 1983. *Learning to care: Classroom activities for social and affective development.* Glenview, IL: Scott Foresman.

A collection of forty-four ready-to-use activities that help children develop three basic empathic skills: recognizing emotions, role-playing, and emotional responsiveness.

Frey, D., and J. Carlock. 1989. 2d ed. *Enhancing self-esteem.* Muncie, IN: Accelerated Development.

Techniques for enhancing self-esteem, presented in a specific sequence and progression. A multitude of activities that can be used with children, adolescents, and adults.

Good Apple Duplicating Masters Series. *Self-concept.* Carthage, IL: Good Apple.

Helps students improve self-concepts, develop better understanding of themselves and others, and enhance interpersonal relationships. Thought-provoking activities emphasizing skills necessary for a happy and meaningful life. Series includes:

1	*Caring*	4–8 years old
2	*Feelings*	3–8
3	*Coping*	2–8
4	*Sharing*	4–8
5	*Belonging*	2–8
6	*Appreciating*	2–8
7	*Communicating*	3–8
8	*Loving*	3–8
9	*A Growing Me*	K–6
10	*Understanding Me*	K–3

Grollman, E. and S . Grollman. 1985. *Talking about the handicapped (Mainstreaming).* Boston: Beacon Press.

A workbook about mainstreaming students with handicaps into a classroom and the resulting feelings and problems.

Knaus, W. 1984. *Rational emotive education: A manual for elementary school teachers.* New York: Institute for Rational Living.

A comprehensive manual containing a series of exercises utilizing the rational emotive concepts. Primarily elementary.

Kreidler, W. 1984. *Creative conflict resolution: More than 200 activities for keeping peace in the classroom.* Glenview, IL: Scott Foresman.

Methods for improving pupils' communication skills, cooperation, tolerance, and positive emotional expression. Helps students deal with anger, fear, prejudice, and aggression in the K–6 classroom.

Kunjufu, J. 1984. *Developing positive self-images and discipline in black children.* Chicago: African-American Images.

Answers some poignant questions about how to educate black youth.

Mattox, B. *Getting it together.* La Mesa, CA: Pennant Press.

A good collection of moral "valuing dilemmas" for elementary through secondary level.

McDaniel, S., and P. Bielen. 1986. *Project self-esteem: A parent involvement program for elementary-age children.* Rolling Hills Estates, CA: Jalmar Press.

A classroom program designed to raise self-concept. Thoroughly tested, inexpensive, and effective.

Myrick, R., and R. P. Bowman. 1981. *Children helping children: Teaching students to become friendly helpers*. Minneapolis: Educational Media Corp.

Guides and teaches elementary school students to become friendly helpers.

Vernon, A. *Help yourself to a healthier you*. Minneapolis: Burgess Publishers.

Preventive mental health program for grades 1–6. Content includes principles of rational-emotive therapy (self-acceptance, feelings, beliefs, challenging beliefs).

Vernon, A. 1989. *Thinking, feeling, behaving: An emotional education curricula for children grades 1–6*. Champaign, IL: Research Press.

A comprehensive, developmental curriculum including chapters on feelings, behavior management, self-acceptance, problem-solving, and interpersonal relationships.

Youngs, B. 1992. *Enhancing self-esteem: A guide for professional educators*. Rolling Hills Estates, CA: Jalmar.

This comprehensive resource delineates ways in which self-esteem is positively or negatively charged in our workplace, and provides tools for rebuilding and nourishing the educator's self-system.

Secondary

Adams, C., et al. 1984. *No is not enough: Helping teenagers avoid sexual assault*. San Luis Obispo, CA: Impact.

Offers teens and parents information needed to avoid sexual assaults. Features facts and exercises to help parents talk with their teens; information about acquaintance rape; strategies for rape prevention.

Bershad, C, and N. DeMilla. 1983. *The changes and the changed*. Boston: Learning for Life/Management Sciences for Health.

A manual designed to help students explore the decisions they choose to make.

Clark, A. 1980. *How to raise teenager's self-esteem*. Los Angeles: Eurich.

The authors have found that it is definitely possible to enhance self-worth in young people by creating an environment where self-esteem is a valued attribute.

Dolmelsch, P., editor. 1985. *The kids' book about single parent families*. New York: Doubleday.

Written by kids ages eleven through fifteen. Covers immediate problems of living with divorced parents, long-range problems, and experiences.

Frey, D., and J. Carlock. 1984. *Enhancing self-esteem*. Muncie, IN: Accelerated Development.

Techniques for enhancing self-esteem, presented in a specific sequence and progression. For children, adolescents, and adults.

Herzfeld, G., and R. Powell. 1985. *Coping for kids: A complete stress-control program for students ages 8–18.* Center for Applied Research in Education.

Stress and relaxation activities for coping. Comes with two cassettes and a manual.

Johnson, D. W. 1986. *Reaching out—Interpersonal effectiveness and self actualization.* Englewood Cliffs, NJ: Prentice Hall.

A comprehensive source for exercises in interpersonal relations, goal-setting, self-awareness, and communication.

Kehayan, A. 1983. *Sage—Self awareness growth experience: Grades 7–12.* Rolling Hills Estates, CA: Jalmar.

More than 150 activities emphasizing creativity, problem-solving, social intervention, and other developmental areas essential to the behavioral growth of adolescents.

Rusk, T., and R. Read. 1986. *I want to change but I don't know how.* Los Angeles: Price/Stem Sloan Publishing.

A handbook containing a step-by-step program to bring self-awareness and self-acceptance.

Tindall, J., and H. D. Gray. 1986. *Peer power, Book I: Becoming an effective peer helper.* Muncie, IN: Accelerated Development.

Develops eight peer counseling skills: attending, empathy, summarizing, questioning, genuineness, assertiveness, confrontation, and problem-solving.

Tindall, J .1985. *Peer power, Book II: Becoming an effective peer helper.* Muncie, IN: Accelerated Development.

More peer counseling training featuring four new modules for advanced students: drug and alcohol abuse, intervention and prevention, moving toward wellness through stress management, developing human potential.

Vedral, J. 1986. *My parents are driving me crazy.* New York: Ballantine Books.

A book that helps kids explore ways to get along with parents.

Vernon, A. 1989. *Thinking, feeling, behaving: An emotional education curriculum for children.* Champaign, IL: Research Press.

A comprehensive developmental curriculum including chapters on feelings, behavior management, self-acceptance, problem-solving, and interpersonal relationships. Grades 7–12.

Youngs, B. B. 1992. *Six vital ingredients of self-esteem: How to develop them in your students.* Normal, IL: Preferred Learning Enterprises.

Practical ways to help kids manage school, make decisions, accept consequences, manage time, and discipline themselves to set worthwhile goals. Covers developmental stages from age two to eighteen with implications for self-esteem at each age.

10 Counseling with Families

Larry Golden

Counseling and Guidance Program
University of Texas, San Antonio

W hy work with families? Logistically, counseling with an individual child is easier than bringing in the family. Families are confusing, hard to schedule, and potentially offer powerful resistance to therapeutic change. Nevertheless, the point of view in this chapter is that professionals who seek to help children also must work with families.

Some controlled studies demonstrate that helping a child by counseling with his or her family is more effective than counseling with the child individually (Alexander and Parsons 1982; Gurman, Kniskern, and Pinsof 1986). In all fairness, controlled-outcome studies that would enable comparisons between different psychotherapies are few and far between (Kazdin 1988). Controlled experiments in psychotherapy are thwarted by the small number of cases and infinite number of variables, to say nothing of significant ethical problems. If one can trust the evidence of clinical experience and "n of one" case studies, however, there is ample support for a family approach (Kazdin 1988). The family is in a position to support or sabotage therapeutic goals. Even the most healing counselor-child relationship fails to take into account that this child *lives* with his or her parents and siblings, not the counselor.

This chapter highlights several specific approaches to helping children by working with their families. *Brief family consultation* is a time-limited behavioral approach. *Solution-focused therapy* attempts to build quickly on a family's prior success and future goals. *Strategic family therapy* offers powerful methods for changing aspects of the family system that maintain the child's problem behavior. *Parent education* provides instruction in child development, communication skills, and behavior management techniques. An assessment tool is included here to help the practitioner decide which approach to use.

School counselors historically have gotten short shrift in family "therapy." School counselors are neither trained nor, in most cases, permitted to do family therapy. In addition, most schools close their doors by 4:00 p.m. when evening hours are more convenient for families.

This chapter presents an assessment model and a specific methodology, brief family consultation, that public schools have used since 1987. Both solution-focused therapy and strategic family therapy are brief approaches that offer useful techniques, given the time limits imposed by the school counselor's caseload. Regardless of the method or technique, school counselors are advised to be available to parents in the school at least one evening per week. Otherwise we will persist in the futile practice of ignoring the child's most important allies, the parents.

The traditional nuclear family idealized in yesteryear television sitcoms ("Leave It To Beaver," "Father Knows Best," "Ozzie and Harriet") is becoming a minority if not a vanishing species (Bundy and Gumaer 1986; Carlson 1992). Today's children come from a variety of home situations including blended, single-parent, dual-career, and gay and lesbian families.

In some respects, the basic dynamics between parents and children are the same now as they have always been. Parents are still responsible for protecting children and preparing them for autonomy. Today's parents, however, are hard-pressed to provide children with a stable launching platform. For example, divorce and its concomitant stressors frequently have a negative impact on children despite parental intentions (Carlson 1992; Goldman 1986).

Today's children conceivably may reap unexpected benefits from their disordered family lives. Children exposed to the stress of living in blended families, for instance, may develop extraordinary interpersonal skills. These complex families require children to become flexible and alert in relationships. They will have much to offer a world that predictably exposes human beings to rapid change. Regardless of the long-term possibilities, today's families will continue to need support and guidance from mental health professionals during this transitional social and economic era.

ASSESSMENT

Not everyone wants or needs long-term psychotherapy. In physical medicine, treatment of health problems corresponds to their severity. The doctor prescribes an aspirin for a headache but employs surgery or radiation against a brain tumor. Likewise, functional families may benefit from short-term behavioral intervention; dysfunctional ones may require long-term psychotherapy that gets to the root of individual or systemic pathology.

The difference between a functional and a dysfunctional family is a values-laden and complex issue. Who is to say which behaviors are functional and which are not? Some of the ambiguity can be eliminated by defining a functional family as one that can benefit from a short-term and relatively nonintrusive approach. Conversely, a dysfunctional family is likely to require a longer term of more intensive therapy. With these definitions in mind, five variables can enable the counselor to differentiate between a functional and a dysfunctional family: parental resources, time frame of problem behavior, communication, hierarchy of authority, and rapport between helping adults (Golden 1988).

Parental Resources

A relatively simple decision must be made: Can these parents provide for the child's basic needs and still have time and energy left over to follow through on a behavioral plan? A strong marriage, supportive extended family, gainful employment, and financial security are conditions that predict that a family can hold up its end in a team approach. At the other extreme, very young, immature single parents are likely to have fewer resources at their disposal. Multigenerational poverty, criminality, alcoholism, suicide threats, and child abuse confront the counselor with "survival" issues that may not yield to counseling interventions. Under emergency conditions such as these, a child is best helped when counselors connect families to community resources and public authorities.

Time Frame of Problem Behavior

Is the child's misbehavior of short or chronic duration? Consider two familiar diagnoses. An *adjustment disorder* is "a maladaptive reaction to an identifiable psychosocial stressor that occurs within three months of the onset of the stressor" (American Psychiatric Association 1987, 329). The "maladaptive reaction" caused by a stressor can be resolved if the stressor is removed or if the child can learn to better cope with stress. This can be accomplished quickly in brief family consultation or solution-focused therapy. A *conduct disorder* is "a repetitive and persistent pattern of aggressive conduct in which the basic rights of others are violated" (American Psychiatric Association 1987, 53). This "persistent pattern" demands a strong approach, such as strategic family therapy, to change habitual patterns of behavior.

Communication

Can family members communicate well enough to solve problems? According to Satir (1972), people have a normal tendency to close down communication during periods of stress. In dysfunctional families, however, closed communication is the rule, not the exception. This closed system is maintained by yelling, blaming, sarcasm, or, more ominously, silence.

The following interaction illustrates a closed, defensive posture:

Counselor (to child): Tell your parents how much spelling homework you would do next week to earn television privileges.

Mother (to counselor, angrily interrupting): She would have to change her entire personality!

Father: It seems to me that the teacher is the one who needs a new personality. It's ridiculous to expect a child to do an hour of homework after sitting still in school all day long.

With her critical response, the mother avoids a meaningful dialogue with her daughter. The father reinforces his daughter's dependency by speaking on her behalf against the teacher. His intervention also deflects discussion of the child's problems.

An educational approach can be helpful to otherwise competent parents who simply need to improve their communication skills (e.g., use of "I" messages). Persistently disturbed communication patterns, however, indicate a need for family therapy.

Hierarchy of Authority

Are parents effective in asserting authority? Imagine an organizational chart that illustrates the decision-making structure. Parents in functional families hold an "executive" position in the family organization. Children are granted freedom commensurate with their demonstrated responsibility. In dysfunctional families, parents surrender authority, often in the hope they can avoid conflict with a child. Children in these families often are out of control. Strategic family therapy would be a satisfactory approach for families that score "low" in this category.

Rapport Between Helping Adults

Can parents and helping professionals work together as a team to resolve a child's behavior problem? Dependability is a factor. Do these parents return phone calls? Are they punctual for conferences? Central to the issue is follow-through. The functional family does its homework. For example, there may be an agreement that the parent will telephone the teacher to make sure the child turned in an assignment. A functional parent probably will complete this task; a dysfunctional one will not. Without this kind of follow-through, a behavioral plan will fail.

A breakdown can occur at the professional level as well. For example, a burned-out teacher may be more invested in documenting a difficult child's "ticket" to special education than in assisting in a plan to improve the child's classroom behavior.

At the risk of overgeneralizing, counselors tend to establish rapport most easily with parents who are verbally skilled and psychologically sophisticated. Some parents who seem to be unresponsive may feel intimidated by professionals or may lack fluency in English. These parents can be quite effective if counselors will reach out.

Figure 10.1 provides a form in which the counselor can quickly rate family functioning according to the five variables.

BRIEF STRATEGIES WITH FAMILIES

Before considering a brief strategy, counselors should examine their own biases. Counseling and psychotherapy originated in psychoanalysis (Corey 1991). Much of what counselors-in-training learn in graduate school is a variation on this Freudian theme. Freud, Jung, Adler, and even Carl Rogers share the humble onion as a metaphor for understanding psychopathology. The presenting symptom is merely the outer representation of unconscious motivation. The therapist has to peel away these successive layers of defense to expose the root cause, (e.g., negative self-concept, inferiority complex, Oedipal fixation). *This takes a lot of time.*

There is little argument with the "onion" as a metaphor for personality development, but there is good reason to challenge the assumption that counselors must peel it! Most parents can't pay for "depth" psychotherapy, and third-party payers such as insurance companies can't either. In fact, today's mental health professionals see clients an average of only five or six sessions (Budman and Gurman 1988). This is not surprising to school counselors or agency counselors, who carry enor-

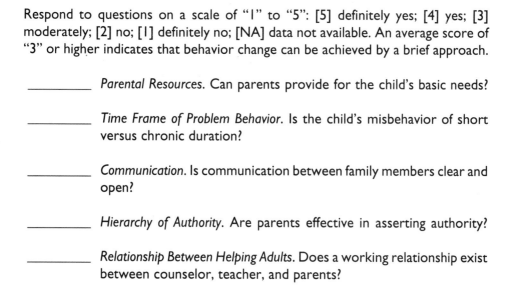

Respond to questions on a scale of "1" to "5": [5] definitely yes; [4] yes; [3] moderately; [2] no; [1] definitely no; [NA] data not available. An average score of "3" or higher indicates that behavior change can be achieved by a brief approach.

_____ *Parental Resources.* Can parents provide for the child's basic needs?

_____ *Time Frame of Problem Behavior.* Is the child's misbehavior of short versus chronic duration?

_____ *Communication.* Is communication between family members clear and open?

_____ *Hierarchy of Authority.* Are parents effective in asserting authority?

_____ *Relationship Between Helping Adults.* Does a working relationship exist between counselor, teacher, and parents?

Figure 10.1
QUICK ASSESSMENT OF FAMILY FUNCTIONING

mous caseloads. Further, there is no evidence that long-term or depth approaches are more effective with children and families than time-efficient strategies.

Brief Family Consultation

Brief family consultation is a time-limited behavioral model that can be implemented in a school or agency setting (Golden 1986). The brief family consultation model was developed at the Parent Consultation Center, a collaborative project of the University of Texas at San Antonio and a local school district. Features of the model are as follows:

1. *The intervention is limited to a maximum of five conferences.* The time limit conserves resources, permitting a large number of families to be served. The time limit also encourages an intensive "do-or-die" effort. Families should be made aware that they will not receive "therapy." To make this distinction explicit, client contacts are termed "conferences," not "sessions," and practitioners call themselves, "consultants," not "counselors."

2. *Only functional families are referred.* Referrals for brief family consultation should be made by professionals, such as school counselors, who understand that a dysfunctional family is unlikely to benefit from such a limited approach. Of course, dysfunctional families could be referred mistakenly. If so, the behavioral objectives should be narrowed to increase the chance that they can be achieved. When expectations for behavior change are unrealistic, everyone is the loser. And dysfunctional families can be referred for therapy.

3. *The goal is behavior change.* The parents, child, and consultant sign a contract specifying behavioral targets and consequences. Progress is reviewed at each conference so targets and consequences can be fine-tuned. The best laid plans are defeated by ambivalence. The motto is "Go for it!" The brief family consultation form presented in Figure 10.2 is used at the Parent Consultation Center in San Antonio, Texas, where brief family consultation has been operational for several years.

4. *The consultant coordinates a team effort that includes parents, teachers, and the child.* A brief strategy works best when all of the key players are involved. Counselors who believe they are doing a good job of helping children without contacting other significant adults are laboring under an illusion: We need all the help we can get! As a general rule, parents and teachers should be included in any attempt to solve a child's behavior problem.

5. *The consultant supports parental authority.* The distressed child likely is making a plea, albeit indirect, for parental control. Out of feelings of guilt and confusion, even competent parents may permit the child more freedom than is appropriate. Parents should be encouraged to take charge of resources that could serve as reinforcers. For example, a child who is "independently wealthy," sporting a big allowance and a roomful of electronic games, is in a position to disregard his parents' demands for behavior change. These parents would be well-advised to terminate the allowance and remove the games. The child *earns* these rewards by achieving behavioral goals.

Family group consultation is a variation of brief family consultation (Golden and McWhirter 1975). Several families are seen together, with the advantage of mutual support and social reinforcement. Counselors function as group facilitators and behavioral consultants. A one and one-half hour conference is broken into three half-hour segments.

Conference #_____

Child _____ Parent(s) _____

Date_____ Consultant(s) _____

1. _____

This target behavior is being achieved now. Circle the number that best describes your opinion:

definitely not   1   2   3   4   5   definitely

2. _____

This target behavior is being achieved now. Circle the number that best describes your opinion:

definitely not   1   2   3   4   5   definitely

What will happen during this coming week? _____

What will parent do? _____

What will child do? _____

What will consultant do? _____

Next conference date _____ Time _____

Figure 10.2
BRIEF FAMILY CONSULTATION FORM

During the first portion, families report on progress during the past week. The second segment requires two counselors as the large group breaks into separate subgroups for parents and for children. The subgroups analyze the reasons for the success or failure of the prior week's plans. Finally, the large group reassembles and each family commits to specific goals for the coming week. A family support group meets for about five weeks because establishing a new behavior takes at least that long. If the group meets for more than five weeks, families start dropping out.

Brief family consultation does have limitations. The behavioral approach works well with elementary-age children. Typically, young children trust that the adults in their lives know what's best for them and respond eagerly to rewards and praise. Adolescents, on the other hand, are likely to regard adults as agents of oppression and resent the manipulation inherent in "carrot-and-stick" tactics (Golden and Sherwood 1991). Teenagers respond better to a cognitive approach that endorses their compelling drive for independent decision-making and action.

Solution-Focused Therapy

Steve de Shazer and Imsoo Berg of the Brief Family Therapy Center in Milwaukee, Wisconsin, developed solution-focused therapy based on the view that *what is* and *what is not* a problem is relative (De Shazer 1988). Therefore, some problems can be solved by deciding they aren't problems. For example, a parent might attribute a child's underachieving to deep-seated pathology or focus , instead, on those areas where the child is working to the best of his or her ability. Why not assume that solutions can be found easily and naturally? Why not capitalize on what families already are doing that works?

This approach may seem naive, but it certainly is refreshing. De Shazer (1984) declared the "death of resistance" to therapy, suggesting that when clients don't follow the counselor's directives, it's their way of teaching the counselor the best way to help them. He opposes the notion that the child's problem serves an ulterior purpose (e.g., a child wets the bed to keep his parents from fighting with each other). The presenting problem is taken at face value, not as a symptom of underlying pathology.

The efficacy of this model has some support. About 85 percent of clients report full or partial success (Wylie 1990). Major features of solution-focused therapy are as follows:

1. *The focus is on solutions, not problems.* Parents become discouraged when they believe they are unable to help their troubled child. This pessimism generates rigid, "more-of-the-same" attempts at problem-solving. The solution-focused counselor emphasizes the family's past and current success as a starting point toward a solution (Nichols and Schwartz 1991).

2. *Certain "formula tasks" are effective with all clients regard-*

less of the presenting problem. De Shazer (1985) and his colleagues found they could initiate change without much knowledge of their clients' problems or personalities. One of these universal formulas is called the *miracle question:* "Suppose one night while you were asleep, there was a miracle and this problem was solved. How would you know? What would be different?" (Nichols and Schwartz 1991, 484). Then there's the *exception question:* "When did you *not* have the problem when by all rights you should have?' Still another of these "skeleton keys'' is the *task:* "Between now and next session, notice what you or your child or both are doing that you want to see continue."

The obvious intent of these formulaic questions and prescriptions is to give full attention to the family's preexisting resources for solving problems. There is a relentless pursuit of the positive. For example, a parent who wishes to control her temper is directed to observe what she does when she is successful in overcoming the urge to "lose it" with her child. If this successful strategy worked once, why not again?

3. *Parents are encouraged to be content with small changes.* Under the assumption that a small change can snowball into bigger ones, solution-focused counselors reinforce the child for being "on track" in solving a problem. They see any movement in the proper direction as a more realistic goal than a complete "cure."

Solution-focused therapy has much to offer school counselors and others who face severe time constraints. Laser-like focus on small successes and disregard for excavation of root causes brings rapid change.

By way of limitations, for the solution-focused therapist, if there is no complaint, there is no problem. The "power of positive thinking" has its limits (Wylie 1992). Focusing on successes and solutions rather than failures and problems may help the overanxious parent of an underachieving child, but what does this approach offer a child who is being sexually abused? Solution-focused therapy minimizes a client's problems (Wylie 1992). Parents, too, tend to deny serious problems such as child abuse or alcoholism. These dangerous conditions demand alarm bells, not positive reframing. At the least, solution-focused therapy is a good beginning, a way to start therapy on a positive note. Counselors, however, must recognize when stronger interventions are needed to break through denial.

Strategic Family Therapy

Family therapy has various schools—Bowenian, experiential, humanistic, psychodynamic, strategic, structural, and systemic. For our purposes, strategic family therapy comes nearest to the vital center of the field. Strategic family therapy exposes how a child's symptoms serve to maintain a dysfunctional system.

Strategic family therapy is associated with the Mental Research Institute in Palo Alto and with certain individuals, most notably Jay Haley and Cloe Madanes (Duncan 1992; Nichols and Schwartz 1991). Strategic family counselors attempt to change only those aspects of the family system that maintain the child's symptomatic behavior. If the presenting problem is resolved, the counselor is content, an attitude shared by the solution-focused counselor. If the problem is recalcitrant, however, the strategic counselor attempts to change the family system so the symptom no longer serves a function. The child's symptom is seen as serving a larger purpose, usually on behalf of the system as a whole. For Haley (1963), the symptom is a strategy for controlling a relationship when all other strategies have failed. The symptomatic person, however, denies any intent to control by claiming the symptom is involuntary (Goldenberg and Goldenberg 1991). This powerful collaboration among family members calls for energetic therapeutic tactics. Some of the major features of strategic family therapy are as follows:

1. *The goal is to eliminate the presenting problem.* Sometimes the presenting problem can be solved with a straightforward behavioral contract. Frequently the child and family have an unspoken investment in maintaining the child's symptom. In those instances the counselor must design and implement a strategy (hence, "strategic" family therapy) to change the family system so the symptom no longer serves a purpose. The counselor does this by directing family members to communicate differently or to perform therapeutic tasks that will change the way they work together (Goldenberg and Goldenberg 1991). Insight is "frosting on the cake" and not necessary to resolve the presenting problem.

2. *The strategic counselor is active and directive.* Families bring a contradiction to therapy: Help us change, but don't upset the apple cart. Homeostasis, the tendency of a system to maintain the status quo, works against change. Haley openly acknowledges that change can be painful and that counselors are justified in using their power to bring it about (Haley 1984).

3. *Paradoxical injunctions are used to defeat resistance.* Some children (as well as parents) are so oppositional that they defy the counselor. The strategic counselor makes use of this tendency by telling the child *not* to change. For example, the counselor could tell an oppositional child to continue to be rebellious against his or her parents. If the paradox works, the child will obey the parents to defy the counselor.

4. *Reframing is used to bring about cognitive shift.* Perception is relative. Because you can't be sure of a child's motive, why not choose one that supports health and control rather than pathology and despair? For example, a father accounts for his teen's running away from home: "She's incorrigible, irresponsible, and downright stupid!" These words describe an individual who probably is incapable of change and would not even if she could. A more useful explanation would be: "She's chosen a 'gutsy' but dangerous way to strike out on her own." This reframe, though not necessarily more true than the first, invites possibilities. An effective reframe forces a cognitive shift that reduces resistance to behavioral change. Even though strategic family therapy finds few adherents among school counselors, reframing as a strategy has relevance to their work.

Opponents of the strategic approach have charged it with a "blame the family'' bias (Wylie 1992). In some cases a youngster's symptom my have an intrapsychic basis that strategic therapists could too easily ignore. Richard Schwartz, a therapist, told about such a case with a bulimic patient:

> A young woman had been "detriangulated" from her family. She had given up her role as family protector, had moved into her own apartment, and was enjoying her job. Her parents had accepted the change and, according to the standard theory that her symptom served the function of keeping her stuck, she should have been, by then, no longer bingeing and purging. Alas, she remained bulimic, apparently "unaware of her cure." (Wylie 1992, 23)

The paradoxical injunction, a favored method of strategic therapists should be used sparingly. A paradox is a way to trick someone into behaving the way the counselor thinks best. This reverse psychology is somewhat disrespectful. On occasion it backfires in an unpleasant way, such as a double reverse. For example, the counselor could direct an oppositional student *not* to study for an exam. The student could confound the strategy by (1) not studying and failing the exam and (2) telling the counselor that he had tried his best.

Parent Education

Although it is not a "counseling" approach, parent education deserves mention as the ultimate preventive strategy. Parent education has an "efficiency" advantage over counseling because relatively large numbers of parents can be instructed in a classroom format.

The goal of parent education is to impart knowledge and skills to parents. Typically, parents learn about child development, communication skills, and techniques for managing childhood behavior problems. Parents, too, are likely to feel encouraged by sharing their experience and receiving support from other parents.

Competent parents are likely to complete a parent education program and benefit from it (Fine and Jennings 1992). The major limitation is obvious: Parents most in need of information about parenting are the least likely to attend parent education activities and most likely to drop out if they do attend. Further, lessons learned in class do not necessarily generalize to the home (Fine and Jennings 1992). If a child's misbehavior serves a useful purpose in the family system, parents won't implement the new skills they've learned. These parents are candidates for family therapy.

CONCLUSION

The overwhelming need for mental health services and sharp limitations on economic resources combine in favor of brief approaches to working with children and families. The simple decision to include the family is in itself a brief strategy. Family approaches, however, are more than a "quick fix." Family strategies recognize the role parents play in maintaining and solving childhood behavior problems and affirm parents' capacity to assist their children with the next and inevitable developmental crisis.

Thirteen-year-old Katrina was referred to my private practice by her mother, Alicia. Alicia was worried about Katrina's declining grades and constant fighting between Katrina and her stepfather, Cliff. At the first interview I asked to see the entire family, including two-year-old Brian.

Cliff, age forty-eight, is a successful, hard-driving insurance executive. His own father, now deceased, was an alcoholic. Cliff has two adult children by a previous marriage. Alicia, thirty-five, is a housewife. Brian is the offspring of Alicia and Cliff's three-year marriage.

Katrina, the offspring of Alicia's previous marriage, rarely sees her father, who lives in another sate. Although her declining grades are a recent phenomenon, she always had been a "below average" student and had been "moody," at least since her parents' divorce when Katrina was four years old. On one occasion she told her teacher about "being better off dead."

Alicia and Cliff seemed committed to each other, but Katrina's misbehavior was the trigger for escalating stress. Cliff blamed Alicia for being overly permissive in her approach to discipline. Alicia acknowledged this but saw Cliff as needlessly harsh. They polarized, effectively neutralizing their attempts to discipline Katrina.

Following is my evaluation of Katrina's family, using the *Quick Assessment of Family Functioning* criteria:

Parental Resources: A score of "3" reflects the family's healthy financial status weighed against any blended family's inherent vulnerability (e.g., another divorce, legal challenges to child custody).

Time Frame of Problem Behavior: A score of "2" indicates that at least some aspects of Katrina's presenting problems were observed since she was four years old. A long-term problem predicts a lengthy intervention.

Communication: A score of "2" reflects the rift between Cliff and Katrina, as well as the strain on marital communication.

Hierarchy of Authority: A score of "I" indicates that Cliff and Alicia antagonize each other when disciplining Katrina, eroding their ability to control her behavior.

Relationship Between Helping Adults: A score of "4" results from Alicia's willingness to seek professional help and her rapport with school authorities. Cliff, however, is distrustful of any potential dependency on a counseling relationship.

This was a complex and difficult case. From a strategic point of view, Katrina's declining grades and moodiness could have several ulterior motives: (1) to bring marital problems to the forefront, (2) to force Alicia to take her side against Cliff, (3) to propel her out of a household in which she did not feel wanted.

My work with Katrina was a three-ring circus with the "fifty-minute hour" usually divided into three segments: (1) family counseling, (2) individual counseling, (3) parent education/marital counseling. I arranged a conference at the school to include Alicia, Katrina's teachers, and the school counselor. It was agreed that Katrina would bring home a daily report indicating whether she had or had not turned in assignments. Further, Alicia and Cliff decided on chores they wanted Katrina to do at home—washing dishes, cleaning her room, and so on. Katrina's ten-dollar per week allowance was eliminated, but she could earn as much as fifteen dollars by turning in assignments and doing chores. She could earn additional bonuses by acting on her own initiative instead of requiring parental nagging. Katrina's behavior improved a little, but her mood remained sullen.

In a typical episode involving Cliff and Katrina, Cliff saw dishes in the sink and Katrina lounging on the couch watching TV. Cliff said, "What about the dishes? Or do you think you're some kind of royal princess?" Katrina stormed into her room and slammed the door. Cliff charged in after her: "I want you out of this house! Do us all a favor and run away!" Later, Cliff and Katrina told Alicia about the incident. She was sympathetic to Cliff's feelings but infuriated by his outburst inviting Katrina to run away. Cliff responded, "As usual, you don't back me up." Alicia snapped back with, "As usual, I've got two children on my hands."

I asked Cliff how he explained to himself Katrina's storming into her room and slamming the door. He identified two possibilities: (I) her mother has raised her to be irresponsible, and (2) she's trying to break up our marriage. I pointed out that thoughts such as these could lead to violent emotions. I asked him to mentally substitute another statement before confronting Katrina again: "She doesn't like being in the same room with me when I call attention to her failings." This relatively moderate statement resulted in Cliff's temperate emotion and rational behavior.

Like many adolescents, Katrina was a poor candidate for psychotherapy. She assumed that a counselor was in the business of helping her parents and teachers exercise control over her behavior—not far off the mark! I acknowledged that I wanted her to improve her grades and get along better with Cliff and her mother. I also wanted her to know I was interested in her as an individual, separate from her family. I asked her if I understood her goals: (I) to convince her mother and stepfather that she was nobody's puppet, and (2) plan for leaving home on her own two feet. She concurred. We talked about the ways a girl her age could rebel strongly against parental authority only to become even more dependent. With a little prompting, Katrina identified pregnancy, drugs, and school failure as being "bogus" paths to freedom! I wondered outloud if a teenager could *secretly* pursue a goal of leaving home on her own two feet.[1]

Although Katrina started making small gains, the marriage was slipping downhill. Marriages in blended families can be easily destabilized by misbehaving stepchildren. Cliff assumed that Katrina was purposely misbehaving to wreck the marriage, paving the way for a reconciliation between her mother and father, a commonly held myth about stepchildren. My experience is that stepchildren are ambivalent about the new marriage. They rebel against a stepparent out of loyalty to the noncustodial parent. They may entertain fantasies of reconciliation. The last thing on earth Katrina wanted, however, was to go through another divorce. I shared this point of view with the entire family.

I also told the family that Katrina was now more able to manage her life and advised Alicia and Cliff to attend to their marriage. Thus, the stage was set for marital counseling.

The procedures of marital counseling are not germane to this chapter. Suffice it to say that eventually the marital format gave way to individual psychotherapy for Cliff. His disturbed childhood with an alcoholic father and his first divorce had left him fearful of dependency, unable to commit, and chronically depressed. I used Rogerian counseling to help Cliff gain insight into the etiology of his condition and cognitive therapy to assist him in achieving mastery over impulsive behaviors.

In summary, this case study illustrates the ways a child's problems are woven into the fabric of the family. It also demonstrates several techniques (e.g., behavioral, cognitive, marital) that can be used in counseling with children and their families.

SUMMARY

This chapter discusses ways to help children by working with their families. The author advocates *brief* strategies because most counselors, whether employed in school, agency, or private settings, must work within time constraints. Brief or time-efficient approaches assume that not everyone needs, wants, or can afford long-term psychotherapy. It is important to recognize, however, that brief approaches are best suited to functional families that face situational difficulties. Dysfunctional fami-

[1]Jay Haley's (1980) book *Leaving Home* offers strategies to get families to support a youngster's goal of independence.

lies with a long history of disordered behavior, on the other hand, may require a long-term intervention that gets to the root cause of the presenting symptom.

The simplest of the strategies is *brief family consultation,* which is limited to a maximum of five "conferences" (the preferred term). The consultant coordinates a team consisting of parents, teachers, and the child in order to achieve the goal of rapid behavior change. A variation of brief family consultation, family group consultation, incorporates several families into one group, with the advantage of mutual support and social reinforcement.

Solution-focused therapy rejects a "problem" focus. Instead, the therapist builds quickly on a family's prior success. Certain reliable "formula tasks" are used with all clients regardless of the presenting problem. The goal is to achieve small steps in the right direction rather than a complete "cure."

Strategic family therapy is more powerful than the other approaches discussed. The goal is to eliminate the presenting problem. However, a dysfunctional family system may serve to maintain this problem. In that case, the therapist may try to change destructive patterns of communication or to redistribute power among family members. To this end, the strategic counselor is active and directive. Paradoxical injunctions are used to defeat resistance and reframing is used to bring about a cognitive shift.

Finally, *parent education* is presented as an alternative to counseling. Parent education programs provide instruction in child development, communication skills, and behavior management techniques, usually in a classroom format.

An assessment tool is provided that helps the practitioner decide what approach would be most appropriate. This tool differentiates between functional and dysfunctional families based on five variables: parent resources, time frame of the problem behavior, communication, hierarchy of authority, and rapport between helping adults.

The major thrust of this chapter is to encourage counselors to include families in their efforts to help children. Why ignore the enormous power of a family to assist or hinder the development of any of its members?

REFERENCES

Alexander, J. F., and B. V. Parsons. 1982. *Functional family therapy.* Pacific Grove, CA: Brooks/Cole.

American Psychiatric Association. 1987. *Diagnostic and statistical manual of mental disorders.* 3d ed. rev. Washington, DC: APA.

Budman, S. H., and A. S. Gurman.1988. *Theory and practice of brief therapy.* New York: Guilford Press.

Bundy, M. L., and J. Gumaer. 1986. Families in transition. In L. Golden and D. Capuzzi, eds., *Helping families help children: Family interventions with school-related problems.* Springfield, IL: Charles C Thomas.

Carlson, C. 1992. Single parenting and stepparenting: Problems, issues, and interventions. In M. Fine and C. Carlson, eds., *The handbook of family-school intervention: A systems perspective.* Boston: Allyn and Bacon.

Corey, G. 1991. *Theory and practice of counseling and psychotherapy.* 4th ed. Pacific Grove, CA: Brooks/Cole.

De Shazer, S. 1984. The death of resistance. *Family Process* 23: 11–17.

De Shazer, S. 1985. *Keys to solution in brief therapy.* New York: W. W. Norton.

De Shazer, S. 1988. *Clues: Investigating solutions in brief therapy.* New York: W. W. Norton.

Duncan, B. L. 1992. Strategic therapy, eclecticism, and the therapeutic relationship. *Journal of Marital and Family Therapy* 1: 17–24.

Fine, M. J., and J. Jennings. 1992. Family therapy's contributions to parent education. In M. Fine and C. Carlson, eds., *The handbook of family-school intervention: A systems perspective.* Boston: Allyn and Bacon.

Golden, L. 1986. Counseling children and families in the schools. In L. Golden and D. Capuzzi, eds., *Helping families help children: Family interventions with school-related problems.* Springfield, IL. Charles C Thomas.

Golden, L. 1988. Quick assessment of family functioning. *School Counselor* 35: 179–184.

Golden, L., and J. McWhirter. 1975. Practicum experiences in family group consultation. *Arizona Personnel and Guidance Association Journal* 1: 44–46.

Golden, L., and A. Sherwood. 1991. Counseling children and adolescents. In D. Capuzzi and D. Gross, eds., *Introduction to counseling: Perspectives for the 1990's.* Boston: Allyn and Bacon.

Goldenberg, I., and H. Goldenberg. 1991. *Family therapy: An overview.* 3d ed. Pacific Grove, CA: Brooks/Cole.

Goldman, R. K. 1986. Children and divorce. In L. Golden and D. Capuzzi, eds., *Helping families help children: Family interventions with school-related problems.* Springfield, IL: Charles C Thomas.

Gurman, A. S., D. P. Kniskern, and W. M. Pinsof. 1986. Research on the process and outcome of marital and family therapy. In S. L. Garfield and A. E. Bergin, eds., *Handbook of psychotherapy and behavior change.* 3d ed. New York: John Wiley & Sons

Haley, J. 1963. *Strategies of psychotherapy.* New York: Grune and Stratton.

Haley, J. 1980. *Leaving home: The therapy of disturbed young people.* New York: McGraw-Hill.

Haley, J. 1984. *Ordeal therapy.* San Francisco: Jossey Bass.

Kazdin, A. E. 1988. *Child psychotherapy: Developing and identifying effective treatments.* New York: Pergamon.

Nichols, M. P., and R. Schwartz. 1991. *Family therapy: Concepts and methods.* 2d ed. Boston: Allyn and Bacon.

Satir, V. 1972. *Peoplemaking.* Palo Alto, CA: Science and Behavior Books.

Wylie, M. S. 1990. Brief therapy on the couch. *Family Therapy Networker* (March/April): 26–35, 66.

Wylie, M. S. 1992. The evolution of a revolution. *Family Therapy Networker* (January/February): 17–29, 98–99.

Consulting with School Staff
11 and Administration

Brooke B. Collison

Counselor Education Program
Oregon State University, Corvallis

Counselors have long used the word *consultation* as one of the three "Cs" describing their primary role. Counselor education programs frequently include course work in consultation as part of the curriculum for masters' level students. In fact, Brown, Spano, and Schulte (1988) cited studies showing that nearly 40 percent of the masters' level programs include at least one course in consultation. We do not know, however, the number of counselors who regularly use consultation procedures or the number of different procedures that are called "consultation." Further confusion is generated—particularly on the part of consultees—about what consultants actually do in a consultation process.

Consultants have been called "experts," "outsiders," "people who do some work and then leave," "helpers," "good teachers," or "counselors." Other terms reflect either positive or negative experiences people have had with consultants. Terms describing consultants or consultation are characteristic of:

- the consultant's personal effectiveness
- the nature of the problem on which consultation focused
- the consultant's philosophical orientation
- the consultant's degree of receptivity to consultation
- the degree of success achieved as a result of consultation

The word *consultant* can mean many different things. We cannot assume that one consultation experience is like all others or that all consultants are alike.

The consultation process also varies according to the setting in which consultation takes place. What common elements are found in most consultations? This chapter is limited to an explanation of consultation with teachers, administrators, and parents. In addition, it extends the consultation concept to selected staff development functions within school settings and describes some case management techniques utilizing consultation skills.

School counselors should study consultation for a variety of reasons:

1. More students in schools need special services.
2. Many areas of the country have a shortage of counselors.
3. A number of issues facing youth demand good counseling and consultation service.
4. Schools are called upon to move into the third-party consultant role to manage services in a time of declining resources.
5. A growing body of research indicates that consultation is an effective method of addressing a variety of school-related issues.

The justification for consultation should not be based only on economics and shortage of resources. It is important to study because it is effective, not just because it is cost-effective.

This chapter does not include the kind of "consultation" counselors are expected to engage in when cases or situations potentially pose problems. The ACA Code of Ethics (American Counseling Association 1988) calls for counselors to "consult" [Sections B (4, 11) and E]. That is a different process than is covered here, even though consultants are expected to "consult" on the same kind of problem issues that face counselors: questions of professional methodology, appropriate role, conflict of interest, assessment of personal effectiveness or professional limitation, questions of client risk, and the like (Dougherty 1992b). Consultants need their own consultation to assure the client that they are providing appropriate service within reasonable boundaries and that they are not practicing in isolation from a professional colleague community.

CONSULTATION DEFINED

Consultation is defined as a process whereby one person, the consultant, works with a second person (or persons), the consultee, to have an effect on a third person, the client—in this case, students. Kratochwill and Van Someren (1985) explained a triadic model of consultation as an indirect process of attaining positive behavior change in students by engaging teachers or others in collaborative problem-solving.

Consultation relationships are different from teaching relationships, parenting relationships, or supervisory relationships. Teaching carries with it a body of content as the focus of teacher-student interaction;

parenting is a lifelong tie bound up in a myriad of biological and emotional investments; and supervision begins with an unequal power basis as a given. Most theorists describe the consultation relationship as egalitarian in terms of power differentials as well as voluntary in nature (Reschly 1976; Kurpius and Robinson 1978). Although many of the skills are the same—interpersonal processing, communication skills, problem definition processes, empathic listening, clarification, ability to see multiple solutions to problem situations, high tolerance for ambiguity, low need for dominance and control, and effective written and verbal communication skills—the collaborative consultation relationship is not the same as counseling.

For the purpose of this chapter, *consultation* will be considered voluntary (on the part of the consultee) and egalitarian with respect to power (though perceptions of power differences may alter the egalitarian relationship). The goal of consultation is to assist students in some indirect way by working directly with teachers, administrators, or parents. Consultation can be conducted by a variety of education personnel who may utilize different knowledge bases for the consultation, especially in situations requiring technical expertise. Idol and Baran (1992) identified some of the potential role conflicts present when different school professionals consult with the same consultees (although I define "consult" as more than "confer with," as in the Idol and Baran article). Consultation procedures differ, but the consultation process has common elements that cut across goals and settings.

PERSONAL EFFECTIVENESS

To function in a consultation role requires a high level of personal effectiveness. Most of the skills required of an effective counselor also are required of an effective consultant. Consultation is more complex, however, as the client (e.g., the student) is one step removed from the process because the consultant works directly with the consultee (e.g., teacher). Although the focus of consultation is the student, the consultee may have unresolved personal issues that relate to the student or the topic of consultation. In the consultation process, the consultant might see a new client emerging—the teacher, parent, or administrator—with his or her own issues to work through relative to the student client. This creates an ethical dilemma for the consultant if he or she has a consultee who wishes to go beyond the limits of the initial student-based contract to undertake personal work. An expanded discussion of consultation dilemmas and related ethical issues can be found in Dougherty (1992b).

As in all human endeavors, consultants' levels of effectiveness differ, even if they have the same theoretical orientation and work in similar settings. An effective counselor who works with one person at a time possibly may not be an effective consultant when the parameters change in terms of focus and number of variables to consider.

NATURE OF THE CHALLENGE

The situations that consultants work with in schools can be observed from the point of view of the student, the teacher, the parents, other students, building administrators, or systems as a whole. In general, school-based consultation deals with the behavior, achievement, or attitude of individual students or groups of students that, in some way has become a problem to others. In some instances, consultation may focus on behavior, achievement, or attitudes identified by students themselves and not a problem to others; the procedure for addressing the situation, however, is through others (consultees).

In this chapter, consultation is defined as a process that originates in response to the consultee's concern (or the concern of a third party) about an individual student's behavior, attitude, or achievement. A second emphasis is on the consultation process with a group of students as the identified client. Some attention will be given to self-identified issues in which consultation is an appropriate procedure. Consultation to systems (classrooms, building, or communities) will be addressed briefly.

PHILOSOPHICAL ORIENTATION

The various approaches to consultation are frequently described along a continuum. Lippitt and Lippitt (1978) illustrated different kinds of consultant activities and philosophies. Visualizing a "nondirective" to "directive" continuum with the nondirective consultant at one end and the directive consultant at the other, one can easily picture the client-centered observer and reflector at one end and the active initiator, director, problem-solver at the other. In between are various styles reflecting a mix of these two behaviors or approaches. None of the positions is pure, and no consultant operates within a narrow philosophy 100 percent of the time; however, the simple continuum illustrates quite well the variation in philosophy and approach.

The consultant who works from a more nondirective philosophy may meet with consultees and listen to comments about a client. Using the techniques of reflection, clarification, support, empathic responding, and gentle probes, the consultant may have a goal of helping the consultee gain new understanding of the client, and the consultee may gain new understanding of self in the process. The consultant might express little in terms of prescriptive behaviors on the consultee's part. Encouraging consultee-described strategies or solutions to the problem client behavior might be the limit of a nondirective consultant's interaction with the consultee.

The consultant positioned further along the continuum toward a directive philosophy might work with the same consultee (assuming a teacher with a pupil who has a classroom behavior problem) by listening, clarifying, and reflecting the teacher's concerns. The more directive consultant, however, is likely to focus the conversation on two areas: (1) definition of the problem behavior, and (2) identification of strategies used in the past to deal with that behavior. The consultant might offer specific suggestions, consistent with his or her philosophical orientation, for working with the client (the student). The suggestions might be prescriptive from an Adlerian point of view (Joyce 1990), from a rational-emotive therapy point of view, or from a behavioral orientation.

The more directive the consultant, the more likely he or she will be to provide alternative strategies to the consultee after the problem has been identified. The most directive consultant on that continuum might even offer prescriptions for consultee action without spending time in problem definition. For example, the consultant who assumes that pupil behavior is a problem in nearly all classrooms might initiate the conversation with several prescriptive solutions for teacher-pupil interaction, without determining the level of the problem that is perceived to exist.

RECEPTIVITY FOR CONSULTATION

In the most ideal of consultant situations, a consultee (e.g., teacher) asks for or invites consultation and is open to discussion of all issues and possibilities relative to a client (e.g., student). The ideal consultee has information about the student and the situations that pose problems and shares that information easily in dialogue with a consultant. As the consultation dialogue continues, the consultee gets a better grasp of the problem situation, identifies alternative strategies, and commits to use those strategies with accompanying methods of assessing their effectiveness. Upon completion of the process, the consultee reports to the consultant the relative success in reaching the desired goal or goals.

Few consultations move as smoothly as this ideal scenario. By definition, a consultant is someone from "outside." Even internal consultants are outsiders to some extent. They may be viewed as having some kind of power whether it is real or not (French and Raven 1959), and their ability to bring some solution to the problem at hand can range from highly probable all the way to a pessimistic view that the consultant will only make things worse.

Every consultant must realize that the consultee's previous experience with consultants will color his or her expectations about consultation, the consultant, possible outcomes, and consequences for them as a person and as a professional. Even if they have had no direct prior experience, a set of expectations about the consultant will arise in the same way that expectations about counselors shape the initial process of counseling. Therefore, the consultation process must first address client or consultee expectations, the source of those expectations, and what has to be done to utilize the positive possibilities or to assuage the negative implications associated with those expectations. In an ideal case, the consultee welcomes the consultant and the ideas that emerge from the consultation. In a worst case, the consultant intentionally defeats the efforts of consultation in an effort to demonstrate that the consultant is not effective.

SUCCESS OR FAILURE

A counselee came into the office of one of my practicum students one Monday and announced enthusiastically, "I did exactly what you said, and now everything is wonderful with my parents." The counselor-in-training was chagrined. She said she had not given any direct instructions to her youthful client. We listened to the audiotape of the session in which she supposedly had given instructions on "exactly what to do." Nowhere in the taped session could we find a counselor response that remotely sounded like a suggestion or an instruction. True, family stress and the difficulties related to a demanding parent had been discussed, but even in those instances, the counselor gave no discernible "suggestion." Nevertheless, the client had acted upon the understanding that she was carrying out instructions.

As a result of consultation, the consultee may or may not take action, depending in part on how invested the consultee is in the process, the degree to which the problem is affecting them and the client, and their knowledge and self-confidence in addressing the issues.

Consultants can increase the probability of perceived failure just in the language they use in the consultation process. "Do this and you'll succeed'' is a set-up for probable failure. "Try this and see what the outcome is" leaves the discussion open if efforts fall short of the desired goals. "What strategy do you plan to implement?" places control with the consultee and leaves the consultant as a processor.

Successful consultations usually have several parts:

1. A pre-entry planning session by the consultant. The consultant needs to understand as much as possible about the consultee and the situation in which the consultation is likely to take place (e.g. a classroom, a student group).
2. An initial contact or meeting, in which the collaborative nature of the consultation activity is defined and mutually understood.
3. The consultation activity, including data collection, problem identification, and exploration of previous efforts at remedy.
4. Generation of alternatives to resolve the problem. This should be done collaboratively.
5. The intervention, usually by the consultee or others identified in previous stages.
6. A planned assessment of the intervention, with agreements on whether the consultation will continue or if it has concluded.

If the consultant attends to each of these steps, the probability for success increases. To begin making suggestions without determining the nature of the problem or the attitude the consultee brings to the consultation is tantamount to having a mechanic begin to repair a car before determining if the person who brought it in wants it fixed or wants to trade it in.

Similarly, to have preliminary consultations with a consultee and never return to determine if strategies were implemented or to discover what the outcomes were demonstrates an absence of care that eventually will destroy the consultation relationship. Follow-up assessment, however, must be done for the benefit of the consultee, not the consultant. Saying to a consultee, "Be sure to tell me how successful my suggestions have been," conveys the wrong message. Saying "I'll come by next week to talk with you about the effect of the interventions and see whether we need to consider a second stage" conveys a sense of commitment to the consultation process as well as an acknowledgment that additional steps are called for.

As in counseling relationships, consultants have to exit the consultation process at some point. Preferably, that point has been defined in advance, perhaps at the initial contact stage. At the very least, the consultee needs to understand, in the early stage of consultation, whether the consultant is to become a permanent fixture or just a passing interlude.

I had completed a consultation project with an agency around the topic of internal decision-making. I had interviewed employees in the agency and worked with the director to improve the language of decision requests and the communication methods of informing employees about decisions that had been made The director enjoyed the consultation relationship and extended the contract for additional work. I declined a second extension of the contract, for I concluded that the director was becoming dependent on me to function as director. In declining, I stated, "Declining doesn't indicate my level of care for you or the agency, but if I remain in a consultative relationship, you may not move off on your own in effective decision-making. After all, that was the original goal I agreed to facilitate." One of the consultant's goals should be to not be needed.

Declining a continued consultation because I believed the client was becoming dependent on my services might be viewed as failing to assist the client in reaching goals. In retrospect, I may have failed to define the nature of the consultation process at the entry point and to come to agreement on a desired end goal of the client becoming an effective decision-maker. The consultation postmortem could continue, and I might conclude that the two of us had merely failed to assess how long it would take to reach the goal. My decision to exit may have been premature.

The case study illustrates the necessity of spending time with the consultee early on about the nature of consultation:

- What is consultation?
- How will the consultant and consultee work together?
- What is the problem or situation to be addressed?
- What has been tried in the past?
- What is needed to address the current situation?
- How will the consultant and the consultee assess the effectiveness of interventions?
- When and how will the consultation end?

Important to consider in the consultation process—particularly with new consultees who may not have a good understanding of how the consultant works—is what happens to information that emerges in the process. As a result of the consultation referral or through the problem definition stage, the consultant may acquire confidential information or even incriminating information relative to things such as teacher performance, family behavior, and the like. In particular, in school settings, teachers may think they are the object of critical review by a consultant— especially if the consultation originated from some external suggestion.

CASE 1: A FIFTH-GRADE CLASS BEHAVIOR PROBLEM

Ann, an elementary school counselor, is informed by the school principal that a new teacher, Fred, is having difficulty with three students' behavior in his fifth-grade classroom. The principal and others have observed these pupils "out of control" in the halls, on the playground, and in the lunchroom. The principal says to the school counselor, "You need to get in there and help him get control of those kids or he won't survive the first year of teaching."

For Ann, this creates several dilemmas:

- How should the consultation be initiated?
- Who is the consultee?
- Who is the client?
- What expectation does the principal have about the outcome of the consultation?
- What expectation does the principal have about information to be shared during or after the consultation?

Ann has to begin her consultation carefully. This is not the time to approach the teacher in the lounge and, in front of other teachers, say, "The principal says you have a big problem in your class, and I need to get you straightened out." Even though a counselor would not say or mean that, a new, insecure teacher might perceive that message. Whether the problem is the teacher's or the student's is an esoteric question that can be debated only if a person feels secure enough to accept either option as an answer.

Ann must decide if she should approach this teacher with an honest introduction ("I'm aware that some pupils in your class have behavior problems around the school"). If she believes the teacher is somewhat insecure and may become defensive if he thinks the principal is questioning the teacher's behavior, Ann would take a different tack. She would most easily initiate the consultation by putting herself in a place to observe the pupils in question (e.g., the halls, the lunchroom) and thus be in a less threatening (less evaluative) position to initiate/ bring up the conversation to the teacher. She might say, "I observed three fifth graders yesterday on the playground whose behavior could easily be a problem to deal with. Do you observe the same thing? Are these students disruptive to your teaching?"

In Ann's statement, she identifies that her information about the fifth-graders' behavior is firsthand (honest statement). She doesn't put the teacher on the defensive, and tries to be supportive, extending an offer of consultation that he can accept or reject. This open-ended question may be less threatening, but it does give the teacher an opportunity to reject the offer, leaving Ann in a dilemma with the knowledge that the principal has asked her to help the teacher.

The consultant's language is critical. Ann might say, "I observed three fifth graders yesterday on the playground, and their behavior could be a problem to deal with. I would be glad to work with you to find alternative ways to deal with those three if you are having problems with them too.'' Another statement might be, "Part of my job as school counselor is to function in a consulting role with teachers in pupil or classroom behavior situations. I would like to meet for a few minutes at your convenience this week to discuss ways we could work together to make things better for these pupils."

This last statement carries a veiled implication of power differential ("I would like to meet...") and power differential, whether perceived or actual, implies an inequity. The theoretical model of consultation most often described in the literature does not include inequity. Obviously, Ann's first task is to develop a relationship with the teacher that approaches an egalitarian point of view.

At some point, Fred has to know that the principal noted the pupils' behavior and asked Ann to intervene. The most authentic posture is to develop a set of consultation norms within a school that lets teachers, parents, and administrators know what happens to information transmitted by colleagues. The consultant's ethical practice has to be known. Ann also must develop a relationship with the principal that will let the two of them understand what will happen with the information she acquires in the problem definition and intervention strategy sessions. If the principal's expectation (and Ann's) is that at some future point Ann will inform the principal about Fred's teaching strategies that may or may not be effective, she is involved in the personnel evaluation role. It is appropriate to be in the personnel evaluation role only if all parties understand that it is one of the functions. Obviously, that eliminates the foundation of an egalitarian consultation relationship.

If Fred accepts Ann's offer to consult, the initial session is critical in defining role and expectation of both the consultee and the consultant. In this kind of situation, Fred possibly has some skill deficiencies as a new teacher. Fred may have some feelings of inadequacy about his performance as a new teacher. Those inadequacies could translate to personal anxiety, stress, or other intense feelings that could be uncovered in the consultation process. The question that Ann must address at this point is whether to focus only on the pupils' observed behavior and emphasize strategies to deal with those pupils or to respond to the affect represented in the new teacher situation and possibly open an area best defined as an issue that Fred might address with a counselor—Ann or someone else. Consultants frequently face this dilemma in the process of data collection within an organization. Becoming a willing listener often opens a flood of associated feelings resembling catharsis in some instances. The consultant must decide whether to listen and process those feelings or to intervene during the interviews and emphasize the parameters of the consultation process.

As a consultant, I have had employees confess intense depressive conditions, including suicidal ideation they had not revealed to anyone before. They made these revelations in an information-gathering interview of a consultation process that had been defined verbally in a group meeting and presented in writing as being just a collection of objective information about reporting and communication lines within an organization. I promised confidentiality of information and assured these employees that I would summarize the information in general terms rather than by names of individuals or units. This was enough for some of them to believe they had found their own therapist (often confounded by their knowing that I carried the title of "counselor" or "counselor educator" as well as "consultant").

After Ann and Fred have talked about what consultation is and how the two of them might work together, they can more easily discuss the clients in this case, the fifth-grade pupils. Ann can focus her questions and comments on their behavior. If Ann begins quickly to "tell" Fred what to do with them, she will have communicated dramatically that she has all the answers and Fred has no ideas of his own. One of the most effective opening stems for the consultant is to ask, "What sort of things have you used with these students so far, and which seem to work best?" Fred then has an opportunity to describe his procedures.

Ann can help Fred understand that the situation with the fifth graders is not unusual. After generating a list of strategies and ideas that he has not tried yet, Ann might suggest her own ideas for Fred to consider in the spirit of collaboration she has created. These ideas most likely will be based on her own philosophy about behavior management for fifth-grade pupils. If she has observed that they receive more criticism than praise, she might make behaviorally oriented suggestions that Fred watch for opportunities to reward behaviors and to ignore minor behaviors that may be functioning only to draw attention. If she has an educational psychology background, she might discuss developmentally appropriate behaviors and help assess the level of classroom tasks for the pupils under consideration. If she is a serious Adlerian, she might assess the goals of misbehavior by examining the teacher's (or other's) reactions to student interactions. The way the consultant approaches problem analysis and development of intervention response always has a philosophical foundation.

Ann and Fred need to talk about which efforts will be made, who will make them, and how long they will be tried (the tendency is for new interventions to be tried once and, if they don't work, to abandon them). They also need to talk about how they will evaluate the effectiveness of outcomes.

Several conversations probably will center on the precipitating event, the principal's suggestion that Ann intervene. Ideally, the new teacher will discover an ally in Ann, one with whom he can discuss classroom situations and explore suggestions. The teacher should be able to view Ann, over time, as a person with a body of knowledge to be used in the classroom situation, as a person the teacher can trust, and as someone who is available when needed, but not in a protective or continual manner.

If, through the course of consultation, Ann concludes that Fred is not well-prepared for teaching, that he does not take suggestions well, that he seems to be personally abrasive with students, and that in general his motivation for being in teaching is not healthy, she faces a consultant dilemma mentioned earlier: What is she to do with information that emerges from the consultation after she has pledged confidentiality. The larger question for the school-based consultant is: "Who is your client?"

CASE 2: A NON-NURTURING PRINCIPAL

Bill, a school counselor recently transferred to a new middle school, doesn't know most of the staff and administrators. In the first months of his work in the new school, he schedules conversation with each teacher—individually during planning sessions, in small groups in the staff lounge, and by inviting himself to meetings of grade-level faculty members who meet to develop plans for the integrated curriculum. Over time, Bill observes a generally low level of staff morale, lack of enthusiasm for teaching, and teachers' reluctance to be involved with the building principal or assistant principal. Through additional observation, Bill concludes that the principal initiates contacts with the faculty only in cases of errors or problems. Faculty meetings usually consist of a litany of things that have gone wrong, and the principal often concludes that "things need to improve in this building." Bill has not observed the principal making any significant rewards or commendations—through either spoken words or written comments—even though Bill has observed qualified staff functioning well within their own classrooms.

Bill can approach this situation in at least two ways: (1) he could begin to work with the teachers individually and collectively to have them define the problem as they see it and determine how best to obtain what they need from the principal [teachers as consultees, principal as client], or (2) he could begin to work directly with the principal [principal as consultee] to benefit the system [system as client]. As Bill is new to the scene, the second option may be more natural.

· Bill can schedule a meeting with the principal to discuss his observations, having recently come to the system. He can state that he needs time with the principal to develop a better understanding of how the principal operates in the building, how the principal views the staff and student body, to exchange ideas about how counselors can function in the building, and about the principal's goals for the system. In this kind of meeting, the consultation function can be discussed. The norms the previous counselor established should be clarified. Just as prior experience shapes expectations for counselees and clients, they shape expectations for counselor-consultants in principal-counselor relationships. Issues of information sharing must be defined, and procedures for referral and problem initiation must be articulated.

Bill should be able to determine rather quickly whether the principal is open to hearing Bill's observations about the building environment, morale issues, and the manner in which the principal's style may contribute to some of the negative morale. Most likely, Bill can state the obvious: "Since I'm new to the building, let me share some observations I've made since arriving. I see a lot of well qualified teachers working hard in their own rooms, but they don't seem to interact much or collaborate, and morale seems low.'' Bill might add, "I don't see the teachers getting a sense from you that they're doing things right; there don't seem to be many rewards or positive strokes coming from you or your office about the good things that they are doing."

If the principal accepts that this is the situation, Bill is in a good position to develop strategies, through discussion, of how the principal might make more positive comments. Bill's task for the consultation could be to help the principal become more nurturing. Bill's ideas may be rejected. Or Bill might acquire distressing information—for example, that the principal believes adults need no positive reinforcement for their performance and that the principal's job is to monitor the system to discover errors and omissions. If this is the case, Bill has to assess the degree of success he might have in trying to evoke change in the principal's deeply rooted behaviors. Possibly, the client-consultee relationship would shift at this point, and Bill would work with the teachers to find a way to supplement what they do not get from the designated administrator. This might be viewed as enabling behavior, permitting the principal to continue doing an inadequate job—not an unlikely situation.

Finally, Bill may identify a situation in which the principal needs a counselor, not a consultant. Bill must decide if he is able to be that counselor or if working toward referral is more appropriate.

CASE 3: CONSULTANT AS CASE MANAGER

Team approaches as a strategy for working with student issues are becoming more common in contemporary school settings. Professional and lay personnel can combine in permanent or ad hoc teams to address problems of a specific student, a group of students, or a school or community. In these staffing situations, the school counselor-consultant can function as an individual member of the team of people promoting their own information and their own interests. A second way teams can function is to utilize their process consultation skills (Schein 1969, 1978) with the goal that the group will function effectively to reach a common end. Pupil service teams (various names denote these groups) composed of highly trained professionals who may not have a history of working together, staffings, or other groups are often called upon to address student or school issues. Professional rivalries or personal agendas of team members may erode the group's effectiveness.

Many school counselor-consultants serve as case managers for individual students or groups of students identified as the client. As more and more direct services for students are delivered by people who are outside the school setting but who may work within the schools, the school must designate at least one person as a case manager, to see that services are appropriate and complementary, rather than individually designed with the possibility that they may be contradictory.

In either role—process consultant or case manager—the school counselor-consultant must utilize personal skills to make sure that diverse members of a staff group function effectively or that the specialized services available for students are managed effectively and efficiently.

Suppose that several teachers have identified a student, Mary, as probably alcohol-dependent. The counselor-consultant might schedule a meeting of staff members who have contact with Mary, to ascertain her probable alcohol use. At some point, more members may be added to the group, alcohol intervention specialists from outside the school, and possibly Mary's parents or friends. As specialists enter the group, they might see themselves as having the sole expertise to handle the issues identified. The consultant role at that time is to assist the group in targeting Mary's alcohol use and treatment. In the process, more information may be discovered, such as levels of achievement or educational deficits that may need to be remedied, in the order of priority the group decides is best. The counselor-consultant/case manager may have to draw upon a great deal of professional skill to see that the diverse and highly trained group of professionals from both inside and outside the school system come together to efficiently and effectively develop a treatment program.

CASE 4: CONSULTANT AS STAFF DEVELOPMENT SPECIALIST

In most schools, the counselor can serve as consultant to the faculty and other staff in the role of staff developer. In these instances, the counselor/consultant must be able to respond with training modules in content areas that are uniquely part of the counselor's content expertise.

Assume that a school district has adopted the *National Career Development Guidelines* (NCDG) (National Occupational Information Coordinating Committee, n.d) as part of the overall curriculum design for the school system. The counselor should be able to identify content areas within the guidelines for staff development training sessions. In addition to the obvious areas dealing with occupational and career information, on which the school counselor should be expert, additional areas within the guidelines apply to the counselor's expected area of expertise. As an example, one of the student competencies identified in the NCDGs is for the student to be able to demonstrate "skills to make decisions." The skills competency is included in the "Career Planning" category but is certainly a skill which pervades all areas of a student's life and requires attention at all levels of education.

A school counselor/consultant could organize a series of staff development activities with the end objective of having teachers function with students in a way that increases the number and kind of decisions students make for themselves rather than being made for them. This could be accomplished through demonstrations with groups of students, preceded by a mini-lecture in a faculty meeting on the topic of interaction styles that facilitate this goal.

As a simplistic illustration, teachers should understand the difference between a verbal style in which they would say "What assignment are you going to do first?" rather than "Do your math assignment first and then your English assignment." This assumes that the goal of educational instruction is for students to be responsible rather than obedient, and consultants can conduct staff development training to shift in-class methodologies toward effecting responsibility rather than obedience.

To function as a staff developer with one's colleagues, the counselor/consultant first must clearly understand the problem (e.g., teachers may not be providing as many opportunities as they could for students to make decisions). The counselor/consultant must have a sense of how consultees can design experiences to respond to the problem situation (e.g., they must see themselves as capable of working as expert consultant with their adult professional colleagues (e.g., peers) in an area in which they have specific professional knowledge). They must be able to deliver the training in a nonthreatening manner as an equal who happens to have specific knowledge. And they must be able to exit the situation after evaluating the effectiveness of the training.

Most counselor education programs cover these skills. Frequently, counselors' own self-image limits the extent to which they consider themselves capable of being a staff developer.

SUMMARY

School counselors should consider consultation as one of their roles.

Although it demands many of the same skills required of effective counselors, it is different, and more complex in many respects. It is not something that "just happens." Even in the role of internal consultant, the school counselor needs to understand that effective consultation requires planning. The stages of consultation, in the simplest form, insist that the counselor/consultant plans effectively, enters the consultation deliberately, works with the consultee to have an effect on the third-party client, evaluates the results of the consultation, and avoids long-term dependency relationships.

Among the consultative roles of school counselors are consultations with teachers to reach students, consultations to impact school principals, staff development procedures, and case management techniques. An overview of consultation is provided by Dougherty (1990); an extensive explanation of the mental health consultation model by Caplan (1970); a discussion of school consultation in counselor education programs by Brown, Spano, and Schulte (1988) and a discussion of counselor-consultant effectiveness by Bundy and Poppen (1986); as well as issues of *The School Counselor* or *Elementary School Guidance and Counseling* (Dougherty, 1992a) and a survey article in the *Journal of Counseling and Development* (Borders and Drury 1992).

REFERENCES

American Counseling Association. 1988. *Ethical standards of the American Counseling Association.* Alexandria, VA: ACA.

Borders, L. D., and S. M. Drury. 1992. Comprehensive school counseling programs: A review for policymakers and practitioners. *Journal of Counseling and Development* 70: 487–498.

Brown, D., D. B. Spano, and A. Schulte. 1988. Consultation training in master's level counselor education programs. *Counselor Education and Supervision* 27: 323–330.

Bundy, M. L., and W. A. Poppen. 1986. School counselors' effectiveness as consultants: A research review. *Elementary School Guidance and Counseling* 20: 215–222.

Caplan, G. 1970. *The theory and practice of mental health consultation.* New York: Basic Books.

Dougherty, A. M. 1990. *Consultation: Practice and perspectives.* Pacific Grove, CA: Brooks/Cole.

Dougherty, A. M., ed. 1992a. Consultation and school counseling (Special issue). *Elementary School Guidance and Counseling* 26(3).

Dougherty, A. M. 1992b. Ethical issues in consultation. *Elementary School Guidance and Counseling* 26: 214–220.

French, J. R. P., and B. Raven. 1959. The bases of social power. In D. Cartwright, ed., *Studies in social power.* Ann Arbor: University of Michigan.

Idol, L., and S. Baran. 1992. Elementary school counselors and special educators consulting together: Perilous pitfalls or opportunities to collaborate? *Elementary School Guidance and Counseling* 26: 202–213.

Joyce, M. R. 1990. Rational-emotive parent consultation. *School Psychology Review* 19: 304–314.

Kratochwill, T. R., and K. R. Van Someren. 1985. Barriers to treatment success in behavioral consultation: Current limitations and future directions. *Journal of School Psychology* 23: 225–239.

Kurpius, D., and S. E. Robinson. 1978. Overview of consultation. *Personnel and Guidance Journal* 56: 321–323.

Lippitt, G. L., and R. Lippitt. 1978. *The consultation process in action.* San Diego: University Associates.

National Occupational Information Coordinating Committee. *The national career development guidelines* (Pamphlet). Washington, DC: NOICC.

Reschly, D. J. 1976. School psychology consultation: "Frenzied, faddish, or fundamental?" *Journal of School Psychology* 14: 150–113.

Schein, E. H. 1969. *Process consultation: Its role in organization development.* Reading, MA: Addison, Wesley.

Schein, E. H. 1978. The role of the consultant: Content expert or process facilitator? *Personnel and Guidance Journal* 56: 339–343.

ABOUT THE EDITOR

Ann Vernon, Ph.D., N.C.C., is a professor and coordinator of the Counselor Education Program, Department of Educational Administration and Counseling, University of Northern Iowa in Cedar Falls. Dr. Vernon is the director of the Midwest Center for Rational-Emotive Therapy and has published extensively on applications of RET to children and adolescents. Her *Thinking, Feeling, Behaving* emotional education curriculums, which are based on RET, are being used throughout the country by helping professionals.

ABOUT THE AUTHORS

James J. Bergin, Ed.D., N.C.C., is a professor and chair of the Department of Student Development Programs, College of Education, Georgia Southern University, Statesboro. Dr. Bergin has authored several articles and held several leadership positions in state and national counseling associations, including government relations chair for ASCA.

Loretta J. Bradley, Ph.D., is an associate professor in the Department of Educational Psychology at Texas Tech University in Lubbock. Dr. Bradley's previous publications have focused on counseling women, midlife career changes, clinical supervision, community agency counseling, developmental and career assessment, and counseling ex-offenders.

Brooke B. Collison, Ph.D., is an associate professor of counselor education and director of the Center for At-Risk Youth at Oregon State University, Corvallis. Dr. Collison is a former president of the ACA, has published numerous articles, and has co-authored a book on *Careers in Counseling and Human Development*.

Larry Golden, Ph.D., is an associate professor of counseling and guidance at the University of Texas in San Antonio. Dr. Golden is a licensed psychologist and maintains a private child and family practice. He has published several books, including *Psychotherapeutic Techniques in School Psychology* and *Helping Families Help Children*.

L. J. Gould, M.A., is a doctoral candidate at Texas Tech University in Lubbock. Ms. Gould's previous publications have focused on gender stereotyping and career development of adult women, with specific emphasis on retirement.

Robert J. Nejedlo, Ph.D., is a professor and faculty chair in the Department of Educational Psychology, Counseling, and Special Education at Northern Illinois University in DeKalb. Dr. Nejedlo is the author of numerous journal articles and has presented workshops on topics such as developmental counseling and strategic planning.

Susan E. Reynolds, M.S., is counseling director at Indian Creek High School in Trafalgar, Indiana, where she coordinates a developmental school counseling program with a school-community focus. She has chaired the ASCA Task Force on Developmental School Counseling and has presented numerous workshops on developmental school counseling.

Ardis Sherwood-Hawes, M.S., is a counselor and program coordinator for the Women's Program, Clark College, Vancouver, Washington. She has published journal articles and chapters in several books. She specializes in issues related to women who are disadvantaged and conducts workshops on sexual orientation and educational opportunities for teen parents.

Toni R. Tollerud, Ph.D., is an assistant professor and coordinator of the School Counseling Program at Northern Illinois University at DeKalb. Dr. Tollerud is chair of the IACD Professional Development Committee. With two of her colleagues, she recently completed a statewide professional development survey of school counselors in Illinois.

Thomas V. Trotter, Ph.D., is an associate professor and coordinator of the Counselor Education Program at the University of Idaho in Moscow. Dr. Trotter is the author of *Walking the Talk*, ASCA's major publication on developmental school counseling, and director of a state project to develop a comprehensive evaluation model on developmental school counseling.

James V. Wigtil, Ph.D., is a professor and the coordinator of the Counseling Program at The Ohio State University, Columbus. He has published in several major counseling journals, served as president of seven professional organizations, and has public school teaching and counseling experience.

JoAnne M. Wigtil, M.S., is currently completing her Ph.D. in Family Relations and Human Development from The Ohio State University, Columbus. She has conducted numerous presentations in the areas of mid-life development and family caregiving of Alzheimer's patients.

Author Index

Subject Index